HELICOPTER GUNSHIPS

Deadly Combat Weapon Systems

Wayne Mutza

specialtypress
PUBLISHERS AND WHOLESALERS

Specialty Press
39966 Grand Avenue
North Branch, MN 55056
Phone: 651-277-1400 or 800-895-4585
Fax: 651-277-1203
www.specialtypress.com

Edit by Mike Machat
Layout by Sue Luehring

ISBN 978-1-58007-154-3
Item No. SP154

Library of Congress Cataloging-in-Publication Data

Mutza, Wayne.
  Helicopter gunships : deadly combat weapon systems / by Wayne Mutza.
    p. cm.
  Includes bibliographical references and index.
  ISBN 978-1-58007-154-3
  1. Attack helicopters—United States—History. 2. Military helicopters—United States—History. 3. Gunships (Military aircraft)—United States—History. I. Title.
  UG1232.A88M87 2010
  358.4'3—dc22
                                        2010017825

Printed in China
10 9 8 7 6 5 4 3 2 1

Front Cover:
This U.S. Marine Corps Bell AH-1W Whiskey Cobra is armed to the teeth and looking for trouble. The Cobra carries a nose-mounted 20mm cannon, 38 2.75-inch rockets, and AGM-114 Hellfire and TOW missiles. *(Bell Helicopter)*

Front Flap:
Although designed to replace the troop-carrying UH-1 Huey, Sikorsky's new H-60 Blackhawk qualifies as a gunship as well. Seen here carrying 16 deadly Hellfire missiles, the H-60 series is used by all branches of the U.S. Armed Forces. *(Igor I. Sikorsky Historical Archives)*

Title Page:
Hovering like a rotary-wing bird of prey, this Bell HU-1A is shown carrying a modified XM-3 rocket launcher in March 1960. Improvements to this prototype configuration resulted in the more advanced XM-22 rocket-launching system. *(Bell Helicopter)*

Facing Page:
Although developed after the Korean War and reaching full maturity in Vietnam, helicopter gunships also served in Operation Desert Storm to great effect. Here, a Bell OH-58D Kiowa flies over burning oil wells in the Middle East. *(U.S. Army)*

Back Cover Photos

Top:
The Bell AH-1 Cobra came into being during the Vietnam War, and subsequently evolved into one of the world's most advanced fighting machines. This AH-1R, one of the latest versions of the Cobra, is shown firing a rocket salvo. *(Bell Helicopter)*

Bottom:
The U.S. Navy also played a major role in the development of helicopter gunships. The AGM-119 Penguin air-to-sea missile shown being launched here is just one example of the potent payloads carried by Sikorsky's SH-60B Seahawk. *(U.S. Navy)*

Distributed in the UK and Europe by
Crécy Publishing Ltd
1a Ringway Trading Estate
Shadowmoss Road
Manchester M22 5LH England
Tel: 44 161 499 0024
Fax: 44 161 499 0298
www.crecy.co.uk
enquiries@crecy.co.uk

TABLE OF CONTENTS

DEDICATION

This book is dedicated to Dale Mutza—one could not ask for a better brother.

ACKNOWLEDGMENTS

Throughout my research for this book, I have been in good company. Numerous individuals gave freely of their time and material, while others resurrected memories to provide details that could come only from someone who *was there*. Some of them participated in the events that shaped the proud, phenomenal history of helicopter warhorses.

Special thanks go to Ed Arva, Martin Bach, Don Brabec, Lennart Lundh, and Gary Verver, who consistently provided assistance; often surprising me with useful materials they came across while pursuing their interests. I'm grateful to Mike Machat for his astute editing skills, and for helping to keep this project on track. Former U.S. Army aviator and Bell production test pilot Harry E. "Ned" Gilliand, Jr., whose faithful assistance was endless, passed away during the preparation for this book. Fair winds, Ned.

And I am deeply indebted to Al Adcock; Robert T. Andrews; James Atwater, U.S. Army Transportation Museum; Olaf Bichel; George Bomermann, LtCol USMC Ret.; Robert Brackenhoff; Robert J. Brandt, MG U.S. Army Ret.; Rick Burgess, managing editor, *Seapower*

Magazine; K. C. Carlon, Col USMC Ret.; Giorgio Carini; John P. Conway; William H. Cox; Rich Dann; Robert F. Dorr; Leo Faciane; David Geaslin; John Hairell; Kim Henry, U.S. Army Aviation & Missile Command; Allyn Hinton; Hal G. Klopper; Tony Landis; Yuval Lapid; John L. Little, The Museum of Flight; Terry Love; Stephen Miller; Hugh Mills; Dale Mutza; Rob Neil, editor, *Pacific Wings* Magazine; Mario E. Overall; Yoshihiro Ozawa; Phil Poisson; Santiago Rivas; Raymond L. Robb; Emiel Sloot; LtCol Randy D. Smith, Marine Corps University; Jim Spiers; Robert N. Steinbrunn; Graham T. Stevens; Tamas Szorad; Tommy Thomason; Rick Vaux, The Museum of Flight; Floyd S. Werner, Jr.; Larry Wielgosz; Ray Wilhite; John M. "Doc" Willingham; Mike Wilson; and Seawolf Mike Worthington.

Credit is also due the Igor I. Sikorsky Historical Archives, Inc., Pop-A-Smoke, the San Diego Air & Space Museum, the Vietnam Helicopter Pilot's Association, the American Aviation Historical Society, and the Air Commando Association. Thanks to Allied Digital Photo for its attention to my photo needs. And to Deb, always Deb.

INTRODUCTION

Gunships—the term was first used during World War II when the weapon packages of light and medium bombers were beefed up for interdiction campaigns. The term would not be applied to helicopters until two decades later when U.S. Army helicopters began flying the angry skies of Vietnam. Throughout the history of the helicopter's development, the distinction between a helicopter gunship, an attack helicopter, and an armed helicopter has been clouded. Often, the distinction lay in the amount of firepower a helicopter possessed, the type of weapons it carried, or the degree to which it had been modified to carry weapons.

For the purpose of this book, *armed* helicopters are any aircraft built for utility, observation, cargo, or troop transport roles to which weapon systems were added. Nearly every helicopter that served during the war in Southeast Asia carried some form of armament. Weapons ranged from crew-operated machine guns to awe-inspiring miniguns and anti-tank missiles, and everything in between. By virtue of their submarine-killing power, torpedo-armed naval helicopters are included. The line between defense and offense is thin; often, an armed helicopter assumed both roles.

The *attack* helicopter, on the other hand, is one designed and built solely for the purpose of ordnance delivery, and used in the direct fire support and attack roles. It is more likely to be a helicopter built around a weapon system.

The development of the helicopter as a true weapon changed the face of warfare. Nowhere was that more evident than during the Vietnam War—The Helicopter War. The attack helicopter emerged, arguably, as the most significant development of the conflict. The answer is the same when veterans of the war are asked what they consider the most enduring symbol of the conflict—"the Huey." All Bell Huey models grew from a single prototype, yet over half a century, gross weight has more than tripled. After Vietnam, aircraft companies, like the military, experienced a period of self-analysis and regrowth. Focus shifted toward Europe where the Soviet tank threat loomed, and survivability on the battlefield was considered most essential. Thomas R. Stuelpnagel, then president of Hughes Helicopters, said, "We learned things about survivability, crash safety, maintainability, and reliability that couldn't be learned any other way. These lessons learned in Vietnam have been directly applied in the Advanced Attack Helicopter program." Building a helicopter that could destroy tanks protected by anti-aircraft weapons and also provide suppressive firepower in a variety of scenarios meant rewriting the book on attack helicopter design. The result is the deadliest, most technologically advanced helicopter in the world— the Apache. It is the hunter-killer supreme. With an incredible array of weapons and electronic gear, Apache pilots can detect the enemy from miles away and kill them with a flick of the finger.

Make no mistake—gunships are killing machines, their main purpose being to close with the enemy and kill them. With the potential to do so much damage to human life and property comes awesome responsibility. It is best summarized by Vietnam three-tour Cobra pilot Graham Stevens:

"There is a real bond among air warriors. But since man first strapped a gun on an aircraft, we aerial gunslingers have been different. Oh yes, we're all pilots, but 'gun pilots' take that dashing, daring, death-dealing, devil-may-care, white-silk-scarf image a step further. After my graduation from flight school, I attended the aircraft qualification for the AH-1G HueyCobra. Man had just walked on the moon, and I thought I was a really cool, new 20-year-old Cobra pilot, molded in the image of Chennault's Flying Tigers, and on his way to battle the wily, elusive, yellow hordes of communism. I clearly remember my bus ride from Saigon's Tan Son Nhut airport to the replacement depot at Long Binh. We passed a big airfield, and there were all these Cobras. I needed to be there! Sometimes we did incredible things and overcame unbelievable obstacles and still came home to laugh about them over a beer. Sometimes we weren't so lucky."

There are countless stories of designers who tamed the helicopter, pilots who pushed it to record-setting milestones, believers who fought bureaucracy to arm them, and skilled and dedicated crews who rode them into battle. The new legions of fling-wing soldiers continue to take the war to the enemy. While their helicopters cannot replace high-performance fixed-wing aircraft, advanced technology has allowed them to be built with airplane-like sophistication and performance qualities. Looming obvious is the immortality of unmanned aircraft, including the rotary-wing, whose capabilities have surpassed surveillance to include attack.

There is no precise method to segment the many facets of armed and attack helicopter development. This book focuses on the American helicopter gunship, examining not only its myriad, often interrelated development programs, but peripheral programs as well. The breadth and intensity of helicopter gunship development is germane to the history of the U.S. Army.

Diligent research reveals several little-known facts: A woman pilot's accomplishments influenced the U.S. military's involvement with the helicopter; the French pioneered organized, massed use of helicopters in an aggressive role; the U.S. Army's initial efforts with armed helicopters were based on its artillery capability; and the U.S. Navy not only was instrumental in development and procurement of the helicopter, but also conducted the first test of an armed helicopter.

Read on and discover that there's much more, all of which makes clear America's determination to protect freedom. And through it all, one observation is clear: Over the course of history, the nature of war remains the same— only the warhorses change.

Wayne Mutza
Mequon, WI
June 2010

CHAPTER ONE

REALIZING DREAMS

Sikorsky's VS-300A sired the XR-4, which was the world's first production helicopter, and the only American helicopter to serve in World War II. Three YR-4As and 27 YR-4Bs were followed by an order for 100 R-4Bs. The type also served the U.S. Navy and Coast Guard as the HNS-1 and the British Royal Navy. First flown on 14 January 1942, the XR-4 was powered by a 200-hp Warner R-550-3 Super Scarab radial engine, giving it a top speed of 81 mph. The R-4B serial number 43-46514 ended up in the Royal Navy. (Author's Collection)

While much has been written about the beginning of the helicopter, an overview of its development is helpful in establishing the foundation of vertical flight and its subsequent union with aerial weapons. Wilbur Wright had this to say five years after realizing his dream of flight in 1903:

"Like all novices we began with the helicopter, in childhood, but soon saw it had no future and dropped it. The helicopter does, with great labor, only what the balloon does without labor, and is no more fitted than the balloon for rapid horizontal flight. If its engine stops it must fall with deathly violence, for it can neither float like a balloon nor glide like an airplane. The helicopter is much easier to design than the airplane, but it is worthless when done."

Although the essence of Wright's words would echo throughout the formative years of aviation, a small number of determined men would come to the fore and disprove Wright's flawed assessment of the helicopter. True, the helicopter lagged far behind the development of fixed-wing aircraft; however, the first studies of vertical flight were well in advance of airplanes. The genius Leonardo da Vinci airscrew is dated 1493. His spiral device, in Greek, was called a *helix*, which was combined with the Greek word *pteron*, meaning wing. The combination of these terms, over time, formed the word "helicopter." Da Vinci's obsession with helicopter models, and other aspects of manned flight, proved that he, like other visionaries who would follow centuries later, was far ahead of his time.

It is easy to understand why the inventors of the American helicopter were philosophers, for the line between philosophers, visionaries, and dreamers has never been clearly drawn. What these pioneers understood and accepted was that traveling the road to success meant getting past its many roadblocks of failure. Risk became their friend. Their goal was not so much achieving greatness as it was fulfilling a dream. Greatness would come but only after others found reason in their impracticality.

While still in his teens, Igor I. Sikorsky had a vision— to design, build, and fly a vertical lift machine. Da Vinci's helix design, and having witnessed flying machines in France and Germany, was all the encouragement young Igor needed. With only his imagination and the flight of birds to turn to for information, 19-year-old Sikorsky built his first helicopter. In Sikorsky's words, "I started my activities in aviation by building a helicopter in 1909, with a small Anzani 25-horsepower engine with two crude propellers rotating in opposite directions on concentric shafts. The first machine achieved little results except mainly to teach me how things should not be done."

Although his second machine left the ground, Sikorsky quickly realized that the helicopter was more complex than the airplane. He was ahead of his time, and his dream of a rotary-wing machine would have to wait. He redirected his focus on designing and building fixed-wing aircraft, resulting in a long line of a variety of airplanes. Despite record-breaking achievements, Sikorsky

never lost touch with his dream of vertical flight, which he quietly pursued.

Sikorsky admired and was impressed with work done by Spanish inventor Juan de la Cierva, whose autogiro first took to the air in 1923. The autogiro was basically an airplane with a rotor that was powered only for jump takeoffs. In flight, the rotor free-wheeled, allowing very slow flight. Harold Pitcairn obtained license to build autogiros in the United States, and along the way, granted sub-license to the Kellett brothers to build them as well. Although the U.S. Navy evaluated the jump-takeoff machine for operations from carriers and rough fields, and the Army Air Corps put it to the test, it was outclassed by a new generation of light liaison airplanes that cost less to operate and could fly almost as slow as the autogiro. Meanwhile, in Germany, Professor Heinrich Focke, who had gained experience license-building Cierva autogiros, teamed with Gerd Achgelis to create the Fa 61 tandem rotor helicopter. The Fa 61 made its first flight in June 1936; however, the previous year the Breguet Gyroplane had accomplished the first helicopter flight in Europe with less fanfare. In February 1938, the Fa 61 generated

Inspired by American ideals, Igor I. Sikorsky came to America to design and build aircraft. While pursuing his dream of building the helicopter, Sikorsky often expressed his wish that the helicopter be used to save lives rather than destroy them, yet he accepted the necessity of the armed helicopter concept. Here, Sikorsky poses with his company's successful Model S-55.
(Igor I. Sikorsky Historical Archives, Inc.)

The U.S. Army Air Corps' first helicopter, the Platt-LePage XR-1A (S/N 42-6581), was based on the German Fa 61. While being repaired following a crash at Wright Field, an order for seven YR-1As was canceled. The aircraft was sold to Helicopter Air Transport, which overhauled it and sold it to Frank Piasecki, one of its designers. (Author's Collection)

The Army's second rotorcraft was Kellett's KD-1 Autogiro, procured as the YG-1 (S/N 35-278). This aircraft, along with a YG-1A, crashed, leading to an order for seven YG-1Bs powered by 225-hp R-755-3 engines. The sustained power of an autogiro's rotor made it one step from being a helicopter. (Author's Collection)

Although the autogiro's performance did not surpass that of light liaison airplanes, the Army, in its search for an aircraft with near vertical takeoff capability, in 1942 ordered seven Kellett XO-60s, which were improved YG-1Bs. This YO-60 (S/N 42-13609) was powered by a Jacobs R-915-3 engine. The auxiliary shaft from the engine to the rotor accelerated the rotor to allow jump takeoff. In flight, the rotor was disengaged to prevent torque from spinning the aircraft. The YO-60's maximum speed was 125 mph at its gross weight of 2,250 pounds. (Author's Collection)

The beginning of the long line of Army helicopters continued with Kellett's XR-8, which followed Sikorsky's XR-4, -5, -6, and -7 models. The Kellett brothers favored German helicopter designer Flettner's intermeshing rotor, which ruled out the need for a tail rotor to counter torque. This aircraft (S/N 44-21908) was one of two prototypes built before rotor stability problems ended the program. (Author's Collection)

Kellett's final helicopter design for the Army was this XR-10. An enlarged version of the XR-8 able to carry six litters, it was powered by two 450-hp R-985-AN-5 engines. External engine mounting allowed full use of the cargo area. This example (S/N 45-22793) was one of two prototypes built before a production order for 10 machines was canceled. (Author's Collection)

interest worldwide when the media showed renowned pilot Hanna Reitsch flying exhibitions in a Berlin auditorium. Reitsch would later set records flying the Fa 61. Engineer W. L. LePage, who had worked with Pitcairn and Kellett, was intrigued enough to travel to Germany to study the Fa 61. Upon his return to the USA, he teamed with H. H. Platt to form his own helicopter company.

When the Committee on Military Affairs convened during late April 1938, the bill that was drafted to fund development of the autogiro ended up instead advocating development of the helicopter. The death knell was sounded for the autogiro when Navy Assistant Secretary Charles Edison testified that the machine couldn't hover. It didn't help that the dean of New York University's Aeronautical Engineering School, Professor Alexander Klemin, while emphasizing Hanna Reitsch's exploits with the Fa 61, suggested the word "autogiro" be changed to "rotary-wing." But rotary-wing it became, prompting the Army in late 1939 to determine its aviation requirements and send them to the nation's aircraft manufacturers. Nine firms submitted bids.

The timing couldn't have been better for Igor Sikorsky, especially since airplane orders had been filled. When told by management of impending closure of his plant, Igor presented his proposal for the helicopter in which he stated, "Unlike the airplane, the helicopter will be used, not to destroy lives, but to save them." On 14 September 1939, he lifted his VS-300 craft off the ground to record the first helicopter hover performed in the western hemisphere. Sikorsky proposed a helicopter for the Army Air Corps, as did the Platt-LePage team. Kellett proposed two modified autogiros, and the remaining five bids were rejected.

On 19 July 1940, Platt-LePage's XR-1 was selected as the Army Air Corps' first helicopter. Its selection was obvious since it was based on the Fa 61 that Hanna Reitsch had so convincingly demonstrated. Next was Kellett's XR-2 (YG-1 and YG-1A), both of which were destroyed during testing, with funds diverted to a modified version, the XR-3 (X/YO-60). Improvements in Sikorsky's S-47 design resulted in the XR-4, for which the U.S. Army Air Corps awarded a contract as the R-4, the only allied helicopter to serve in World War II. Orville Wright may not have shared his brother Wilbur's skepticism, for he attended the formal acceptance ceremony for Sikorsky's XR-4. America's helicopter industry had been born. Sikorsky's follow-on models, the XR-5, -6, and -7, were funded during the war. Kellett had switched to helicopter design and developed the XR-8. Pitcairn, which was purchased by Firestone, came in with the XR-9, and Kellett submitted the XR-10. A single XR-11, S/N 45-9478, was a tandem rigid-rotor design built by Rotor-Craft. All were canceled shortly after the war's end, except Sikorsky's H-5. What followed was the development of a long line of helicopters, throughout which Sikorsky stressed that the best use of his designs was saving lives. His vision to better the lives of others while fulfilling his own was realized when, at the height of the Vietnam War, Sikorsky said, "For me, the greatest source of comfort and satisfaction is the fact that our helicopters have saved over 50,000 lives and still continue with their rescue missions. I consider this to be the most glorious page in the history of aviation." At the same time, the humane Sikorsky sympathetically accepted the necessity of armed applications of his helicopter.

Sikorsky's vision was shared by another philosopher and inventor, Arthur M. Young, who during the late 1920s challenged his inventiveness and eventually became intrigued with work done by German inventor Anton Flettner. Flettner's first helicopter flew in 1932, and in 1942 his FL 282 Kolibri (Hummingbird) joined the Luftwaffe, becoming the first helicopter in operational military use. Ignoring that he would be labeled eccentric for pursuing helicopter design, Young set off down the road of success, and failure, testing countless flying models to solve the pervasive rotor control and stability problem. More of his designs failed than succeeded, yet Young reasoned, "These crackups were teaching you something."

After a decade of research fraught with failures, Young invented the rotor stabilizer bar, and he was ready to demonstrate his idea to aircraft manufacturers. In 1941, Young met Larry Bell, who was turning out Airacobra pursuit planes. They signed an agreement for the construction of two helicopter prototypes, the first of which flew on 26 June 1943. Demonstrations with Ship No. 1 drew many visitors, one of whom was Igor Sikorsky, who came to see the vertical engine mount. Five years earlier, Young had attended a conference after which Sikorsky sold him on the tail rotor principle following a presentation. Two additional prototypes led to Bell's Model 47, which was rolled out on 8 December 1945. With war production at a standstill, Larry Bell turned to helicopter production; it was a wise decision, for the Model 47, known in the military as the H-13 and HTL, would enjoy a 27-year production run.

Other American inventors who shared the dream, and took risks, had built successful helicopters. Larry Bell was on friendly terms with, and even assisted, competitor Stanley Hiller, who would secure large Army contracts. Since early helicopter design centered on the rotor system, helicopter pioneers, while relying upon Cierva's findings of rotor control and stability, were identified by their rotor configurations. Arthur Young of Bell and Igor Sikorsky pursued the single main rotor with tail rotor system, Frank Piasecki the tandem rotor system, Charles Kaman the intermeshing rotor system, and Peter Papadakos the coaxial rotor system. This core group of visionaries—dreamers, if you will—brought the helicopter to the threshold of becoming a practical machine.

The North Korean invasion of the Republic of Korea on 25 June 1950, although tragic, marked the beginning of the helicopter's success. The demand for helicopters soared as the machine once considered a foolhardy invention proved itself in combat. In the hands of skilled and dedicated aircrew, their rescue of an estimated 25,000

Helicopter pioneer Arthur M. Young in 1944 flies the first of three Model 30s, which led to his union with Bell Aircraft. (Bell Helicopter)

wounded soldiers and civilians spoke volumes about their usefulness. A lesser use as a weapons platform would not be as easily embraced. But, given the tenacity of the American soldier, it was only a matter of time before he began shooting back; no one would have expected anything less.

As experimentation and development of the helicopter continued into the 1950s, interest in their military applications grew. Manufacturers who would become the *big names* in the American helicopter industry began earning their reputations, along with big contracts. Besides Bell, Sikorsky, Piasecki, Hughes, Kaman, and Hiller, other manufacturers competed in designs that ranged from tiny one-man copters to giant lifting machines. Sikorsky's

single rotor design and Piasecki's tandem contra-rotating configuration took the lead in fulfilling military contracts. Others were close behind.

In Korea, Bell's H-13 and Sikorsky's H-5 had earned the small helicopter a place in the military's ranks. Legendary Howard Hughes would meet the growing military and commercial demand for a light helicopter by turning his fancy for huge helicopters and jet propulsion research to the Model 269. Sikorsky's H-19 was built early enough to serve in Korea, and its success led to the larger, more powerful H-34. Piasecki, meanwhile, was turning out H-25s for the Army and Navy, and met even greater success with its H-21.

CHAPTER TWO

FLING-WING SOLDIERS

This JH-34C (S/N 54-0932) shows the original 10-tube 4.5-inch rocket system intended for use as indirect artillery fired from the ground. Rockets were also air-launched in direct fire mode; however, the 2.75-inch rocket replaced them. (U.S. Army)

Since the Korean War, low-intensity conflicts flared across the globe—in Asia, Africa, South America, and the Middle East. These Cold War hot spots gave rise to the use of helicopters in combat. The U.S. military had become comfortable with the helicopter and, true to its purpose, began devising ways to arm them.

Although the United States had policies in place that advocated counterinsurgency (COIN) efforts, France, aware that mobility and, subsequently, airpower was crucial to COIN, put into play the strategies of limited warfare to offset large armies. Wary of the threat of worldwide communist domination, Washington initially was content to supply France with air assets. As the United States stepped up its involvement in French Indochina during the 1950s, it gave the Central Intelligence Agency (CIA) a free hand in intervention, which included the use of helicopters.

At the collapse of French colonial rule at Dien Bien Phu, the French had already opened a new insurgency front in Algeria. When war broke out in French North Africa, French forces relied upon Piasecki H-21s and Sud-built Sikorsky H-34s. Quickly realizing the helicopter's vulnerability and the need to protect assault forces, the French armed their Bell H-13s, Sikorsky H-19s, Piasecki H-21s, and small non-U.S. types. U.S. military leaders watched closely. Thirty-caliber machine guns, along with 37mm rocket launchers holding 18, 36, or 54 rockets were tried. Since the H-21 proved to be less maneuverable and the H-19 was underpowered, the H-34 proved to be the best gunship. Called Pirates, they were fit with German 20mm MG.151 cannon, 12.7mm machine guns, and 37mm and 68mm rockets. Even clusters of 73mm bazookas were tested. French-armed H-34s would again go to war in Chad in 1969.

Since the armor-dominated battlefields of Europe placed demand on anti-armor weapons, the French Army experimented with anti-armor missile systems. The French SS-10 ground-to-ground anti-tank missile of the early 1950s was followed in 1956 by a larger, longer-range version called the SS-11. The air-launched AS-11 was tested on the Alouette in 1958. Since armor presented a better target from the air, the Nord wire-guided AS-11 was added to the armament mix. It was an ideal tactical concept. The weapons proved effective in guerilla war, clearly indicating the need for a dedicated helicopter gunship. For the French, that came in the turbine-powered Sud Aviation Alouette. For the American military machine, that opened up an entirely new and controversial dimension in aerial warfare, which would culminate in the mother of low-intensity conflicts.

Experimentation with armed helicopters in the U.S. military amounted to little more than studying the possibility of mounting a 20mm cannon in the nose of a Sikorsky R-5 near the end of World War II. Since the Navy had acquired Bell's Model 47, its Electronics and Armament Test engineers wanted to see if a bazooka could be fired from the aircraft. The job went to Marine Experimental Helicopter Squadron One (HMX-1), whose

In Algeria during 1959 and 1960, France operated at least five of these H-34s armed with .50-cal. machine guns and a 20mm cannon. This example, S/N 58-875, served with EH.3 of the French Air Force. (French Army Air Service History/Lennart Lundh)

The French Navy also modified the H-34 for attack. This example of No. 20 squadron carried a pair of SS-11 missiles mounted forward, and what appears to be a firebomb. On the opposite side of the aircraft is a launcher for six 5-inch High Velocity Aerial Rockets (HVARs). (French Army Air Service History/Lennart Lundh)

As the French military learned the value of the H-34 as a gunship, it expanded testing with a wide variety of systems. Most unusual was this 20mm manual turret tested from June 1964 to March 1966 on Sud-built SA-69. (French Army Air Service History/Lennart Lundh)

U.S. Army testing with helicopter weapon systems overshadowed the Navy's earlier involvement with armed helicopters. In early 1950, HMX-1 was assigned the task of determining if a bazooka could be fired from a Bell Model 47. In May, this 3.5-inch launcher was designed and installed on Model 47 (reg. N237B) at the Naval Air Development Center, Johnsville, Pennsylvania. The pilot-controlled launcher was attached to a pipe forward of the skid gear to clear the cockpit. Later, a blast shield was added to protect the engine area. (Bell Helicopter)

Grenades are loaded into a makeshift launcher mounted to an H-13 of the 24th Infantry Division in Japan in January 1953. (U.S. Army)

personnel successfully fired the bazooka on 29 August 1950. On 6 October the unit added another first to its list by dropping a bomb hung from a Piasecki HRP-1 from 8,000 feet. Then, in 1953, the Army experimented briefly with a multiple grenade launcher attached to an H-13. Little came of these tests and the war in Korea came and went without the helicopter gunship concept seriously acted upon. But inventive, imaginative minds were at work. These were, after all, the *armed* forces, and maximizing the emerging helicopter's potential was too tempting to ignore.

The limited performance of the helicopter itself was partly responsible for its stunted development as an aerial weapon platform. Since no engines had been designed specifically for helicopters, reciprocating engines used to power fixed-wing airplanes were used. Their weight-to-horsepower ratio, a critical factor in helicopter design, left rotary-wing aircraft severely underpowered. Some bulky engine configurations reduced a helicopter's payload to the extent the aircraft's usefulness was questioned. The turbine engine was seen as the solution. Engineers at Kaman Aircraft Corporation showed a keen interest in Boeing's Model 502 (T50) turbine engine, which had seen use in various applications since 1947. The turbine produced 300 hp, which was enough for Kaman to sell the Navy on a proposal for an experimental installation in a K-225 helicopter. On 11 December 1951, the craft flew into the record books as the world's first gas turbine helicopter. Kaman made another breakthrough in March 1954 by flying the first twin-turbine helicopter, an HTK-1 powered by two Boeing 502-2 engines.

Similar events took place in Europe. Among the foreign helicopter manufacturers that began establishing themselves at the end of World War II were France's Sud-Est and Sud-Ouest, the result of France having nationalized its aviation industry prior to the war. Both companies developed a wide variety of rotorcraft before merging in 1957 to become Sud Aviation, and Aerospatiale a decade later. The fourth model of Sud-Est's 3000 series helicopters was the most revolutionary since it was the world's first turbine-powered production helicopter. Introduced in 1955, the SE.3130 Alouette II was powered by the new French-built Turbomeca Artouste II. The Alouette II not only broke altitude records, only Bell's Model 47 matched its production quantity. The Alouette soon entered French military service, with some armed with torpedoes and others with wire-guided anti-armor missiles. Not to be outdone, in 1955 Bell recorded its first turbine-powered flight with an XH-13F powered by a 220-hp Continental-Turbomeca XT51-T-3 turboshaft engine.

New doors had been opened, triggering a period of experimentation and growth that resulted in a vast array of helicopter designs. While many designs never left drawing boards, some provided basis for successful designs, and still others became highly successful. All would, in some way, contribute to the U.S. armed helicopter. The most thorough and lasting program of arming helicopters was interwoven with the genesis of the Army's air cavalry. This concept was the key to opening the door to a new dimension on the battlefield. But opening that door did not come easy, for the pervasive impression was that battles were fought mainly on the ground, by ground soldiers led by ground commanders.

Despite the perception by Army leaders that Air Force support of ground forces was lacking, the Army was bound by the provisions of the Key West Agreement, which outlined air roles for the services. Drafted during 1948, the agreement allowed the Navy to retain its own combat air arm; the Army could retain air assets for reconnaissance and medical evacuation, and the Air Force would control all strategic air assets. Cavalry, as applied to U.S. forces, harks back to the Indian Wars in which highly mobile horse-mounted infantry scouted for the enemy, then dismounted and engaged and held them until larger forces arrived. Just as the horse cavalry resisted replacement by mechanized cavalry during the 1930s, the armored cavalry threw up the same resistance to air cavalry two decades later. Despite the proud history of airborne units, some Army officials were certain there was a better way to quickly place troops on the battlefield than by parachute.

During the early 1950s, that belief led to the expansion of tactical doctrine to include helicopters, and the formation of an experimental unit called Sky Cav, which

While not operationally feasible, Hiller's YH-32 ULV, which is called the first helicopter gunship, was successful as a proof-of-concept vehicle and paved the way for future armed helicopters. Nicknamed "Sally Rand," three ULVs were built and tested with a variety of armament at Fort Rucker in 1957. Modifications included twin-canted tails to accommodate recoilless cannons, and a modified windscreen. This Sally Rand is fitted with six anti-armor rockets. (U.S. Army)

combined armor, infantry, and helicopters. The Sky Cav concept is attributed to MG James M. Gavin, who, in an article he wrote in 1954, lamented the absence of air cavalry during the Korean War. BG Carl I. Hutton, the first commander of the Army Aviation School at Fort Rucker, agreed, vowing to examine all possibilities with helicopters. He appointed COL Jay D. Vanderpool leader of a group to study the helicopter's capabilities. The group, called "Vanderpool's Fools," made arming the helicopter high priority. Training Memorandum 13 issued by the Army in June 1956 encouraged "experimentation in new concepts in mobility." While not mentioning specifically helicopter weapons, the directive was loosely interpreted by proponents of the armed helicopter as approval, although indistinct, of their efforts. Meanwhile, the Infantry School at Fort Benning was studying offensive use of the helicopter, and the Command and General Staff College at Fort Leavenworth was writing helicopter doctrine. There was little coordination between the lot, and whatever they recommended was subject to budget approval—more likely disapproval—in Washington.

The aerial component of Sky Cav comprised mainly Sikorsky's H-19, the Army's first transport helicopter, which made its combat debut late in the Korean War with the 6th Transportation Company. Although tests with the Sky Cav did not produce the desired results, in 1956 Sky Cav airborne reconnaissance troops were assigned to the 82nd and 101st Airborne Divisions. With the advent of the Combat Arms Regimental System the following year, both units were placed under the famed 17th Cavalry. Soon, these and other nebulous units were experimentally arming helicopters, some of which were test models only.

Such experiments were not lost on helicopter manufacturers, some of which entertained their own weapon designs. As Army aviation leaders waded into the business of rewriting airmobility doctrine with armed helicopters, the first live fire tests took place in July 1956; an H-13 anchored to a platform fired two .50-cal. machine guns and four Oerlikon 8cm rockets. Meanwhile, GEN Hutton and his staff at the Army Aviation Center's Combat Development Office at Fort Rucker were busy drawing up blueprints for an armed helicopter strike force. The group met stiff opposition not only from Army senior commanders with traditional mindsets, but also from U.S. Air Force leaders who opposed bitterly any infringement of their domain. But Vanderpool's Fools persevered, and on 24 March 1958, formed the 7292nd Aerial Combat Reconnaissance (ACR) Company from the Sky Cavalry Platoon formed one year earlier. Combining weapons, scout, and infantry sections, the ACR was a helicopter-oriented strike force that served as the model for future air cavalry units.

With free reign given the ACR to experiment with a wide range of weapon systems and tactics, although a stretch of the Key West Agreement, the field was wide open. Most of the helicopter types in the Army inventory were modified for weapons tests, with emphasis placed on

This gun system, the XM-2, which consisted of an M-60 machine gun mounted to skid cross tubes on both sides, became the standard for the H-23D and later the OH-13G. This Hiller OH-23D Raven was serial number 57-2988. (U.S. Army)

The Swiss-made 8cm Oerlikon rockets mounted to this OH-13E were surplus from a previous unfunded program. Mounted above the skids are .30-cal. machine guns fed by ammunition drum canisters. (U.S. Army)

The ACR experimental weapons kit seen on this H-13E in 1957 incorporated AN/M2 .30-cal. machine guns and six 4-foot-long 2.75-inch rocket tubes. The straight skid cross tubes of early model Sioux helicopters proved ideal for mounting weapon kits. (U.S. Army)

This General Electric kit was the first armament system designed for use on helicopters. Originally designed to fire eight 89mm anti-tank rockets made by Redstone Arsenal, it was later modified to fire 2.75-inch rockets from four center tubes. Rockets could not be fired from outboard tubes because they would not clear the M-60 barrels. This combination kit was damaged when the H-13 landed on uneven ground. The inboard gun was mounted inverted to allow the ammunition belt to feed without jamming. (U.S. Army)

Early gun sights were crude or nonexistent, with tracers often being used to adjust streams of bullets. This dated ring and post sight in an H-13G eventually was replaced by reflecting sights obtained from the Air Force and Navy. The Air Force Mark VIII sight became a favorite. (U.S. Army)

This Bell-manufactured firebomb mounted on an H-13 at Fort Bragg in 1962 featured a simple fuse and serrations to ensure the casing split upon impact. (U.S. Army)

Mounted to this H-13D (S/N 51-2511) are 20 89mm T-290 anti-tank aerial rockets, called ACR Kit L. The rockets were fired remotely while the aircraft was secured to a platform at Fort Rucker's Matteson Range in September 1957. The rocket was cleared for area fire but not anti-tank use. (U.S. Army)

Aircraft manufacturers often ran in-house programs of weapons development. As a private venture in 1966, Bell modified this Model 47G-3B (Reg. N8522F) to accommodate a machine gun in the cockpit. GEN Hamilton H. Howze is seen firing the gun, which poked through an opening in the Plexiglas bubble, severely limiting its travel. (Bell Helicopter)

This was one of two H-13Hs modified by Bell to fire four SS-10 missiles. The Army took delivery of the pair in August 1958 and by year's end the missiles were ruled excessive for the suppressive fire role. (James T. Emmerson)

Two-inch Weevil rockets developed by Redstone Arsenal were tested on this H-13H from 1957 to 1958. Long tubes were used during dispersion pattern tests. Mounted above the tubes on each side was a .30-cal. machine gun. Huntsville, Alabama, which included Redstone Arsenal, became known as "the rocket capitol of the world." The rocket was named after the boll weevil, a destructive insect that plagued Alabama crops. In Vietnam, these weapon systems were replaced by an observer with an M-60. (Bell Helicopter)

The XM1E1 armament kit, which incorporated twin M37C .30 cal. machine guns, is mounted to this H-13K. The aircraft was a nonstandard test helicopter used at the Aberdeen Proving Ground. It was kept at Aberdeen for continued tests so that production aircraft destined for combat units did not have to be used. (U.S. Army)

Sikorsky's H-19 and H-34, Piasecki's H-25 and H-21, Bell's H-13, and Hiller's H-23. Prototype and one-off types were included, as well as conceptual configurations from private design teams. Noteworthy is a small helicopter that marked a major milestone in Army aviation history. An early attempt by Hiller to build a jet-powered helicopter resulted in the YH-32 Hornet, of which the Army ordered 12 in 1953. The small two-place rotorcraft featured ramjets on its rotor tips; however, the design suffered from high fuel consumption and, subsequently, poor range, which was only 28 miles.

Important to this study was an outgrowth of the Hornet called the YH-32 ULV, (ultra-light vehicle), which was billed as the first helicopter gunship. When Hiller received the contract in 1955, it was the first ever issued for an armed military helicopter. Named after Sally Rand, a nude dancer, since it was stripped bare of non-essential equipment, the ULV successfully tested armament packages consisting of rockets, wire-guided missiles, and a 75mm recoilless cannon. The Sally Rand was to travel with the infantry in a self-contained trailer that also served as the launch platform. The concept, unfortunately, "died on the vine."

Other observation helicopters that underwent more extensive testing as weapons platforms were Hiller's H-23D and Bell's H-13E, G, and H models. The H-23 Raven was evaluated with machine gun mounts, the maximum number being six .30-cal. guns tested in 1956. The H-13 Sioux was tested with a hodgepodge of systems that included machine guns, rockets, fire bombs, smoke generators, and anti-armor missiles. On 15 August 1958, Bell Helicopter delivered to the Army two H-13Hs mod-

ified for firing four SS-10 missiles. The system was given the designation Kit K. Although missile firings were successful, in December the Army ruled them too offensive for the suppressive fire role. The missile program was dropped in February 1959 but not before another ruling was made to convert to the SS-11 missile for use on Bell's new turbine-powered HU-1 Iroquois.

After many brainstorming sessions and countless spent cartridges, standardized kits for both aircraft were developed, although they were interchangeable. The kit settled upon at Aberdeen Proving Ground for the H-13 was the XM1E1, which consisted of two M37C .30-cal. machine guns, with one mounted to the skid cross tubes on each side. A total of 1,300 rounds were carried for the guns, whose rate of fire was 700 to 800 rounds per minute (rpm). Maximum range was 3,200 meters. The XM2 for the H-23D was similar; however, it used a pair of M-60 7.62mm machine guns, firing at 500 to 600 rpm. Range of the XM2 was 3,720 meters. The guns of both systems could be elevated nine degrees, and were fired by controls on the pilot's flight controls.

The Sikorsky H-19 Chickasaw was one of the first Army helicopters tested with weapons. Former Army helicopter pilot Bob Brandt noted:

"While I was a student at Fort Rucker in 1960, the folks who were experimenting with arming helicopters flew several H-19s. The H-19C/D helicopters were too limited and the idea of using them was dropped. Loaded and above 80 knots, one was in danger of entering 'blade stall,' which was a terrifying experience for most pilots who encountered its sudden and violent pitch-up to what seemed to be a near vertical attitude. The H-19 was a lot of fun to fly as long as you were not in a hurry to get anywhere."

Besides weapons, the H-19 tested techniques, which later formed the basis for military doctrine, such as troop support and special operations. During a 10-year period, Sikorsky produced 1,281 Model S-55s. Additional aircraft were built under license in Great Britain, France, and Japan.

One of the lesser-known aircraft types tested with weapons was a unique low-cost, easily maintainable craft powered by a 240-hp *cold-jet* engine. Once again, with an eye toward French developments, the Army acquired three Sud-Ouest SO 1221 Djinns, which the Army labeled YHO-1s, with serials 57-6104 through -6106. Based on earlier success with Ariel model helicopters, Sud-Ouest first flew the Djinn in December 1953. Although the Army found the radical design a superb weapons platform, the project was abandoned due to political opposition to the purchase of foreign aircraft.

Piasecki's twin rotor H-21 also underwent extensive testing as a gun platform since it was considered to be less vulnerable to ground fire than the H-34. However, the French, and later, the U.S. Army in Vietnam, would prove that false. The Shawnee entered the Army as the H-21C beginning in 1954. Given the H-21C's versatility and lift capability, Vanderpool's Fools were quick to acquire them for weapons tests, assigning them to the 7292nd ACR

The amount of armament attached to the H-19 was limited since the aircraft was underpowered. A shield was added to this H-19C Chickasaw's rear cabin fuselage for protection from the blast of anti-armor rockets. Long tubes were commonly used to increase the accuracy of rockets. (Igor I. Sikorsky Historical Archives, Inc.)

A total of 66 1.5-inch NAKA rockets were carried in this launcher mounted to this H-19D. Rockets weighed only 1/2 pound each. The pilot could control elevation of the launcher. Inboard of the launchers were .30-cal. machine guns. Two H-19Ds were fitted with ACR kits, which consisted of two .30-cal. machine guns and two 12-tube 2.75-inch rocket launchers. This aircraft was S/N 55-3197, while the other was S/N 55-3191. (U.S. Army)

Although the Army favored the Sud-Ouest YHO-1 Djinn for weapons delivery, the three machines it had acquired from France were returned in 1958. Compressed air ejected through rotor tip ports aided propulsion, while engine exhaust deflectors provided directional control and stability. After the French successfully fired SS-10 missiles from Djinn, this U.S. Army machine was similarly equipped. (U.S. Army)

Helicopter Gunships: Deadly Combat Weapon Systems

based at Fort Rucker's Tiger Port. Like other helicopters experimentally outfitted with weapons, nothing was considered too outlandish, including a remote-controlled .50-cal. turret borrowed from a B-29 bomber.

This system was labeled Kit O and used 500 rounds of ammunition. The idea was to lay down suppressive fire while the Shawnee approached a landing zone in a nose-high attitude, a tactic not possible with fixed guns. The 650 pounds that the turret added to the Shawnee's nose proved unwieldy, but it foreshadowed the standard use of chin turrets on armed helicopters. Most successful was the flexible quad machine gun system, which would quickly be adopted for the emerging HU-1 Iroquois helicopter. Augmenting the H-21C's armament were crew-operated machine guns mounted in the cabin doorways. Only these guns would be retained for combat in Vietnam. Seven H-21Cs known to have been involved with weapon tests are serial numbers 52-8647, 55-4172, -4203, -4213, -4214, 56-2018, and -2128. The latter, during April 1961, fired 200 modified 2.75-inch rockets for the Army Aviation Board and Ballistic Research Laboratories, Aberdeen Proving Ground to verify the weapon's suitability as helicopter armament.

Like the French, the U.S. Army found the H-34 the best gunship. Powered by a 1,525-hp Wright R-1820-84 radial engine, the Choctaw's brute strength and durable airframe made it a favorite as a weapons platform. Accordingly, it was tested with the largest number and most powerful array of weapons. Nothing illustrates better the Army's notion of aerial artillery than the 4.5-inch

While most machine gun systems installed on H-21Cs were fired by aiming the aircraft at the target, the .30-cal. guns of this quad system could traverse and elevate, giving the pilot more firing latitude, especially during landing flare. The system was developed at Aberdeen Proving Ground in 1961 and led to a similar system for the UH-1. (U.S. Army)

Only one or two Piasecki H-25s are known to have been included in armament tests. This example carries two launchers for firing a total of 132 1.5-inch NAKA rockets. Inboard of the launchers are .30-cal. machine guns. (Robert Brandt Collection)

The H-21C (S/N 55-4213) fires one of the most unusual weapon systems tested on Army helicopters, a remote-controlled .50-cal. machine gun turret removed from a B-29 bomber. (Robert Brandt Collection)

The 2.75-inch rocket system tested by H-21C (S/N 56-2128) comprised two 12-tube launchers built around the nose landing gear. The April 1961 tests led to larger units installed on H-34s and UH-1s. (U.S. Army)

One of the weapon systems tried on the H-21C was this .30-cal. machine gun, which traversed around the nose landing gear strut. (U.S. Army)

A pair of .30-cal. machine guns was mounted around the Shawnee's fixed-nose landing gear. Next to each gun is an ammunition box containing 250 rounds. Farther aft are 12-tube 4.5-inch launchers, the largest rocket units tested on the H-21C. Extensive bracing kept them clear of the aircraft. (Robert Brandt Collection)

This sturdy platform became standard during weapon tests. Rocket launchers, such as these 7-tube Mk 7s, were mounted below, while .30-cal. and .50-cal. machine guns occupied the top portion. Few of these launchers, which were built by Pachmeyer of Los Angeles for the Air Force and Navy, were made available to the Army. (U.S. Army)

Long-tubed 2.5-inch rocket launchers were a familiar sight during Army helicopter weapon tests. These 6-tube units are positioned low to minimize blast damage to the H-21C's underside. (U.S. Army)

Surrounding this H-21C's nose landing gear is ACR Kit P, which comprised eight Oerlikon 8cm rockets, two .50-cal. machine guns inboard, and two .30-cal. machine guns outboard. The Shawnee also had a .30-cal. machine gun mounted in each doorway. When the supply of 8cm rockets was exhausted, the kit was converted to fire 24 2.75-inch rockets. (U.S. Army)

rocket systems installed on the H-34. The Committee for Aerial Artillery Test and Evaluation saw the H-34 as the ideal highly mobile "move-and-shoot" artillery system to provide fire support to mobile assault units that advanced beyond the range of ground artillery.

Original launchers dating back to World War II were fashioned into 10-tube, and later 12-tube, launchers for each side of the aircraft. The M16 and T38 High Explosive (HE) rockets came from Navy stocks that were earmarked for dumping in the ocean. The system used a sight from a 4.2-inch mortar or Little John missile, along with a gunner's quadrant mounted to the left side launcher. Within two minutes after landing in the direction of fire, the launchers could be elevated and the aircraft traversed to adjust deflection by means of a track-roller device attached to the aircraft's tail wheel. The pilot then fired the rockets electrically. Although the system delivered the same firepower as one volley of a battalion of 105mm howitzers, the debate over its use versus direct fire with air-launched 2.75-inch rockets was settled with the Infantry School standing firm on the latter.

School officials based their decision on the results of four months of tests conducted by the U.S. Army Avia-tion Board, beginning on 27 September 1961. Continued use of the 4.5-inch rocket system did not meet the Army's helicopter area fire mission requirements since the system was too heavy and the rockets were no longer in production.

The 2.75-inch rocket, by comparison, was lighter, and not only was in production, but was a standard item in U.S. Air Force, Navy, and Marine inventories. However, the rocket, which was a standard Navy Type Mark IV Mod VI, was designed for firing from high-speed aircraft, and had to be modified by nozzle scarfing to slow its launch and give it instant stability. Following successful H-21C tests, H-34 S/N 56-4299 was equipped with a system designed and built by the Army Ordnance Missile Command at Redstone Arsenal, Alabama. The kit comprised two 24-tube launchers on MA-4A bomb racks, with rockets fired by the pilot using a Navy Mark 17 sight. During testing, a total of 464 HE and anti-tank rockets were fired at Fort Rucker and Fort Sill. The Army had begun acquiring H-34s in 1955, and from 1956 to 1962, eight H-34As and JCH-34Cs are known to have been used for weapons tests. They are serial numbers 53-4481, -4482, -4493, 54-0925, -0932, -3031, -3045, and 56-4299.

This view of S/N 53-4493 shows the twin .30-cal. machine gun window installation, .50-cal. and 20mm ammunition boxes, and Aero 14 mount for the 5-inch rockets. (Igor I. Sikorsky Historical Archives, Inc.)

Armed to the teeth, S/N 53-4493 strikes an imposing view while assigned to the 8305th Combat Reconnaissance Squadron at Fort Rucker in 1962. The Choctaw's armament consisted of 40 2.75-inch rockets, two 20mm cannon, two .50-cal. machine guns, four .30-cal. machine guns, and two 5-inch HVARs. (U.S. Army)

The four-gun XM-6 system mounted far forward on this H-34C would become standard on the UH-1B Huey. This Choctaw features the three-stack, flame-dampening exhaust, which replaced the single-stack configuration. In 1959, when the Army began upgrading its H-34As to H-34Cs with an automatic flight stability system, the nose tripod antennae were added. (U.S. Army)

Number 4482 was still in use as a gunship in 1966 with the 1st Aerial Artillery Battery at Fort Sill, Oklahoma.

Many weapon kits were designed and fabricated by unit members and given simple number or letter designations from A through V. Weapon development for helicopters expanded beyond Fort Rucker, with many of the Army's test offices and armories becoming involved. By late 1959, most kits had been standardized and the ACR went about the business of selling themselves, most often by means of demonstrations; over time, the sales approach had senior officials accepting the ACR concept. It would take three years for the ACR to evolve into an Aerial Reconnaissance and Security Troop.

As Vanderpool's Fools forged the gunship's future, similar endeavors were taking place, both militarily and in

During a firing test, a short circuit caused all 25 of the 2-inch rockets on this H-34 to fire, which starved the engine of air and caused engine failure. This rocket saw little use since its exhaust severely corroded the aircraft's skin. The 10-foot-long tubes seen here were tried with different types of rockets. Although they increased accuracy, their use did not justify the added weight. (U.S. Army)

This weapon arrangement on H-34A (S/N 53-4493) was called ACR Kit V. Above the long six-tube rocket launcher are two .30-cal. machine guns, the inboard one of which is fit with a flash suppressor to minimize damage to the aircraft's skin. (U.S. Army)

the private sector. It became obvious to helicopter manufacturers that armed helicopters were moving closer to gaining wide acceptance. It was only a matter of time. As armament testing moved into the 1960s, it led to the expansion of the ACR to a larger unit, and tactics for employing armed helicopters were formalized. Conceptual gunship artwork was coming off of drawing boards at Bell, and Kaman helicopters were tested with heavy armament, although on a limited basis. Even Sikorsky's twin-turbine S-61, first flown in 1959, was fitted with launchers for firing 40 4.5-inch rockets. All were part of the big push toward an armed helicopter force, but none would match the success of the ubiquitous UH-1 Huey helicopter.

The original 10-tube 4.5-inch rocket launchers were changed to 12-tube systems, above which was mounted a .50-cal. machine gun. Serial number 54-3045 seen here at Fort Rucker has the original single-stack, low-positioned exhaust. This H-34A later went to the South Vietnamese Air Force. (U.S. Army)

From 1962 to 1966, the Army Aviation Board tested this JH-34 (S/N 56-4299) with 20mm cannon on both sides of the aircraft. (U.S. Army)

The H-34 (S/N 56-4299) was mated with this experimental launcher on both sides of the aircraft to test the 2.75-inch rocket. Existing forward hard points were used, with two rear attaching points added. Total weight of this system loaded was 1,350 pounds. This system evolved into the XM-3 launcher for the HU-1 Huey helicopter. (U.S. Army)

Among the many weapon systems tried from H-34s were mine dispensers, which were designed for specific trajectory of the explosives. (U.S. Army)

One of Bell's many proposals for armed helicopters included this drawing of rocket-armed aircraft based on its Model 47. (Ned Gilliand Collection)

Keying in on the Army's quest for gunships, Bell presented concept art showing various gunship designs. During the late 1950s, Bell designers came up with this proposal for a ducted fan vehicle intended for the anti-armor role, then deemed a priority in helicopter design. (Ned Gilliand Collection)

Although none were built during the late 1950s, Bell proposed to the Army this D-230 Aerial Jeep with folding rotors and artillery piece. Although it appears airborne in the illustration, closer examination reveals that it is parked on the ground with an operator standing at the rear. (Ned Gilliand Collection)

In response to the Army Transportation Corps' search for a VTOL platform Flying Jeep, Curtiss-Wright in 1957 built two prototypes designated VZ-7APs. Whether or not the 106mm recoilless weapon mounted to S/N 58-5508 was fired, this combination is unique among the imaginative designs of the period. (U.S. Army)

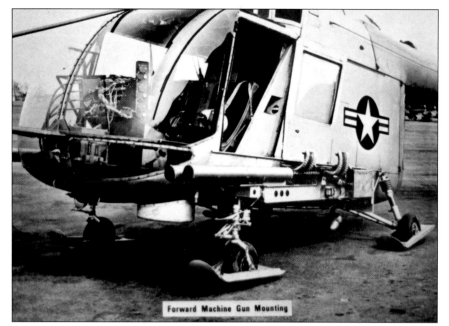

Forward Machine Gun Mounting

Although Kaman Aircraft Corporation designed its turbine-powered H-34 Huskie for the Air Force Local Base Rescue mission, the company, to stay competitive, offered a weapon system consisting of four .30-cal. machine guns. The most armament the Huskie would carry throughout its history was a Browning Automatic Rifle suspended in the rear cabin opening for rescue work in Southeast Asia. (Kaman Aircraft Corporation)

This unusual apparatus served as a combination training tool at Fort Rucker, the home of Army aviation. Added to the L-19 Bird Dog engine test stand are oversize Browning 1919A4 .30-cal. machine guns that made up the XM-1 gun system of H-13s and H-23s. Mockups of SS-11 missiles and an engine run-up control console complete the unit, which is manned by instructors as a tongue-in-cheek display of their capabilities. (U.S. Army)

The Huey

The Huey needs little introduction, having become the very symbol of the Vietnam War, and beyond. Seldom mentioned is the fact that the Huey was the result of the Army's search for a turbine-powered medical evacuation helicopter to replace the H-13 and H-19. Its secondary roles were instrument training and liaison, and it was not intended as a troop transport, and certainly not an attack helicopter. The advent of the turbine engine is largely responsible for the Huey's inception and its ensuing success.

The Army had long sponsored development of Lycoming's XT53 engine. Spearheading the effort to power Army helicopters with turbine engines was COL John Oswalt, the senior Army aviation officer in research and development. Gas turbines had proven superior to piston types because they are lighter, more powerful, have simpler drive systems, and can be mounted horizontally. Oswalt drew up the design characteristics for a turbine-powered utility helicopter in conjunction with the Army's announcement in February 1954 for a design competition. The aircraft was to carry an 800-pound payload for 100 nautical miles at a constant speed of 100 knots. It had to be able to hover out of ground effect in 95-degree temperature, and it had to be transportable in cargo aircraft and be easily maintained in the field.

One year later Bell's design was selected among entries from 20 competitors. In 1955, Bell flew its Model 201 (XH-13F) with a Turbomeca Artouste turbine engine to establish a baseline for mating a turbine with the new helicopter. In June, Bell was awarded a contract to build three prototype XH-40s, the first of which flew on 22 October 1956. To the Army's delight, the XH-40 not only accommodated four litters, but a medical attendant as well. The first of six YH-40 test beds flew in August 1958, with deliveries to the Army beginning the following month.

Phil Norwine of Bell noted: "In 1959, a group of us took a pre-production Huey to visit the 101st Airborne Division at Ft. Campbell. The first thing they did there was to tell us to take the litters out of the Huey and see how many troops we could get strapped down in the ship. We finally settled on nine."

The Army's seriousness about turning the Huey into a combat aircraft became even more apparent when one of the first production machines was scheduled for weapon tests. Bell made quick work of a March 1959 contract for 100 production machines, delivering the first aircraft in June. That month, the Army ordered the improved UH-1B Model, which already had gone beyond the design stage. An even more advanced model, the UH-1C, reached the mockup stage by the end of 1959. Initially, the Bravo model retained the T53-L-5 engine. It differed from the A model in having wider main rotor blades, a heightened rotor mast with counterweights relocated above the rotor head, and a longer fuselage that increased cabin size to accommodate more litters and crewmen.

The new aircraft was designated HU-1A, for Helicopter, Utility, Model 1A. In keeping with Army policy of naming aircraft after Native American tribes and woodland animals, it became Iroquois; however, that was seldom used after GI ingenuity soon transformed HU-1 into Huey. And Huey it became, even receiving Bell's

The XH-40 mockup presented the basic profile that Bell would retain throughout the long life of its Model 204. The designation H-40 was the sequential design number assigned by the Air Force, which handled Army aircraft acquisitions. Included in the mockup's data block is the weapon system designation 443L, foretelling its intended use as a gun platform. (Bell Helicopter)

The Army's first test of the SS-11 occurred in March 1960 at Redstone Arsenal using this modified XM-3 rocket launcher fitted to an HU-1A. Bell Helicopter installed the system, which initially used a sight from a World War II-era Northrop P-61 Black Widow. An improved sight and launcher resulted in the XM-22 system, which became standard on the UH-1B and C model Hueys. (Bell Helicopter)

endorsement by embossing the name on the right directional control pedal. Never has a name become more identifiable with a helicopter, and, as the future would tell, never has the utility designation been more understated.

The first 14 machines left the production line with Lycoming 770-shaft-horsepower (shp) T53-L-1A engines, with the switch made to the 960-shp T53-L-5. Most of the initial production machines went to the 57th Medical Detachment, and the 82nd and 101st Airborne Divisions. After the Army's Transportation Aircraft Test and Support Activity completed a five-month, 1,000-hour flight evaluation, Hueys assigned to airborne divisions under Strategic Army Corps were put to the test in a tactical situation. The Hueys proved the airmobility concept during the war game dubbed *Operation Dragon Head,* which ranged over the states Virginia, North Carolina, and South Carolina during early November 1959.

As expected, Vanderpool's Fools waited eagerly to get their hands on the Huey, first mounting a four-gun system to a prototype in 1957, and then arming the first HU-1A released to them with the SS-11 missile system. Although Army aviation leaders were fast becoming sold on the Huey, they kept their options open, aware that they tread the same ground as aircraft engineers whose imaginative designs often led to formalized development programs. Keenly aware of the Army's interest in armed helicopters and wisely anticipating the need for gunships in world trouble spots, aircraft manufacturers put their engineers to work. The bizarre nature of the designs that left their drawing boards was matched only by the Army's armament experiments. From Bell came conceptual artwork showing everything from sleek gunship designs to ducted-fan air vehicles armed with artillery pieces and rockets. Even Kaman in 1958 subtly offered weapons packages to the Air Force for its dedicated rescue helicopter, the H-43B Huskie. Months later, Kaman unveiled its heavily armed Huskie III, designed for both rescue and counterinsurgency.

In July 1960, Army pilots set seven world records in an HU-1A, and the Huey was off to a good start. That same year, five HU-1As, which would become UH-1As under the September 1962 revised designation system, were committed to armament tests. Air Force officials, expectedly, took a dim view of the potential for an Army attack helicopter, citing its development as an infringement of their jealously guarded air support mission. The Army downplayed the issue by maintaining that armament was for defensive purposes only; the Air Force was not convinced.

For comparison tests, an AS.10 missile is mounted outboard of an SS-11 on this Huey's XM-22 system. Differentiating the two is the SS-11's greater length and more angular fins. (U.S. Army)

Tested on Army Hueys, the 40mm XM-94 ended up on Air Force special operations Hueys in Southeast Asia. The system's XM-129 gun could fire 400 grenades per minute at a range of 1,500 meters. (U.S. Army)

One of the first weapon packages tried on Bell's universal mount was this arrangement comprising flex M-60C machine guns and a 4-tube rocket launcher. The mount would be improved to incorporate a bomb rack that placed rocket launchers inboard of the guns. (U.S. Army)

The Army's priority for large caliber weapons with a high rate of fire resulted in tests with 20mm cannon configurations. Although this arrangement, installed in YUH-1B (S/N 58-2078), had tremendous punch and latitude, it proved unwieldy. (U.S. Army)

Although this installation of a 20mm XM-61 Vulcan cannon gave the Huey awesome firepower, the system was too big and too kinetic for the aircraft. The Vulcan fired at a rate of 2,400 spm and had a maximum effective range of 1,500 meters. (U.S. Army)

Mounting the XM-6 quad M-60 system to this forward position on the UH-1B proved impractical for a number of reasons. Not only did the ammunition belts stretch farther, the guns ruled out a quick egress from the cockpit, and firing noise severely affected pilots' flying activity. (U.S. Army)

After this externally mounted 20mm M-24 cannon underwent extensive testing on a UH-1B at Rock Island Arsenal in late 1965, a podded version was combat tested in Vietnam. The external armament created minimal aerodynamic drag. (U.S. Army)

This is the 20mm M-24 cannon encased in a fairing. Positioning of bracing and ammunition routed above the cabin door permitted use of the door. (U.S. Army)

The first standardized gun kit for the Army Huey was the XM-6, which was called the XM-16 when mounted on the XM-156 universal mount. The XM-6 used two 7.62mm M60CA1 machine guns, which fired 550 spm; muzzle velocity was 2,805 feet per second. A motor slued the guns 10 degrees inboard, 70 degrees outboard, 10 degrees upward, and 85 degrees downward. Flexible chutes fed ammunition from containers secured to the cabin floor. A triangle on the cabin door indicates the Army's early use of geometric symbols to identify units. (Bell Helicopter)

Bell advertised its military Model 205, the UH-1D, as having gunship capability. Accordingly, this prototype (S/N 60-6032) served as an armed demonstrator with a quad 7.62mm machine gun system mounted on forward hard points. Also advertised were SS-11 missile systems and other weapon kits. (U.S. Army)

Although designed specifically for helicopter use as an Army research and development project, the XM165 Canister Cluster Subsystem, a tear gas dispenser, ended up in Air Force use as the CBU-19, nicknamed "Vodka." The unit was dropped from A-1 and A-37 aircraft in Southeast Asia until 1969. The 100-pound device contained 528 CS (tear gas) canisters. When dropped, an electrically fired explosive bolt sheared a rod holding spring-loaded end clamps. The package then split into two clusters forced downward by strong-back leaf springs, releasing and igniting the canisters. (Bell Helicopter)

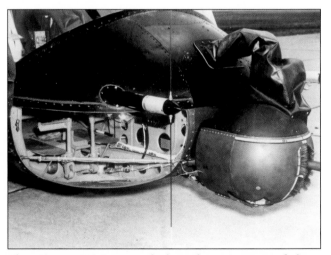

The 40mm XM-5 grenade launcher was one of three major weapon systems approved for the UH-1 series helicopter. Developed by Springfield Armory and built by GE, the weapon fired 220 to 240 spm. The turret traversed 60 degrees, elevated 15 degrees, and depressed 35 degrees. Recoil braces are apparent in the chin bubbles. At the lower portion of the turret is a spent cartridge ejection port. Bi-pole antennas flank the turret. (U.S. Army)

Weapon systems evaluated by A model Hueys consisted mainly of 2.75-inch rocket launchers, 7.62mm machine guns, and a 40mm grenade launcher. The latter satisfied the desire for a large caliber weapon with a high rate of fire.

Since an anti-armor mindset prevailed, a great deal of attention was given to mating the Huey with the SS.11 missile. The U.S. Army purchased its first SS.11B1 missiles from France in 1959. Although heavier than the AS.10, the SS.11 was preferred because it was better designed for air launch, it had a greater range of 9,800 feet, and a heavier warhead of 15 pounds. Built by Nord Aviation (later Aerospatiale), the anti-armor missile, after gaining approval for use on the HU-1B in 1961, went into licensed production by General Electric as the AGM-22B.

For firing, the pilot aimed the aircraft, while the left-seat copilot used an XM-58 sight to fly the missile by wire to its target. A two-stage solid-fuel rocket powered the 66-pound missile to a speed of 425 mph, while thrust vector nozzles adjusted the missile's path on command.

Since the Huey proved to be a good fit for the Army, it underwent rigorous armament testing not only with available weapons, but also with those designed specifically for the aircraft. Weapons appeared on the airframe anywhere there was room to accommodate them; some were so cumbersome or packed such a wallop that bracing had to be added. Machine gun and rocket combinations became the early standard. Since the HU-1A had no structural attachment fittings, called hard points, 2.75-inch

This Delta (S/N 65-9565) was the first of the largest UH-1D production batch totaling 571 aircraft. The XM-3 rocket system mounted to its rear hard points was not used operationally. Instead, the most common system at that location was the XM-23 door gun system with M-60D machine gun. (U.S. Army)

The third-built HU-1A (S/N 57-6097) ground-fires an SS-11 missile during initial test of the system mated with the Huey. The missile was derived from the SS-10 ground-fired missile. (U.S. Army)

This early armament system is seen on UH-1C (S/N 66-635) at Fort Rucker in April 1967. The flash suppressors on the M-60C machine guns were seldom used operationally. Flexible ammunition chuting was pioneered by Hughes Aircraft Company during World War II. (Charles B. Mayer)

A prototype AGM-114 Hellfire missile mounted to a UH-1B during early tests at Fort Rucker. The Bell-developed XM-156 universal mount was the most common weapon attachment point on the Huey. A flat plate normally covered the circular attachment face where horizontally mounted weapons were added. (U.S. Army)

rocket launchers and Browning M37 .30-cal. machine guns were mounted to the skid landing gear. Usually, these were within reach of crewmen in the cabin if they malfunctioned. The M37 typically used a 250-round ammunition belt, allowing only 30 seconds of firing time at the gun's firing rate of 500 rounds per minute. Although the nose-mounted 40mm grenade launcher developed at Springfield Armory proved successful, it would appear on later-model Hueys. The same held true for the XM-22 missile system.

Although deliveries of the production HU-1B to the Army didn't begin until March 1961, prototypes were tested with armament during late 1960, concurrent with HU-1A tests. Since the Army had developed a standardized weapons package for the Huey consisting of an 8-tube MA-2 rocket launcher and 7.62mm XM-6 machine gun unit, Bell built the B Model with hard points on the lower fuselage, aft of the cabin. Bell went one step farther by designing and building the XM-156 universal mount, to which a wide variety of ordnance could be attached.

Army aviation officials wasted little time in seeking a larger transport version of the Huey. It had already become apparent that weapons systems would bring the UH-1B up to gross weight, nullifying its use as a transport. And it was becoming more obvious that helicopters would be flying over Southeast Asian jungles. The decision to seek approval in the Pentagon for upgrading the UH-1B coincided with a search for a medium transport helicopter. Some Army officials insisted that they not venture beyond the UH-1B and instead procure a "filler" aircraft between the UH-1B and a new medium transport. The decision to proceed with an enlarged Huey was an easy one, and the medium transport selected was Boeing Vertol's CH-47 Chinook. Since the Chinook was deemed too heavy for the assault role, the new Huey would get the job, with the Chinook committed to re-supply, artillery movement, and non-combat troop movement.

Bell's B Model, then, would serve not only as the basis for the Army C, Marine E, and Air Force F models, it spawned the first of the long-fuselage Hueys, the UH-1D. Since the Delta was built around the proven B Model, Bell was able to forego much of the development process and lead-time necessary for new mass-produced aircraft. A contract was awarded to Bell in July 1960 for seven YUH-1D prototypes, the first of which flew on 16 August 1961. The stretch of the UH-1D allowed 10 troops, or six litters, to be carried, twice that of the UH-1B. Its 1,100-shp T53-L-9 turbine was soon replaced by the L-11, and later the L-13.

Despite its intended use as an assault transport, both prototype and early production UH-1Ds were tested as weapons platforms. With hard points at the front and rear of the fuselage cabin area, a number of interesting armament systems was seen. However, besides having crew-operated weapons in cabin doorways, Army UH-1Ds, along with the follow-on H Model, seldom served operationally as gunships, earning them the nickname Slick.

The 24-tube XM-3 was widely used during the early days of the Huey helicopter. It is seen here mounted to a UH-1B wearing markings of the Aerial Reconnaissance and Security Troop, D Troop, 3rd Squadron, 17th Cavalry at Fort Benning, Georgia, in 1963. An auxiliary fuel tank is under the troop seats, the red fabric of which was later changed to sage green. (U.S. Army)

The UH-1C (S/N 64-14102) was a weapons training aircraft, seen here mounting the XM-21 system. Attached to the universal mount is an XM-157 rocket launcher with the M134 minigun mounted on a pylon extension. (U.S. Army)

Outfitted with test instrumentation, Serial Number 64-14102, the second-built UH-1C, is armed with the XM-21 and XM-5 systems. This weapon combination was not used operationally since ammunition loads for both systems exceeded weight and space limitations. Later visible changes in the Charlie model line included a revised engine air intake unit, armored pilot seats, and relocation of the FM homing antennae on the nose. The aircraft's constructor number, 1226, is worn on the vertical blade-type VHF/UHF antenna. (U.S. Army)

CHAPTER THREE

THE CRUCIBLE

Pilots and crew chief of HML-367 prepare their AH-1G for a flight from Marble Mountain Air Facility (MMAF) in Vietnam. The pilot stands on the ammunition bay door, which, on rare occasion, was the perch for downed crewmen rescued by Cobras. Marine AH-1Gs in Vietnam were painted Marine Field Green and were armed with rockets. (Col James Sexton, USMC [Ret.]/Mike Wilson)

The arrival of the escort carrier USNS *Core* (ACV-13) at Saigon's dock on 11 December 1961 marked the first major commitment of U.S. helicopters to Vietnam. Aboard the *Core* were H-21Cs of the 57th and 8th Transportation Companies (TC) that soon would be airlifting South Vietnamese soldiers into battle. While the crews of these Shawnees were learning the hard lessons of helicopter warfare, major changes were taking place in the United States that would establish doctrine for future arriving helicopter companies.

Until communism posed a threat in Southeast Asia, Army aviation was focused on the atomic battlefield, and tank wars, not guerilla warfare. Responding to Russian Premier Khrushchev's proclaimed support of wars of liberation, and the likelihood of communist insurgency in developing countries, President Kennedy called for greater emphasis of COIN programs. Yet, Kennedy, mindful of the French experience in Indochina, and heeding the words of GEN Douglas MacArthur that the United States not become involved in an Asian land war, had decided not to go down a road that had no end. But Kennedy's subsequent order to withdraw from Vietnam would be canceled by newly sworn President Lyndon Johnson even before Kennedy's body was removed from the Capitol Rotunda. In conjunction with Kennedy's policies, Secretary of Defense McNamara and his staff in late 1961 had re-examined the Army's air arm. He had already proposed cutbacks in Army aviation, but surprisingly, he relented, calling the Army's program too conservative. He directed Army leaders to re-evaluate their requirements, and within days, the Army Tactical Mobility Requirements Board was formed and given the job.

After three months, the group, called the "Howze Board," after its leader GEN Hamilton H. Howze, arrived at a single major conclusion: A test air assault division should be formed. Approval of the board's final report paved the way for integrating an air cavalry troop into each division's armored cavalry squadron. Intensive studies of airmobile organization, equipment, and tactics against an enemy force of irregulars were begun, and the board's final report was submitted on 20 August 1962.

Meanwhile, to establish tactics doctrine, the Army had established the Utility Tactical Transport Helicopter Company (UTTHCO) at Okinawa on 25 July 1962. The unit deployed to Vietnam and its 15 HU-1As arrived in September. These were armed with two 8-tube clusters of 2.75-inch rockets and two .30-cal. machine guns. The UTTHCO operated from Tan Son Nhut Air Base and flew its first CH-21 escort mission on 16 October. In November 11 UH-1Bs arrived sporting factory-installed XM6E3 7.62mm machine gun systems, which were augmented in country by the 8-tube rocket launchers fabricated for HU-1As. Until the UTTHCO's arrival, Shawnees had only defensive crew-operated weapons, with armed escort provided by USAF T-28s and A-26s. Rare exceptions were the 57th and 81st Transportation Companies, whose members rigged some of their H-21Cs

Various combinations of rockets and machine guns were tried on the first Hueys flown in combat in Vietnam. The XM-6 quad system, which used four M-60C guns, was factory-mounted to UH-1Bs shipped to the war zone; however, the MA-2 rocket system was added in country, having been used on HU-1As. (U.S. Army)

Reversing the XM-6 and MA-2 rocket tubes allowed crewmen to maintain the guns in flight. Smaller types later replaced large igniter arms on the rear of rocket tubes. Ammunition feeding the guns traveled a great distance through chutes leading to ammunition containers in the cabin. (U.S. Army)

with XM-1 systems intended for Scout helicopters. Guns were mounted at downward angles on both sides of the Shawnee's nose landing gear.

Although the ad hoc arrangement gave crews a defensive capability in the landing zone, the practice was soon discontinued. Robert J. Brandt, a Shawnee pilot with the 33rd TC stated: "The 33rd in Vietnam received several quad M-60 systems for mounting under the cockpit. We decided that the system's weight over protection was not worth the trouble of installing them on our H-21s." On 6 November 1962, the Army Concept Team in Vietnam (ACTIV) was formed to closely watch the UTTHCO and evaluate the helicopter's role in counterinsurgency.

By 1965, the 2.75-inch Spin-stabilized Folding Fin Mighty Mouse Aerial Rockets were held in 7-tube XM-157 launchers on Bell UH-1Bs. Success with these launchers led to the larger 19-tube series. The Mighty Mouse rocket was originally developed for air-to-air use with North American F-86D and Lockheed F-94C jet interceptors in the early 1950s. (Bell Helicopter)

Only two Aerial Rocket Artillery (ARA) battalions existed in the Army during the Vietnam War period: the 2/20 ARA of the 1st Cavalry Division, and the 4/77 of the 101st Airborne Division. This UH-1B of C Battery, 4th Battalion/77th Artillery (C/4/77) Griffins carries the Maxwell system comprising half of an XM-3 rocket launcher and one SS-11 missile launcher from the XM-22 system. Each ARA battery had one of the hybrid systems. The 4/77 arrived in Vietnam in 1968. All ARA units started with UH-1B and C model Hueys, which were exchanged for Cobras. Armor was added to the pilot's window frame. (Author's Collection)

Dubbed Why Not Two, this UH-1B of the UTTHCO was experimentally fit with four LAU-3 19-tube rocket launchers. Initial Army tests of the LAU-3 led to the XM-159 and then the slightly longer XM-200. The UTTHCO experimented with camouflage as much as it did with weapons. The unit's assets were assumed by the 68th Assault Helicopter Company. (U.S. Army)

To capitalize on the helicopter's tactical mobility, the UTTHCO pioneered Eagle Flights, which consisted of at least four UH-1Bs, each carrying up to 10 South Vietnamese Army of the Republic of Vietnam (ARVN) soldiers. Accompanying the Slicks were four or five UH-1B gunships. Not only did Eagle Flights keep the Viet Cong off guard by swooping down on their positions, they taught the ARVN to work in small units. Eagle Flights eventually were flown with U.S. and South Vietnamese Air Force fighter bomber escort. During the UTTHCO's five-month evaluation period, it flew 1,779 combat hours and suffered one gunship heavily damaged by enemy fire.

Back in the States, the findings of the Howze Board led to activation in February 1963 of the 11th Air Assault Division (AAD) at Fort Benning, Georgia. As Hueys left the production line, most were channeled to the division, and to light helicopter units in Vietnam. The number of U.S. Army aviation units in Vietnam steadily increased, with the first all-Huey assault unit, the 114th Aviation Company (Airmobile Light), arriving in May 1963. The 114th "Knights of the Air" would set the standard for the basic structure of Assault Helicopter Companies (AHC) by dividing its 25 UH-1s among two lift platoons and an armed gun platoon. The first production UH-1Ds went to the 11th AAD in August 1963, and shortly thereafter, they began replacing UH-1B Slick transports in Vietnam. The last CH-21C combat mission was flown in June 1964, and by September of that year, 250 Hueys were in country. The assets of the UTTHCO were turned over to the 68th Armed Helicopter Company in August 1964.

When the 11th AAD study was finalized on 1 July 1965, it had become obvious that Vanderpool's Fools had pioneered one of the most tactically innovative and efficient concepts in Army history. The massive unit was re-designated the 1st Cavalry Division (Airmobile), having been resurrected for its third, and longest, war. Known as the "First Team," the 1st Cav began immediate deployment to Vietnam. Complete deployment would span two months and involve the shipment of its authorized 428 helicopters, half of which were UH-1Bs and Ds. Within weeks after establishing a base at An Khe, South Vietnam, the 1st Cav would draw first blood in the Battle of the Ia Drang Valley.

Army aviation units in Vietnam were organized into one of four categories: the airmobile division, either the 1st Cavalry Division or the 101st Airborne Division; infantry divisions, each of which had an aviation battalion and an air cavalry troop; the 1st Aviation Brigade, formed in May 1966 to embody all non-divisional aviation units; and numerous flights, detachments, and sections that served various commands and support units. The exception was the 11th Armored Cavalry Regiment, to which an air cavalry troop was assigned. A total of five air cavalry squadrons and 15 air cavalry troops would serve in Vietnam, and nearly 40 AHCs would come under the 1st Aviation Brigade—all would fly helicopter gunships.

Army helicopter crews wrote the book on airmobile operations, with tactics varying according to unit policy, terrain, and lessons learned. Hueys in the combat zone flew with a crew of four, comprising pilot, copilot, crew chief, and gunner, the latter two covering fields of fire with mounted or hand-held M-60 machine guns. A number of units increased their firepower with crew-operated .50-cal. machine guns. Standard was the combat assault, which had Huey Slicks inserting troops with gunships providing covering fire.

Enthusiastic about the success of the Huey gunship, Army leaders set their sights on a pure helicopter gunship; one designed and built solely for troop helicopter escort and direct fire support. Stiff opposition from the Air Force had choked off funds for such research, but it took the intensifying war to convince even the most stalwart opponents that gunships were needed. Bell Helicopter was ahead of the game, having begun in-house development of an advanced attack helicopter that made use of Huey components. Pending its arrival, Bell and the Army capitalized on the Huey's potential as a gunship.

A pure gunship, the UH-1C was a transitional aircraft, combining major components of the B Model and the awaited gunship. Basically an uprated B Model, the "Charlie" model offered enhanced overall performance, making it an ideal weapons platform, able to keep up with UH-1Ds replacing B Model Slicks in Vietnam.

The major feature that set it apart from the UH-1B was a simpler and stronger 540 rotor head with blade chord increased from 21 to 27 inches. The rotor head had been tested on a YUH-1B and, when experimentally installed on a UH-1D in 1964, accounted for several world speed records. The new rotor system, combined with the L-9, and later the L-11, engine, not only boosted gross weight to 9,500 pounds, it offered superior lift and maneuverability. The L-11 engine gave the UH-1C a top speed of 140 knots. To counter the extreme torque of the

Among many armament experiments conducted by the 25th Aviation Battalion in Vietnam, those involving a Mortar Air Delivery system resulted in this simple, yet effective, mortar launch device. As many 60mm mortar rounds as the aircraft could carry were loaded into the tray, which dropped them clear of the skids. (U.S. Army)

engine-rotor combination, the Charlie model's vertical tail fin was cambered and its horizontal stabilizers enlarged.

Production began in 1964, with a total of 766 produced over the next two years. Noteworthy changes that occurred during production included the addition of dual hydraulic systems, replacing the bell mouth engine air intake with a screened, removable particle separator section, and avionics changes. Beginning in 1970, a number of UH-1Cs became UH-1Ms with the switch to the L-13 engine. The L-13's 1,400-shp eliminated earlier reservations about the UH-1C's marginal performance when fully loaded in Vietnam's heat and humidity.

Armament for the UH-1C paralleled that of the B Model Huey, with one major exception: Beginning in 1966, the XM-16 quad M-60C machine gun system would be replaced by the M134 minigun. After General Electric had designed, tested, and built a basic electric-powered 7.62mm rapid-firing gun, based on the rotary Gatling design, Army and Air Force weapons labs began testing aerial applications of the minigun. The standard armament

package for the UH-1C became the XM-21 system, which combined the minigun with the 7-tube XM-158 rocket launcher. Three variations of this launcher replaced the cylindrical XM-157 and XM-157B, beginning in 1966. Also standard was the 19-tube XM-159 or XM-200 rocket launchers. Although a carryover from the UH-1B, the rectangular 24-tube XM-3 launcher was also used.

Nicknames identified aircraft armed with specific combinations of these systems. "Frog" referred to use of the 40mm XM-5 grenade launcher and 7-tube rocket launchers, while "Heavy Hog" and "Heavy Frog" referred to the XM-5 and larger XM-3 or XM-159/XM-200 launchers. "Hog" identified any combination of rocket launcher and quad M-60 or minigun. Until the arrival of the UH-1M, the minigun was not mated with the grenade turret due to ammunition weight and storage limits.

Numerous other systems would be combat tested, some of which were Army-developed, or simply the result of GI ingenuity. Early in the war, a small number of UH-1Bs and Cs were armed with the XM-31 system,

The XM-22's missile boom was attached to an XM-156 universal mount, which was braced to the airframe. With the aircraft in trim and pointed at the target, a booster motor fired the missile. After traveling 200 meters, another booster motor engaged, allowing the copilot to fly the missile to the target. Signals sent through two wires that played out from the missile controlled directional thrust through three metallic-green vectoring nozzles. If a missile malfunctioned, it was programmed to go down and to the right. This UH-1C of A Troop, 7th Squadron, 17th Cavalry used the XM-22 system in support of the Special Forces camp at Ben Het in September 1968. (Robert N. Steinbrunn)

comprising a pair of M-24 20mm cannon pods. Used in combat on a limited basis, the cannons fired 700 spm at a range of 3,000 meters. Although the Charlie model was originally intended as an interim gun platform, pending the arrival of the pure gunship, it remained in Vietnam, often sharing missions with AH-1G HueyCobras until the final days of the war.

Never was there any doubt as to the importance of Huey door gunners in combat. Besides serving as extra "eyes and ears" of pilots, their skill and latitude with weapons was irreplaceable. Often, their firepower made the difference in defeating the enemy and saving lives. Crew-operated weapons often went far beyond standard XM-23 M-60 or XM-59 .50-cal. door gun systems, their limits based solely on the amount of ammunition that could be carried, and allowable unit policy.

Basic infantry style M-60A machine guns on early Sagami mounts gave way to M-60D aviation-type guns on simple swivel mounts, or highly modified M-60s that were stripped of non-essential parts and beefed up to increase the firing rate. These Free 60s typically were suspended from straps or bungee cords, allowing gunners, albeit carefully, to fire under the aircraft's tail and belly. In the event the helicopter was shot down, such weapons were easier to handle in ground combat. The ultimate crew-operated weapon proved to be the minigun, called the XM-93 system. Although tested by the Army, more were found on Navy and Air Force Hueys in Vietnam than on Army UH-1s. Personal weapons were abundant, and if the unit armory didn't have what suited aircrew, the black market did a thriving gun business, and special operations troops had exotic weapons for trade.

Hueys and Missiles

When the North Vietnamese brought armor to bear against allied positions, the obvious counter from an aviation standpoint was anti-armor missiles, which had been tested on early model Hueys. Beginning in late 1965, 32 XM-22 missile systems were earmarked for Vietnam, along with a supply of high explosive and anti-personnel AGM-22B missiles. Mounted to UH-1Bs and Cs, the missiles proved effective against hard targets such as bunkers and armor. In combat, the system's drawbacks were its reliance upon fresh batteries and a trained operator's good hand-eye coordination during a steady firing run. Since such ideal conditions seldom existed during a run on a target, the missile's use was limited. This low demand in the 1st Cav's 2nd Squadron/20th Aerial Rocket Artillery meant that the missile system was stored, and when called for, it took three hours to switch from the XM-3 to the XM-22. To eliminate delay, and to avoid committing much needed gunships to missile use only, Chief Warrant Officer Robert Maxwell in 1965 devised a system that created a dual-purpose gunship. The Maxwell System was a hybrid missile/rocket arrangement that combined an XM-3 rocket launcher with an AGM-22B missile. This gave the aircraft the flexibility to attack point targets with missiles, or lay down area fire with rockets. Maxwell built four units, one for each battery of aircraft.

Enemy armor did not present a major problem until North Vietnamese tanks appeared in force during early 1972. Army aviation officials saw this as the perfect opportunity to put to the test a missile system that had long been in the planning; the Tube-launched, Optically-tracked, Wire-guided BGM-71 missile, best known simply as TOW.

The TOW missile system was based on research begun in 1957 at Redstone Arsenal of a Heavy Anti-tank Weapon. Research of the airborne TOW began in late 1963 when the Army Missile Command awarded contracts to Hughes Aircraft and Philco Ford Corporation to develop a sight unit that enabled firing of a TOW or MGM-51 Shillelagh missile from a UH-1B. Their goal was the design of the XM-26 tactical missile system to replace the XM-22. In 1967, five XM-26 TOW airborne launch systems were built for the UH-1B; however, the program was canceled in March 1968 to concentrate on the TOW/CHEYENNE (AH-56A) program.

After Army staff considered for a second time replacing the TOW with the Shillelagh, Congress put the matter to rest in September 1970. That month, TOW training units became operational to replace the 106mm recoilless rifle, and by year's end, the ground-based TOW was deployed to Europe.

When the North Vietnamese Army kicked off its *Easter Offensive* in March 1972, supported by Russian and captured U.S. armor, the Army saw the opportunity to prove the airborne TOW's effectiveness against Soviet armor. It was also hoped that an impressive showing would cinch funding for the Advanced Attack Helicopter (AAH) program.

In April 1972, two XM-26 systems were taken from storage in the United States and loaded aboard three C-141s, along with two UH-1Bs, three crews, Hughes and Bell technicians, and support equipment for the urgent flight to Tan Son Nhut Air Base, South Vietnam. None of the UH-1B pilots had ever fired a TOW missile from a Huey so they were given a crash course. The group, which was designated the 1st Combat Aerial TOW Team, or "Hawk's Claw," set up shop at Camp Holloway in the Central Highlands during late April. On 2 May, the team flew its first combat mission during which it destroyed four M-41 tanks, one truck, and an artillery gun. Throughout May, the Hawk's Claw scored hits with devastating results on armor, vehicles, artillery, and other hard targets.

The 2nd Combat Aerial TOW Team took over on 8 June and carried on the business of destroying enemy equipment. At the cease-fire on 28 January 1973, 162 TOW missiles had been fired in combat, 151 of which were successful firings that scored hits. Army documents indicate that the combat success of the TOW system as a point weapon not only played a role in cancellation of the AH-56A Cheyenne program in August 1972, it rallied Congressional support of the AAH program.

Among the variety of helicopter systems tried by the Army to deny the enemy the cover of darkness was the Lightning Bug system incorporating a .50-cal. machine gun and searchlight cluster on a UH-1D. The Delta (S/N 65-10130) is seen at Tan Son Nhut Air Base in January 1967. (U.S. Army)

The minigun and .50-cal. machine gun mounted to the same side of this UH-1H illustrates the maximum firepower of crew-operated weapons on Army Slicks in Vietnam. In most circles, this would qualify as a gunship. (U.S. Army)

This UH-1B of the 238th Aerial Weapons Company Gunrunners typified the difficulty in differentiating a UH-1B from a UH-1C. This Bravo model (S/N 63-12070) apparently was one of many that had its tail boom replaced with that of a Charlie model, although the synchronized elevators are from a B model. Being based in II Corps, the 238th, an all-gunship unit, wore its unit designation on the pilots' doors. Four kill markings are worn on the doorpost. Unusual is the crew chief's infantry type M-60A on a modified swivel mount. (Larry D. Smith)

Huey Night Fighters

The same amount of effort spent engaging the enemy had to be spent finding him. That proved more difficult at night, requiring that U.S. forces devise ways to deny him the cover of darkness. Helicopter gunships had proven effective at decimating the enemy, and Air Force flareships were sometimes available, but it made more sense for helicopter gunships to possess detection capability for instant engagement. Army aviation leaders, certain that helicopter combat operations could be carried out at night using navigational aids and night vision equipment, in 1966 began night combat assaults.

The first Huey illumination system in Vietnam is credited to CW3 Kenneth Lamonte of the 117th Aviation Company in 1964. On the universal mount, Lamonte attached a pipe to which he secured six bomb shackles for carrying flares. The system used wiring of the XM-6 gun system, allowing the pilot to release flares in any sequence. Other flare systems were tried, the construction of which was limited only by the builders' imagination.

Helicopter crewmen of the 25th Aviation Battalion in Vietnam were an inventive lot, first using 55-gallon drums cut lengthwise to hold Mk-24 flares. Mounted in the Huey's cabin doorway, the flares were released simply be undoing a retaining strap. Members of the unit acquired a Multiple Ejection Rack (MER), which was used by Navy and Air Force aircraft to launch multiple stores. When attached to the Huey's universal mount, the MER held six Mk-24 flares. Eventually, a flare launcher that was tailor made for

Two crewmen on the left side of this Huey operated a minigun and light cluster, which consisted of an AN/VSS-3 Xenon searchlight developed for the M551 Sheridan armored vehicle, and an AN/TVS-4 Starlight scope for night vision. This Nighthawk system was mounted on a UH-1H. (U.S. Army)

This night-flying UH-1D combines a night vision device and a .50-cal. machine gun. The reliable Fifty was often favored over the minigun's 4,000-spm rate of fire since it was more accurate, had longer range, had more penetrating power, and could fire armor piercing ammunition. (U.S. Army)

The UH-1M INFANT night attack system, seen here at Fort Rucker in 1968, combined elaborate night vision sensors with the XM-21 weapon system. (U.S. Army)

The XM30 gun system, which used the XM140 30mm gun, tested on the Huey was the precursor to the Apache's M230 gun system. The test unit was mounted to both sides of this UH-1C, which had cabin doors modified to accommodate ammunition feed chutes. (U.S. Army)

Huey gunships of the 92nd AHC in Vietnam used this popular theme to decorate their 19-tube rocket launchers. The unit Stallions emblem was worn on the universal mount's dust cover. Two other assault helicopter units known to have painted rocket launchers as beer cans are the 189th AHC and the 335th AHC. (Rob Mignard)

all UH-1 models was mounted in Hueys selected by units as its flareship. Mounted forward in the cargo compartment, the XM-19 system stored 24 2-million-candlepower Mk-45 flares, which were ejected out of the cabin doorway. Subsequent experiments with longer lasting and more flexible lighting systems resulted in a cluster of seven powerful landing lights used on Air Force transports.

Fabrication and use of the first operational system is credited to the 197th Aviation Company in 1965. Initially, these were used to find and hold the enemy while gunships engaged. As the tactic caught on, light ship/gunship missions appeared regularly on unit mission boards. Although these missions were called "Firefly" by units in northern regions and "Lightning Bug" in the south, the designations were used interchangeably. A typical Firefly/Lightning Bug mission had a high bird providing target direction to the light ship, which illuminated the target. Next to the light cluster in a UH-1D was a heavy crew-operated weapon, usually a .50-cal. gun. The main element of surprise came from a blacked-out gunship flying relatively low level, while carefully avoiding the powerful light beam. In the Mekong Delta, an OV-1 Phantom Mohawk often worked with the team over flat terrain, spotting targets with its infrared gear and vectoring the light ship onto the target.

In the push to give Army helicopters night-fighting capability, it was decided to use the UH-1C's hard points for the nose turret to mount electronic detection systems. In 1966, five Charlie models were fit with Remote Image Intensifier Systems, which enhanced available light to project images onto onboard video monitors. Four of the Batships, serial numbers 65-9422, -9431, -9437, and -9439, were sent to Vietnam in June for five months of combat evaluation. Although test results were minimal, the Batships brought valuable information back to the labs for the development of electronic night vision systems.

As the light cluster unit was refined and the Cobra gunship entered the combat theater in 1967, a more elaborate night-fighting system was developed, which exploited the cabin space of UH-1D and H model Slicks. Reportedly, the 334th AHC pioneered this system, the basic components of which were an AN/VSS-3 Xenon searchlight (borrowed from a Sheridan armored vehicle), an AN/TVS-4 night observation device (NOD), and a crew-operated minigun with its rate of fire stepped down to 1,500 spm. Completing the package was a twin M-60 in the right doorway and, often, a Free M-60.

The Huey's crew normally consisted of two pilots, light/NOD operator, and three or four gunners. Called "Nighthawk," comprising the Slick and a pair of gunships, the team often was guided by ground-controlled approach radar. The light ship flew low and slow, while gunships flew at a standoff position. When the light ship crew spotted a target with the NOD in infrared mode, it marked the target for the gunships by switching to white light mode, or by firing the minigun, whose tracers marked the target. Sometimes a flareship accompanied the team for broad illumination of the battlefield. Nighthawk was most effective in flat, open terrain, and proved equally effective fending off attacks on bases.

The ultimate Huey night fighter developed for combat in Vietnam was called INFANT, for Iroquois Night Fighter and Night Tracker. Developed by Hughes Aircraft in 1967 under direction of the Army Night Vision Laboratory, this system mated the more powerful UH-1M with the image intensifier/AN/ASQ-132 and the XM-21 armament systems. At the heart of the system was a dual sensor unit mounted to the Huey's nose, which had to be strengthened to accept the assembly. The right sensor was an image intensifier, which was counterbalanced by the AN/ASQ-132 Low-Light Level Television (LLLTV) unit. Both sensors displayed images on monitors in the instrument panel and in the cabin. Mounted atop the INFANT's miniguns were 500W Xenon infrared searchlights to aid in pinpointing targets. The miniguns not only were tipped with flash suppressors, they used dim tracer ammunition, which was developed for INFANT by being chemically modified to produce low intensity light invisible to the naked eye. INFANT Hueys also were given a Navy-developed formation light kit consisting of electro-luminescent light panels, three of which were applied to the cabin roof, one on the tail rotor hub, and one on each main rotor tip.

To demonstrate to the Army the possibility of upgrading its early Hueys, Bell in 1968 modified a UH-1C into a larger, more powerful Huey it labeled Model 211 Huey Tug. Envisioned as a heavy lifter, the Tug was given a larger tail boom, larger main and tail rotor, strengthened airframe, and larger transmission. A stability control system replaced the rotor stabilizer bar. Since improvements brought the Tug's gross weight up to 14,000 pounds, including a 3-ton external load, power came from a 2,650-shp T55-L-7 engine. Although Bell toured Army installations and proposed the modification of UH-1B/Cs during overhaul after Vietnam combat tours, the Army declined. (Dick Van Allen)

Gunship crews paid a high price for low-level operations in Vietnam. While flying a night support mission near Fire Support Base Debbie in November 1970, the tail rotor of this UH-1C of the 174th AHC struck a tree. The crew walked away from the crash, and after a night of keeping the enemy at bay, they and the wreck were recovered by a Chinook and flown back to Duc Pho. (Robert Brackenhoff)

The proliferation of Army Hueys throughout Vietnam resulted in a wide variety of interesting weapon configurations and marking schemes. This well-maintained UH-1C (S/N 65-9555) hailed from the 174th AHC Sharks at Duc Pho in 1970. Prior to adding shark mouths to their gunships, the unit had received the blessings to do so from Robert L. Scott of World War II Flying Tigers fame. (Robert Brackenhoff)

This black-painted UH-1C of the 92nd AHC wears only the last three digits of its serial number (65-12741) on the tail fin in 1970. The gunship was later transferred to the Navy's Seawolves squadron. (Rob Mignard)

Of four INFANT systems built (UH-1M serial numbers 66-511, -584, -703, and -726), three were sent to Vietnam for a three-month combat evaluation by the Army Concept Team in Vietnam. The INFANT was tested with various combinations of aircraft, including gunships, Nighthawks, and Phantom Mohawks. Number 66-726 was lost during one of these combat missions. The INFANT package brought the UH-1M up to its maximum weight, imposing a nose-heavy condition, thereby nullifying the maneuverability vital during gunship tactics. As a result, INFANT systems saw only limited use in four combat units, beginning in late 1970.

Another system that took advantage of the UH-1M's power was the AN/AAQ-5 Forward-Looking Infrared Radar (FLIR). Mounted to strengthened nose hard points, the 260-pound sensor turret produced images onto onboard monitors by comparing thermal radiation characteristics of objects. Used for both day and night missions, the FLIR was integrated with the XM-21 armament system incorporating flash suppressor-tipped miniguns. Five systems were evaluated in Vietnam during 1971.

The Royal Australian Air Force's No. 9 Squadron began operating from Vung Tau in June 1966, supporting the 1st Australian Task Force, especially the Special Air Service. In 1969, four of the squadron's UH-1Ds were converted to gunships utilizing all four of the Huey's hard points. The crew of this "Bushranger" UH-1D pours M-60 and minigun fire on the enemy. (U.S. Army)

This UH-1C is identified only by its large bee motif on the nose, signifying the Stingers gun platoon of the 116th AHC. Assault helicopter companies usually used a theme. The 116th's four flight platoons, for example, were the Stingers, Hornets, Wasps, and Yellow Jackets. (Robert Brackenhoff)

Wearing its unit designation on the pilots' doors, a practice of northern-based units in Vietnam, this UH-1C of the 119th Crocodiles in 1967 also wore its unit emblem on the nose, and a pair of eyes on the XM-5 turret. (Rodger D. Fetters)

Pilots of the Hawks Claw unit at Camp Holloway load a TOW missile in one of the unit's two UH-1Bs, which were specially armed with the XM-26 missile system to deal with North Vietnamese armor. An armor panel protects the engine, while the upturned exhaust resists lock-on from heat-seeking missiles. (U.S. Army)

Guns A-Go-Go

While experiments with arming Hueys fell within the norm, those with cargo helicopters were certain to draw more attention, often unwanted. Such was the case with the foremost of helicopter gunships: Boeing Vertol's Armed and Armored CH-47A Chinook, designated A/ACH-47A, which would later be re-designated ACH-47A, for Armed Cargo Helicopter.

Born of necessity for the Vietnam War, the ACH-47A was indicative of the Army's quest for a helicopter with massive firepower to replace Huey gunships. In view of the success with armed UH-1B gunships since 1962, Army leaders began their search for the behemoth in 1964. Even after Army staff selected Bell's Cobra as its first pure gunship, they sought a large gunship with firepower surpassing that of the Cobra; both were considered interim escort gunships pending the arrival of the ultimate gunship, the Cheyenne. The large gunship concept was opposed by the Commander in Chief, Pacific and the Joints Chief of Staff, not to mention the Air Force, which bristled over any Army plan that hinted at infringement of its tactical domain. All had recommended, as an alternative, expanding the use of fixed-wing aircraft for close support. But the Army, like the Marines, knew what was best for its ground troops.

Some of the support for the ACH-47A came from the grunts' lack of endearment for aerial rocket artillery, especially the ARA's reliance upon notoriously inaccurate rockets. Other helicopter types were tested for the gunship escort role, but the Chinook was coming on line and showed promise as a powerful lifter.

Having examined the Army's concept, Boeing Vertol in June 1965 submitted a formal proposal for modifying 11 CH-47As into gunships. The contract was signed one week later and on 2 July the first test Chinook, S/N 64-13145, was diverted from the production line for conversion to the prototype A/ACH-47A. The payload capacity of the CH-47A allowed Boeing engineers a great deal of latitude in selecting armament systems, ammunition loads, and armor protection. Numerous systems were considered, including manned turrets, miniguns, cannon, grenade launchers, rockets, and stub wings for mounting various combinations of weapons.

After careful study, the optimum mix of weapons was chosen. An XM-5 40mm grenade launcher with 500 rounds of ammunition was mounted on the nose, while M-60 or M2 .50-cal. crew-operated machine guns occupied five stations—forward right side, forward left escape hatch, two rear fuselage waist windows, and the rear cargo ramp. The rear overhead cargo door was removed to reduce weight and expand the rearward field of fire, plus, the four gun window openings were enlarged. The .50s, which were favored for their heavier punch, were belt-fed from ammunition bins of 1,000 rounds each.

Attached to the end plate of each 30-inch stub wing was an M24A1 20mm cannon, which was belt-fed from an 800-round ammunition container in the cabin. Mounted below each stub wing was an XM-10 bomb shackle, which could accept either an XM-159B/C 19-tube rocket launcher, or an XM-18 system containing a minigun rated at 3,000 spm. Total weight of the armament package with ammunition was 3,000 pounds.

The conversion to gunship meant that troop seats, the cargo hook, winch, heater, and soundproofing material were removed for weight reduction; however, a hefty 2,681 pounds was built back into the aircraft in the form of full torso pilot armor seats, and armor plate added inside the aircraft and externally under the nose section and on rotor pylons.

The gunships were powered by uprated 2,850-shp Lycoming T55-L-7 turbine engines for maximum performance, which, for a fully loaded gunship, matched that of a standard CH-47A. Carrying a combat crew of eight, plus full fuel and ordnance loads, the ACH-47A's maximum gross weight was 31,600 pounds. It cruised at 125 knots and gained five knots with its ammunition load expended. The prototype made its first flight on 6 November 1965, with delivery made to the Army the following month. Number 145 was first weapon tested at Aberdeen Proving Ground, and relocated to Fort Benning for unit training in March 1966. Two months earlier at Fort Benning, the Field Evaluation Detachment (Special/CH-47/Provisonal) had been established. On 19 April the unit became the 53rd Aviation Detachment, Field Evaluation (Provisional). By that time, the remaining three aircraft had arrived, a drastic reduction from the 11 airframes originally ordered. This was due to budget constraints.

In May, three of the ACH-47As were shipped to Vietnam: S/N 64-13149, nicknamed "Easy Money"; 64-13151, nicknamed "Stump Jumper"; and 64-13154, nicknamed "Birth Control." While the trio underwent combat evaluation, the first aircraft would remain at Edwards AFB for advanced tests. Combat testing was to last six months, with the first three months at Vung Tau and the remainder at An Khe, home of the 1st Cavalry Division. The 53rd Aviation Detachment came under the 10th Aviation Group, while the ACTIV closely monitored gunship evaluation.

The 53rd, which had become better known as "Guns A-Go-Go," rode a wave of success, destroying every target its ACH-47As encountered. The gunship Chinooks were, however, ill fated, and the first would fall during the evaluation period. On 5 August, number 151 Stump Jumper collided with another Chinook while ground taxiing, and was destroyed. The gunship left behind in the States, number 145, was prepared for shipment to Vietnam as a replacement. Meanwhile, the detachment underwent intense combat trials supporting the 1st Cavalry Division, the Royal Australian Task Force, IV Corps, and the 1st and 25th Infantry Divisions. One of the test missions had the gunships fly into the swath of destruction left by B-52 Arc Light missions. Enemy emplacements sometimes survived the carpet-bombing and Guns A-Go-Go was deemed sufficiently armed and protected to venture into the zone to finish the job.

Besides the Guns A-Go-Go emblem on the rotor pylon, number 64-13145 wears the name "Crazy 8," barely visible forward of the gun position. It would be renamed Cost of Living. Armor plating attached to the rotor pylon protected vital components, while body armor panels were laid in the chin windows. The XM-5 grenade launcher's ammunition chute passed through the cockpit to storage containers in the forward cabin. (Roy Benson)

An XM-18 minigun pod and a 20mm cannon on the gunship Chinook's right side provided the crew with both area cover fire and standoff capability against anti-aircraft guns. Both systems had first been tested on the Huey. (U.S. Army)

The ACH-47A's five machine gun positions gave it a 360-degree field of fire. Side-facing .50-cal. gun stations were designated XM-32 systems, while the rear loading ramp position was the XM-33. Number 64-13154 later would have screens attached to its engine intakes. The gunship was shot down and destroyed during the Battle of Hue in February 1968. (U.S. Army)

Kaman's H-2 Tomahawk gunship, evaluated during late 1965, featured twin turrets housing 7.62mm machine guns. Both could operate in synch or independently to provide vast coverage of targets. The nose doors are opened to reveal drive and feed components of the turrets. Attached to each stub wing is an XM-159 rocket launcher. Breakaway aerodynamic covers for the launchers are on the ground. (U.S. Army)

When Sikorsky competed against Bell and Kaman for the Army's interim gunship, the job went to the company S-61A demonstrator seen here firing 4.5-inch artillery rockets. Four launcher units were mounted to the aircraft, two on each side, for a total of 40 rockets. (Igor I. Sikorsky Historical Archives, Inc.)

At the end of the test period in December 1966, the gunship Chinooks were renamed 1st Aviation Detachment (Provisional) and attached to the 228th Assault Support Helicopter Battalion (ASHB) of the 1st Cavalry Division at An Khe. That month also marked the arrival of number 145, which had been nicknamed "Cost of Living." The assignment proved controversial since the gunships taxed the 228th, whose pilots were flying excessive hours due to a severe pilot shortage.

On the plus side, the enemy quickly discovered that Chinooks no longer were large, easy targets. Unable to distinguish at a distance between standard CH-47s and heavily armed versions, the enemy became reluctant to shoot at them. Even the dreaded radar-controlled quad .51-cal. anti-aircraft gun could not stand up to the ACH-47A's 20mm cannon. Two gunships flew a daisy chain pattern, using their range of weapons to keep targets under merciless fire. Ground troops were awe-struck at the Guns A-Go-Go firepower, making them the favored close support aircraft.

Tragically, the ACH-47A's most effective weapon was responsible for the loss of number 149 "Easy Money". On 5 May 1967, while in a gun run, a retention pin on one of the aircraft's cannons vibrated loose, allowing the gun to elevate and fire into the forward rotors. "Easy Money" crashed, killing all aboard. The two remaining ACH-47As continued flying, while working bugs out of the weapon systems and refining tactics. One of the enemy's favorite tactics was to "bear hug" ground troops, closing the distance to the extent that supportive fire was ineffective. Guns A-Go-Go crews, however, had proven skillful at placing cannon and heavy machine gun fire on enemy troops close to friendly units. This proved embarrassing to aerial rocket artillery units, and spelled trouble for the gunship Chinooks.

The death knell for the Chinook gunship program sounded on 22 February 1968, when number 154 Birth Control was downed by numerous hits while flying support of the battle to recapture Hue during the Tet Offensive. Cost of Living landed while exchanging gunfire with advancing enemy, and rescued the downed crew. Before the area could be secured to retrieve the downed gunship, it was destroyed by mortar fire. Since the Army would not allow an ACH-47A to operate alone, and every Chinook was needed for transport, the ACH-47A program was canceled. Cinching the demise of Guns A-Go-Go was the ever-increasing number of Cobra gunships in the combat theater. The remaining ACH-47A sat out the war as a maintenance trainer at Vung Tau.

Competitors

Two other gunship designs that were considered along with the gunship Chinook also ended up competing with Bell's Cobra helicopter. During the 1960s, helicopter manufacturers, in anticipation of military needs and to keep up with competitors, experimented with and offered weapon kits.

Keenly aware of the Army's interest in gunship designs, Kaman Aircraft Corporation developed a gunship version of its UH-2 Seasprite. Initial tests with Kaman's Seasprite in 1963 to determine its suitability in the Army environment received poor marks. However, two years later, Kaman presented a refined gunship version, which differed significantly from the Navy UH-2. Called the H-2 Tomahawk, the gunship featured stub wings for mounting rocket launchers, along with twin nose turrets, each housing two 7.62mm machine guns. The turrets fired in synch or independently, and could be fired by either pilot. Modifications included a liberal amount of armor protection for the cockpit, engine, transmission, and fuel tanks. The Tomahawk's T58-GE-8 engine, rated at 1,250 shp, allowed a gross weight of 9,000 pounds and a top speed of 162 mph. In Army livery, yet wearing Navy Bureau Number (BuNo) 149785, the Tomahawk competed against Bell's Cobra and Sikorsky's S-61 at Edwards AFB, California, during November and December 1965. The machine fared better than its initial showing; however, it lost to the Cobra design.

Completing the triad was Sikorsky's S-61A, which was fast becoming popular as a military and civilian transport. Prior to the competition at Edwards, Sikorsky had successfully demonstrated its armed S-61A during Army exercises. Sikorsky used its demonstrator, registered N318Y, in a variety of armed configurations, most of which were add-ons to the large aircraft. Its size and twin-turbine engine power, however, gave rise to Sikorsky's claim, "As a weapon system, this aircraft can be armed with more artillery than present COIN helicopters." There was truth in advertising, for the S-61A could carry 40 4.5-inch rockets in four launchers, two on each side, along with a supply of 70 rockets in the cabin. The S-61A's size was also touted as an advantage by being less vulnerable to ground fire than smaller helicopters. Also publicized were the aircraft's dynamic components being high on the airframe, with pilots protected by the airframe, tub structure, electronics, and flooring. Engines were separated by a firewall, and were fed by independent fuel systems, each having fireproof lines and pumps. Armor could be added without significantly decreasing performance.

Besides the large rockets, an armament package offered by Sikorsky included a nose-mounted 7.62mm minigun turret, which was flanked by a quad-60 on each side of the nose, a 20mm M61 cannon under the fuselage to provide a 360-degree field of fire, and fixed-forward or manually swiveling .50-cal. M-3 machine guns in waist positions. An XM-159 rocket launcher was to occupy the left side of the fuselage. A Pontiac 20mm M61 cannon rated at 1,500 spm, and NAKA launchers, which fired 66 1.5-inch, half-pound rockets, were also made available. Although Bell's Cobra was deemed the most maneuverable and most suitable candidate for the gunship mission, despite their cancellation as gunship proposals, both the Sikorsky S-61A and Kaman H-2 went on to establish long and remarkable service histories.

Snakes

Although UH-1B and C model Hueys in Vietnam did a credible job of providing armed escort, the increasing weight of improved weapon systems in the hot, humid climate, along with the speed of transport helicopters, stymied even the best gunship pilots. The fact remained that these were utility helicopters with weapons systems added. The need for a pure attack helicopter was never clearer. An aircraft designed specifically for attack had to be agile and possess great firepower to assume the armed escort role, and free Hueys for medevac and troop transport. Helicopter manufacturers and U.S. military officials alike had watched the 15-year-long French experience in Indochina and Algeria, knowing full well that helicopter developments and military needs would become unavoidably intertwined.

As early as 1958, studies had been done at Bell and models built of a slim helicopter that made use of the Huey's drive and rotor systems. Designated Bell's Model D-245 and unofficially called the Warrior, the design incorporated swept stub wings and a gun in a nose fairing. Noteworthy was the sleek design's slender canopy covering a tandem seating arrangement, which would become the standard of gunships for years to come. Bell went so far as to call the D-245 a Combat Reconnaissance Helicopter to suggest association with the Army's 7292nd Aerial Combat Reconnaissance Company. But the Army wasn't buying it; with no tried and true doctrine governing attack helicopters, support for the concept fizzled.

Undaunted, Bell continued self-funded research and work on an attack helicopter that made use of Huey components. The company completed in secret a full-scale mockup of a gunship design, which was revealed to the Army in June 1962. Labeled the Model D-255 Iroquois Warrior, the design incorporated the trademark tandem stepped seating, stub wings, a nose turret, and a streamlined ventral cannon pod. Attached to the futuristic fuselage was the familiar UH-1B tail boom. The craft's

Bell's continuation of studies during the late 1950s and early 1960s to attain the optimum gunship design resulted in this Model D-261, which featured a pusher propeller. Bell submitted this design, along with its D-262, in the AAFSS competition. (Ned Gilliand Collection)

Bell unveiled its revolutionary Model D-255 Iroquois Warrior mockup in 1962 as its second contender to garner Army interest in a pure gunship. Although the program was temporarily shelved, the design served as the basis for other designs that evolved into the famed HueyCobra. (Bell Helicopter)

Bell test pilots Donald Bloom (rear) and David Lively demonstrate the D-255 mockup in 1963. Besides the spurious serial number 62-00255, the mockup wore military designation HU-1F, and an Iroquois Warrior emblem. The vertically tiered cockpit arrangement, with gunner/copilot in the front and pilot in the rear, would become the standard for attack helicopters. (Ned Gilliand Collection)

The Model 207 Sioux Scout was the result of brain-storming by a group of Bell test pilots and engineers in response to Secretary of the Army's challenge and rigid design requirements for an attack helicopter. Apparent in the 207 is Bell's experience with its Model 47 and gunship mockups. Except for being underpowered, the Scout was a huge success. (Bell Helicopter)

Bell's D-262 mockup for the AAFSS competition was displayed with dummy SS-11 missiles and a minigun in the nose. Its tail boom was the same used on the UH-1B Huey. (Ned Gilliand Collection)

In 1963, Bell's Model 207 was tested with various wing styles after undergoing ground tests without wings. Since the 207 was somewhat a secret project, it was painted white to avert attention from its role as a gunship demonstrator. (Ned Gilliand Collection)

The Sioux Scout's gunner/copilot accessed the cockpit by means of a hinged canopy and collapsible gun sight. This design pioneered the use of armchair flight controls and the TAT-101 machine gun turret. (Ned Gilliand Collection)

slender profile not only presented a smaller head-on target, it offered excellent visibility and aerodynamic qualities.

While the mockup was met with mixed reaction, the Secretary of the Army temporarily shelved the armed helicopter program, challenging manufacturers with newly established technical requirements. His increase of the speed requirement from 155 to 200 knots divided the house into two design philosophies: Bell's new single-purpose gunship, and modifying existing airframes into gunships. This would be an interim machine pending design of a much-advanced helicopter. Meanwhile, a group of Bell test pilots and engineers, knowing that to stay ahead in the game required a proactive approach, in late December 1962 decided to design a flying demonstrator to show what a gunship could do. The brainstorming group came up with a relatively compact machine that combined Bell's proven OH-13S and Model 47J-2, which were reshaped into a slimmer, vertically tiered body that minimized drag and offered all-around visibility.

Called Bell's Model 207 Sioux Scout, the aircraft was powered by a supercharged Lycoming TVO 435-B1A piston engine that delivered 220 hp. Its 37-foot-diameter main rotor came from the OH-13S, while a modified tail rotor, transmission, center section, and tail boom were from the 47J-2. The Sioux Scout had a maximum weight of

3,000 pounds, it cruised at 95 mph, and had a top speed of 125 mph. The multi-purpose stub wings eased rotor loads, had 12 hard points for external stores, and served as a "wet wing" containing 43 gallons of fuel that allowed a range of more than 200 miles.

The Sioux Scout pioneered the use of side-arm controls for the gunner in the front seat. Dual hydraulics was installed, and a unique fuselage combined box beams and honeycomb panels to create a rigid structure. This durable construction feature proved ideal for dampening vibration and minimizing turret recoil, and was carried over into future gunship design.

The Model 207 introduced Emerson Electric's TAT-101, which contained two 7.62mm machine guns. The privately funded turret was a modification of the M-60C gun unit and would qualify for the Marine UH-1E. A total of 1,100 rounds of ammunition were carried for the turret, which traversed 100 degrees sideways, 15 degrees upward, and 45 degrees downward; 2.75-inch rockets in 6-tube, horizontally arranged launcher units could be carried under the wings.

When the Sioux Scout lifted off from Texas soil on 27 June 1963, it became the first pure gunship in the free world to fly. After work on the aircraft was completed the following month, it underwent 65 hours of flight tests, followed by weapon tests at Fort Sill, Oklahoma. Beginning in November, the aircraft was taken on a tour of U.S. Army bases where scores of military and NASA evaluators put the Scout through its paces, logging more than 300 hours on its airframe, and firing 83,500 rounds of ammunition through its guns. Especially important was a month-long evaluation in 1964 by B Troop, 3rd Squadron, 17th Cavalry, 11th Air Assault Division. Besides being underpowered, only the reliability of the turret was found lacking. The overwhelming recommendation by the evaluators was that the Army develop a turbine-powered version that was more heavily armed.

That made good sense to the Army staff, who, in early 1964 began formulating specifications for the advanced helicopter the Secretary envisioned. Under a program called Advanced Aerial Fire Support System (AAFSS), major aircraft firms were invited to submit design proposals. As manufacturers concentrated on the advanced design, less attention was given to the interim design. Convinced that an interim aircraft would be needed due to the time and money the AAFSS would require, Bell engineers went back to their D-255 design. Deciding that it was too large for the T53 engine installation, it was made smaller and its canopy redesigned into a two-section arrangement, undoubtedly to give the pilot in the rear cockpit greater visibility. The design, now labeled the D-262, was rejected by the Army early in 1965, but Bell officials doggedly stayed on with the project.

That year, the situation in Vietnam had worsened to the extent that GEN William C. Westmoreland advised the Pentagon that an immediate AAFSS or an interim measure was urgently needed. The Army was now faced with a decision to halt the AAFSS program, lower its requirements, or select a suitable type for swift production. Bell was in the perfect position, having secretly refined the company-funded D-262 into its Model 209, the mockup of which was completed in March 1965. Not until the project was more than half completed did Bell leak to one Army official what they were building. That individual was GEN George P. Seneff, a strong proponent of the gunship who overcame stiff opposition to persuade senior Army commanders that the Cobra was vital. In August 1965, the "Bush Board," led by COL Harry L. Bush, was convened to study and select the interim design. When the board officially announced that it was seeking an interim armed helicopter, Bell immediately proposed its Model 209.

The Model 209, like the D-255 and D-262, featured the same sleek, tiered-cockpit fuselage. A 1,100-shp T53-L-11 engine drove the same transmission and rotor system of the UH-1C. Such commonality, which significantly reduced production time, maintenance, and costs, included the C Model's tail boom and tail rotor. Stub wings generated some lift, but more importantly, bore ordnance. To save weight, a Stability Control Augmentation System (SCAS) had replaced Bell's trademark stabilizer bar.

After much discussion, it was decided that the Cobra would have retractable skids. Bell official Cliff Kalista said, "The retractable landing gear was one of the keys to the sale of the HueyCobra. It was put on originally to give the ship sex appeal." The penalty for such appeal, however, was heavy, in terms of complexity, cost, and weight. And everyone, including the Army, knew it would only be a matter of time before a pilot landed with the gear retracted. But the unique skids remained and would later pay dividends as a bargaining tool. Besides under-wing munitions, armament consisted of a single GAU-2B/A 7.62mm minigun in an Emerson Electric turret with 4,000 rounds of ammunition.

Competing proposals for the interim gunship came from Sikorsky with its S-61A, Kaman with its UH-2A Tomahawk, Boeing Vertol's ACH-47A Chinook, and Piasecki's Model 16H-1A Pathfinder. The UH-2A and S-61A competed against the gunship ACH-47A Chinook in the concurrent heavy gunship program, while the Piasecki 16H-1A was a stand-alone project. It was the subject of two years of proprietary experimentation with a compound rotorcraft, which came under sponsorship of an Army-Navy test program in 1964. The Pathfinder sported wings in addition to its rotor system, and featured a shrouded propeller in its tail for propulsion. Under Army contract, it was to be tested at speeds up to 230 mph, making it a natural for consideration as a gunship. However, the one to watch, as Bell officials knew, was Kaman, whose engineers were pushing to get their UH-2A up to the 200-knot speed mark.

Among the entries, only Bell's Model 209 and Piasecki's Pathfinder were completely new airframes. The 209 was rolled out and made its first flight on 7 September 1965, three weeks ahead of schedule. On 25 October, it

The first Cobra, the Model 209, was the culmination of Bell's many gunship designs. The retractable skid gear of the 209 was more an aesthetic feature than for speed. Bell engineers knew that with the gear "sucked up," the 209 would have greater sales potential. The ventral tail fin, thought necessary for directional control, was later eliminated. (Bell Helicopter)

Given its size and ability to carry numerous weapon systems, Sikorsky's S-61A was a repeat entry in Army attack helicopter competitions. Here, in rare Olive Drab livery, the S-61A prototype fires an XM-18 minigun unit for the interim gunship competition. Although it never served the Army in an armed capacity, numerous S-61 variants went on to serve successful careers. (Igor I. Sikorsky Historical Archives, Inc.)

In the interim gunship competition, Piasecki entered its Model 16H-1A Pathfinder. Although it showed promise as the fastest of all proposals, it was eliminated from the competition. Wings and a shrouded pusher propeller gave the Pathfinder speeds easily exceeding 200 mph. (Steve Williams)

flew at a sustained speed of 200 mph, breaking the world speed record of 180.1 mph for a helicopter in its weight class. In that same month, Boeing Vertol's ACH-47A and Piasecki's 16H-1A were eliminated from consideration. The odds were turning in favor of the Cobra.

In November, the three remaining contenders flew comparative tests at Edwards AFB, followed by weapon tests at Fort Sill. Since nothing was allowed into production without approval from commanders in the combat theater, the Model 209 was shipped by transport aircraft to Vietnam. There, the 1st Cavalry Division placed it under scrutiny and gave it firm approval after putting it through its paces. The First Team's commander, GEN John J. Tolson, did, however, insist that the 209's L-11 engine be replaced by the L-13. After the Army accepted the Huey Cobra, Congressional approval would come only after Bell agreed to reduce its cost by trimming non-essential items. The retracting skids were immediately raised as an issue and Bell happily agreed to replace them with fixed skid gear.

Finally, on 11 March 1966, the Army announced that the Model 209 was the winner. Within three weeks a development contract, along with a production order for 10 machines, were awarded. Bell Vice President Phil Norwine said, "Between April of 1966 and August of 1967, we completed development, testing, qualification, and manufactured and delivered the first Cobras to the Army in time for them to train pilots and get the helicopters into action in August 1967."

Meanwhile, the best estimates told that the first AAFSS could not be fielded until the late 1960s. Primary entrants in the competition included Sikorsky's S-66 and Lockheed's CL-840 (AH-56), both of which featured pusher propellers to boost speed. Although Bell's Model D-262 did not have the prop, Bell also entered its Model D-261, which did have a pusher propeller mounted in mid-fuselage; however, it did not go beyond the design stage. Unique among the push propeller designs was Sikorsky's Rotoprop tested on the same demonstrator S-61A (N318Y) entered in the interim gunship competition. A conventional tail rotor mounted on the tail pylon swiveled 90 degrees in three seconds to become a thrust propeller. A quad 7.62mm gun turret was mounted to the nose, along with a 40mm grenade launcher turret or 20mm XM12 (M61) cannon. Although the aircraft was eliminated from the AAFSS competition, Sikorsky used the demonstrator as the basis for its S-67. On 16 March 1965, number N318Y became the first helicopter from which a minigun was fired.

Wearing tan and green camouflage, the Model 209 went on to serve as a test platform for a 30mm turret in 1969. The first Cobra also mounts dummy TOW missiles and an associated nose sighting unit. (Bell Helicopter)

What's in a name? The Model 209's first in-house moniker had been HeliCobra, after Bell's P-39 Airacobra of World War II fame. To Bell employees, it was known simply as Ship 1, but to the Army, Bell's Model 209 became AH-1G, for Attack Helicopter, Type 1, seventh in the Huey series. The Army didn't sanction the name Cobra until 16 March 1967. The name identified the Huey gun platoon of the 114th Aviation Company in Vietnam. A Bell representative visiting the unit liked the name and dubbed the 209 the Cobra on his return. Since the name Huey had become popular for the utility helicopter from which the gunship was derived, Army aviation pioneer GEN Hamilton Howze suggested HueyCobra. Bell officials dropped the idea of copyrighting the name Huey when the Army pointed out it couldn't use HueyCobra if the first portion of the name was copyrighted. So it formally became HueyCobra, the first major deviation from the Army's practice of naming aircraft after Native Americans and woodland animals.

Production of the AH-1G brought changes, the most significant of which was compliance with GEN Tolson's insistence that the L-11 engine be replaced by the 1,400-shp L-13. Despite the engine's additional 300 shp, it weighed only 36 pounds more, and was more fuel efficient. Also important was self-sealing fuel tanks, armor shields to protect vital components, and armored seats. The AH-1G cruised at 166 mph, with its dive speed topping out at 220 mph. A 247-gallon fuel capacity allowed a range of 362 miles at an operating weight of 6,070 pounds. Maximum takeoff weight was 9,500 pounds and its service ceiling was 12,700 feet.

Two pre-production machines were built and assigned serial numbers 66-15246 and -15247. The first underwent armament trials at Fort Hood, Texas, and the second was used mainly for evaluating the SCAS.

Built into the Cobra's nose was an Emerson Electric TAT-102A turret with a GE M-134 7.62mm minigun rated at 4,000 spm. It was replaced during production by a TAT-141 turret, which used an M28A1 system incorporating a GAU-2B/A minigun and an M-129 40mm grenade launcher, or two of each. A total of 4,000 rounds were carried for each minigun, which fired at 2,000 or 4,000 spm in six-second bursts; 231 rounds were carried for the grenade

The Model 209 demonstrates the gunner's sighting position and the turret minigun ammunition bay. Dual landing lights in the nose would later be replaced by a retractable light in the aircraft's belly. (Ned Gilliand Collection)

The Model 209 displayed at Le Bourget Airport, Paris, on 3 June 1967, complete with retracting skid gear and rocket launchers. Markings added for the tour included "Bell HueyCobra" on the nose, airshow registration code H-188, and a snake motif on the tail fin designed by Army CPT Robert R. Matlick of the New Equipment Training Team (NETT). The spurious serial number, 47015, suggested an alliance between Bell and the Army. (Author's Collection)

Pilot's cockpit of the production AH-1G HueyCobra, this being S/N 66-15283. The position was a practical layout that gave the pilot good visibility. (Bell Helicopter)

A number of early model AH-1Gs, including the first production aircraft, were converted to TAH-1Gs by installing full controls and instruments in the front cockpit. Turret weapons were faired over. Army trainer aircraft, traditionally, wear large white codes and panels painted International Orange. (Hugh Mills)

Not all Cobras were armed or painted Olive Drab. This was the fifth-built AH-1G (S/N 66-15250). Cobras assigned to test units or the 120th Aviation Company "Arctic Knights" in Alaska wore this high visibility scheme. The black rectangle under the fuselage is a flush-mounted radio altimeter antenna. (Bell Helicopter)

This AH-1G (S/N 66-15283) wears test instrumentation atop its rotor mast. Attached to the bottom of the XM-200 rocket launcher is an XM-8 smoke dispenser. The unit held 12 smoke grenades, which were used for marking targets or laying smoke screens. The last two digits of the aircraft constructor number, 2039, are on the rotor pylon. Seats later had side armor panels added. (Bell Helicopter)

launcher, which was rated at 450 spm. The Cobra's stub wings, which spanned 9 feet 4 inches, were stressed to carry heavy weapon systems on four stations. At least two rocket launchers were always carried, and, initially, were often paired with podded 1,500-round XM-18 SUU-11A/A miniguns. When the dual gun turret came on line, four rocket pods became the favored load. An LAU-10/A 4-tube, 5-inch Zuni rocket launcher was available, but rarely used.

To make the Cobra's bite even more lethal, it was given standoff capability against large anti-aircraft weapons with a 20mm cannon introduced during late 1968. The system, which was called the XM-35, used a modified six-barrel M61A1 Vulcan cannon designated the M195, which had a firing rate of 750 spm. The gun occupied the left inboard station, with ammunition fed from saddlebag containers attached to both sides of the fuselage. Each container held 450 rounds, with 50 held in a crossover chute connecting the two. Heavy panels were added to the fuselage to prevent muzzle blast damage, and structural strengthening of the wing and transmission mounts was necessary.

Few changes were made during Cobra production. Beginning in 1967, the dual nose landing light was changed to a single, retractable unit located in the belly, immediately behind the turret. Other changes were based on lessons learned in the combat theater. Since experience showed that the Cobra's tall tail fin was sensitive to tail winds, especially in a hover, directional control was improved by relocating the tail rotor to the tail fin's right side during the late 1960s.

Prior to deliveries of the first Cobras, which began in June 1967, the AH-1G NETT was formed, whose 36 combat-experienced members began training at Bell in April 1966. Fifty members strong, with specialists from Bell, Emerson Electric, and Lycoming, the NETT set up shop with 12 Cobras at Bien Hoa Air Base, South Vietnam, in August 1967. Six of the aircraft stayed with the NETT,

while the other six soon went to the "Playboys" gun platoon of the 334th AHC, also at Bien Hoa.

The first group of Playboy gunship drivers completed transition to the Cobra on 4 October, and on the 8th flew the first official combat mission. A pair of Snakes recorded seven sampans destroyed, and on another mission scored 13 enemy kills while supporting a combat assault by the 118th AHC. The Cobra had drawn its first blood one month earlier when number 66-15263, flown by CW2 John D. Thompson, attacked an enemy sampan to record the HueyCobra's first kill. Thompson's front seat copilot/gunner was 1st Aviation Brigade commander GEN George P. Seneff. The victory was especially rewarding for Seneff after having fought steadfastly for the Cobra.

The Cobra's arrival changed the face of helicopter combat operations, with Playboy crews writing the book about AH-1G tactics. New chapters were written as the Playboys performed the first medevac mission with a Cobra, and the platoon suffered the first loss of a Cobra. As more Cobras arrived in Vietnam, they were assigned to air cavalry troops, assault helicopter companies, aerial weapons companies, and aerial rocket artillery units.

Assault helicopter companies and air cavalry troops were similar in that they used Hueys for troop transport and a Cobra gun platoon for armed escort. Air cavalry units commonly paired AH-1Gs with OH-6A Scout helicopters to form "Hunter-Killer," or "Pink" teams. A two-Cobra section was called a "Red Team" or "Fire Team," which became a "Heavy Fire Team" with the addition of a third Cobra. The three gunship-equipped platoons of an aerial weapons company were given the more liberal job of providing firepower on call. The aerial rocket artillery battery, with three Cobra platoons, delivered heavy rocket fire in support of troops operating beyond ground artillery range. Cobras were not bound by their unit's basic mission—armed reconnaissance, armed escort, and close fire support was their forte, and they did their best to make that, and more, available to any unit that asked for it.

One of the first Cobras in Vietnam, number 66-15259, wore camouflage while assigned to the New Equipment Training Team (NETT). Few Vietnam-based AH-1Gs wore the scheme, which closely resembled that used on Air Force aircraft. (Floyd Werner Collection)

Each Cobra unit in Vietnam that used the popular shark mouth was identified by different styles of the ferocious marking. This marking was worn by the "Snakes" of D Troop, 1st Squadron, 10th Cavalry, called in Army parlance D/1/10. (William White)

Voodoo Lady was a rocket and minigun-armed AH-1G with the 11th Armored Cavalry Regiment in 1969. The Cobra's large slab fuselage sides provided ample room for artwork. (Manly Barton)

Like many Army helicopter combat units, the 1st Cavalry traces its lineage back to the early nineteenth century Indian Wars when it was called "Dragoons." That history was kept alive by respectfully naming aircraft and units after Native American tribes. This AH-1G belonged to A Troop, 7th Squadron, 1st Cavalry Regiment Blackhawks (A/7/1) in 1969. (Cespedes/Davis)

This AH-1G (S/N 67-15674) belonged to 2/20th ARA. Seen at Tay Ninh in 1971, it is armed with a Heavy Hog configuration of four XM-159 rocket launchers. Besides the name "Murder Inc.," it wears its call sign "Blue Max 33" in the unit geometric marking, and the 2/20 emblem on the rotor pylon, popularly called the Dog House. The Cobra was lost at An Loc in May 1972. (Author)

The yellow square with pilot's call sign, Peacemaker Two-One, identifies B Troop, 1st Squadron, 9th Cavalry, 1st Cavalry Division. The unit's crossed saber design on the nose is repeated on the dog house. Dual landing lights in the nose mark this as an early production AH-1G. (George Sullivan)

While assigned to D Company, 227th AHB, 1st Cavalry Division, number 69-16442 wore a "Mister Olds" caricature as a play on its serial number. Mister Olds was based on the popular Oldsmobile 442 muscle car. The crossover chute to supply the 20mm cannon from the right side ammunition container is visible below the fuselage. The bullet trap to save the minigun is secured to its barrels. (Rich Jalloway)

This AH-1G in 1970 wears a shark mouth similar to that painted on Cobras of C Troop, 16th Cavalry. Unusual is that the mouth does not incorporate the chin turret. An early modification had the nose landing light changed to a retractable type in the belly, seen extended on this aircraft. (Robert Brackenhoff)

This Cobra of C Troop, 1st Squadron, 9th Cavalry, 1st Cavalry Division carries both 7-tube and 19-tube rocket launchers. Painted on the hardback of the XM-158 rocket launcher are the words Pure Hell. (Manly Barton)

Four fully loaded XM-159 or XM-200 rocket launchers gave the Cobra 76 rockets for support missions. All cylindrical launchers featured locking rings for attaching breakaway fairings, which were seldom used operationally. (U.S. Army)

Weapon combinations and tactics varied according to the enemy situation, unit policy, and terrain. The Cobras normally engaged targets between 1,400 and 2,000 feet, beyond the effective range of most small arms fire. Since such altitudes reduced the Snake crew's reconnaissance ability, it was not unusual for crews to drop out of altitude and take on the enemy at much closer range. Where Huey pilots would never think to overfly a target during a gun run, Cobra pilots did it regularly, relying on the aircraft's speed and slim silhouette for safety. Enemy gunners became reluctant to fire on the "skinny" helicopter. A Viet Cong officer who fought in the 25th Infantry Division's area of operations (AO) had this to say about Cobras flown by the division's D Troop, 3rd Squadron, 4th Cavalry, commonly called Three-Quarter Cav:

"... the American's greatest success at that time was two armed helicopters from the 25th ... Cobras ... on the front of which were painted the teeth and red mouth of magical beasts ... just a glimpse of us and they swiveled their guns to shoot and kill instantly; many of our soldiers died ... we made dummies holding rifles so we could attract them and shoot at them ... we buried the victims of the red-headed beasts all in the same place as a warning to

everyone. There were 50 or 60 graves, one added every two or three days."

Three-Quarter Cav's "Centaurs", like most Cobra units, could not resist adding the famed shark mouth and eyes to the noses of their steeds. The ferocious markings not only became the Cobra's trademark, each unit was identified by its own rendition of the redheaded beast.

All-Cobra units typically operated between 9 and 12 AH-1Gs, while 8 assault helicopter companies flew between 4 and 6 Cobras. The three platoons of the 235th Aerial Weapons Company (AWC) flew fire teams mixed with UH-1Cs until January 1968, when it became the first all-Cobra unit, with eight assigned to each platoon. The following month, the 1st Cavalry Division took delivery of its first AH-1Gs. The 361st AWC "Pink Panthers" became the only Cobra unit committed to providing continuous support of classified Military Assistance Command Vietnam – Studies and Observation Group (MACV-SOG) cross-border missions.

As much as the Cobra's participation in the war solved problems, it created new ones. Pilots, who had flown the UH-1B and C and had become accustomed to crew chiefs and gunners, lamented the loss of those extra eyes, ears, and

HELICOPTER GUNSHIPS: DEADLY COMBAT WEAPON SYSTEMS

guns. In the Cobra's sealed cockpit, they found it difficult to detect ground fire and their visibility was limited. They had come to rely upon gunners who had nearly unlimited fields of fire. Even after amassing combat hours in the Cobra, some pilots remained partial to the security and cohesiveness of crewmen, keeping alive the Huey gunship versus Cobra argument. Vietnam's oppressive heat spiked temperatures in the cockpit unbearably high, prompting Bell to come up with a powerful air conditioner. Bell engineers had good intentions when they tinted the Cobra's canopy blue, but this was found to create dangerous conditions by reducing night vision and causing interior glare; canopies were quickly changed to clear glass.

John M. "Doc" Willingham, who flew Cobras in Vietnam and throughout the AH-1G's life, draws from his wealth of experience to provide insight into the Cobra's peculiarities:

"The original SCAS system was based upon small gyros in a box mounted on the bulkhead behind the pilot's seat. It sensed pitch, roll, and yaw, and applied compensation through small control hydraulic servos inline with the mechanical flight controls to enable the pilot to help stay aligned with the target, without a lot of pilot input. It was a 'pilot in the loop' system.

"My most memorable experiences were flying the AH-1G with the 20mm cannon. The ammo feed system from the right chute crossover rarely worked well so we loaded only the left ammo bay. The 20mm required a lot of electrical current to fire. The SCAS was low on the primary electrical bus and prone to vibration. When rolling in on a target and firing, the SCAS would kick off line, requiring large pedal input (the 20mm aircraft had tail rotor bias built into the SCAS). The canopy door would start vibrating open, requiring clinching the cyclic with knees and trying to get the right elbow on the canopy handle and finding the three SCAS engagement switches with the left hand. And the Cobra required the collective to be increased when recovering from an attack dive. I must have looked like a clown when firing the 20 and trying to juggle all the controls and cover the Loach and our troops on the ground, not to mention the reflection in the mirror of my FNG front-seat copilot's large eyeballs. Thank God I never hit any of our guys, even when they called for 'danger close.' The muzzle flashes from the bad guys always stopped when the 20 started firing. Same for the minigun in the turret.

"The solenoid that clicked shut to unload the live rounds of the 20mm sometimes didn't work, which resulted in a jam and stoppage. It was difficult to get the new part, so I would safety-wire the solenoid open, which resulted in wasted ammo, but didn't jam the cannon. I would always tell the pilot flying the aircraft after me. It worked, but wasted some ammo each time it was fired, as at least five rounds of live ammo were dumped overboard. I hated that when I was rolling in on target."

Details of the 20mm XM-35 cannon installation on the AH-1G. Some structural strengthening was necessary for the gun, along with muzzle blast panels to protect the fuselage below the canopy. Ammunition was stored in faired containers attached to both sides of the aircraft. (Hugh Mills)

Another Cobra pilot recalls when in 1969 a fellow pilot of D Company, 158th Aviation Battalion, 101st Airborne Division in Vietnam rolled his AH-1G 360 degrees, demonstrating the Cobra's fighter-like characteristics. Bob Andrews commented: "We didn't believe him. A few weeks later he showed us a film he had taken showing the flight instruments indicating a complete roll and the outside horizon turning 360 degrees. We thought the two pilots were lucky to have survived. Obviously, they didn't show our company commander or our unit instructor pilot the film."

Graham Stevens served three tours in Vietnam, most of which was spent flying Cobras. In late 1969, his unit received the first operational XM-35 20mm system. He shares his recollection of the gun:

"As luck would have it, my new home would be at Bien Hoa in the world famous 334th Aerial Weapons Company. This was like being assigned to Eddie Rickenbacker's 'Hat in the Ring' squadron of WWI. Very prestigious. The 334th was the first fully armed helicopter unit in Vietnam; hence their slogan, 'First With Guns.'

"The gun was basically a modified M61A1 Vulcan with shorter barrels and a declutching feeder. It automatically cleared itself of all live rounds at the end of each burst. The gun was pilot-controlled, but controls were provided so either the pilot or gunner could fire the weapon. The gun's firing rate was 750 spm and sighting was accomplished using the M73 reflex sight. Although the 20mm system brought a lot of firepower to an engagement with the enemy, the first system did, to say the least, have some quirky features. The system used electrically primed ammunition, versus a percussion cap like other types. The weapon was fixed for forward fire only.

"The major trade-off of the system was that it was very heavy, and difficult and time-consuming to load. Crews then rearmed their own aircraft at Forward Area Rearm Points. Crews would first re-fuel, and then hover over and rearm. Based on how much time you had, you might only rearm with 7.62 minigun and rockets. The 40mm and the 20mm took longer to load. Because of the M35 system's weight fully loaded, the aircraft carried only three seven-shot rocket pods. Everything with regards to gunships is about gross weight and trade-offs. Do you want to carry more ammo? Then it might require less fuel. Do you want to remain on station to provide support for a longer time? Then you won't be able to carry as much armament.

"The best engagement technique for the M35 was the use of enfilade fire, which aligns the long axis of the aircraft with the long axis of your target, using the tail rotor pedals to make small adjustments. The weapon was deadly and accurate. The approximately 5-meter bursting radius of HE ammunition could easily decimate bunkers, and sampans as well. Along the rivers and canals, or in the rice fields during the monsoon period, the enemy would sink their sampans by day and refloat them at night. They would remove all their cargo and equipment from the sampans and put them up on platforms at overnight stops. The OH-6A scout aircraft, however, could always find

During a "hot" rearm and refuel at Camp Evans in 1969, armorers load ammunition for the nose minigun of an AH-1G of D Company, 158th Aviation Battalion, 101st Airborne Division. Watching is pilot Capt. James Luscinski, who was shot down and killed near Quang Tri on 8 October 1969 while searching for his Cobra driver teammate, Robert Andrews. Andrews had crashed while covering the recovery of a downed Huey. His copilot was killed and Andrews, severely injured, spent five days on the ground before being rescued. (Robert T. Andrews)

these almost invisible trails. Once marked by smoke from the scouts, the deadly fire from the 20mm would ensure that the sampans and enemy soldiers wouldn't be making the voyage any farther."

The North Vietnamese Spring Offensive set the stage for the first Cobra-versus-armor confrontation. Credit for proving the Cobra's tank-busting ability is shared by D Troop, 1st Squadron, 1st Cavalry; F Troop, 4th Cavalry; F Troop, 9th Cavalry; and especially F Battery, 79th Field Artillery of the 1st Cavalry's 3rd Brigade. The latter is credited with destroying or incapacitating more than 20 armored vehicles, mainly with rockets. Among the battles sparked by the offensive, the battle at An Loc pitched Cobras against intense anti-aircraft fire, including heat-seeking SA-7 surface-to-air (SAM) missiles, necessitating

This was the first of two Army experiments to develop a night-fighting Cobra during the war. The device, called SMASH, for Southeast Asia Multi-Sensor Armament Subsystem for HueyCobra, used an AN/AAQ-5 FLIR on the nose and an Emerson Electric Moving Target Indicator Radar AN/APQ-137 on the right outboard wing shackle. The unit enabled the crew to detect, identify, and engage targets day or night. It could be used to direct-fire all onboard systems. The unit incorporated an Aerojet ElectroSystems AN/AAQ-5 passive IR system. (Ned Gilliand Collection)

Called the CONFICS, for Cobra Night Fire Control System, this is the second night-fighting system, which was developed by Frankford Arsenal from 1968 to 1970. Developed under the ENSURE 100 program to provide the AH-1G with night vision, the unit incorporated Low-Light-Level TV (LLLTV) for target acquisition and fire control. It was integrated with the M28A1 turret sighting system and included a searchlight for low light conditions. The project was disbanded due to its sensitivity to light and its inability to see through fog, haze, dust, and clouds. (Ned Gilliand Collection)

The Naval Ordnance Test Station, China Lake, California, often sponsored system evaluations for other services. For example, this Army Cobra from the first production batch was used at China Lake in April 1968 to test the feasibility of AH-1Gs carrying fuel-air explosives (FAEs). (Via Gary Verver)

hurried modification of the AH-1G's exhaust system. Initial attempts to line the exhaust with heat-reducing thermal elements proved ineffective and gave way to an upturned pipe that directed exhaust into the rotor-wash. The Cobra's infrared signature was reduced at the small cost of a slight reduction in performance and weight penalty. To counter SAM guidance systems, late in the war an ALQ-144 infra-red jamming unit was added to the upper engine cowlings of both Cobras and Hueys.

At the war's peak, nearly 700 Cobras were in Vietnam, serving more than 35 combat units. Nearly 300 AH-1Gs were lost, one third of which are attributed to operational, or non-combat, causes.

An AH-1G of the U.S. Naval Test Pilot School in 1975. Black-painted tail booms were common on Marine Cobras, a practice first used by HML-367 in Vietnam. A dummy turret holds ballast to avoid center-of-gravity shifts, and an instrumentation boom is attached to the nose. Marine helicopters typically wore their aircraft number in two locations. (Via Terry Love)

Cobras for the Marines

Ever committed to bonding its air and ground elements, the Marines closely watched the development of the Army's Cobra. In 1967, the Corps requested 72 AH-1Gs to equip a squadron in each of its three wings. Secretary of Defense McNamara overruled the Secretary of the Navy's approval, downgrading the order to 38 aircraft. Although assigned Navy BuNos 157204 through 157241, the Cobras retained their Army serial numbers since they were diverted from the Army production line.

The first five AH-1Gs arrived in February 1969 and went to Hunter Army Airfield, Georgia, for training Marine pilots. As more aircraft arrived, two were held for study of the attack helicopter, while the remaining Cobras were shipped to Vietnam, beginning in April. There, they joined UH-1Es and OV-10A Broncos of Marine Observation Squadron Two (VMO-2), 1st Marine Air Wing (MAW) at Marble Mountain Air Facility near Da Nang.

The first Cobra mission was flown on 18 April, and by December, VMO-2 had its full complement of 24 AH-1Gs. Marine evaluation reports paralleled those of the Army, extolling the Cobra's vast improvement over Huey gunships. Soon, Cobras were taking over UH-1E missions, freeing them for duties for which they were better suited. On 16 December 1969, Marine aviation units in Vietnam were reorganized, with all Cobras forming a new unit: Helicopter, Marine, Light (HML) Squadron 367.

True to their autonomous nature, The Marine Corps, although satisfied with the Army Cobra, wanted something different; something that was an even better fit. It wanted a Cobra with Marine avionics, a rotor brake for windy and fast-paced shipboard operations, a turret weapon that hit harder, and, most importantly, it wanted a

While assigned to the rotary-wing U.S. Naval Test Pilot School at NAS Jacksonville during the mid 1970s, this AH-1G (S/N 68-15194) wore a striking black and white scheme. (R. E. Kling)

Fitted with test instrumentation, the fourth AH-1J, BuNo 157760, leaves the confines of a ship's deck for sea trials. The Sea Cobra wears its constructor number on the rotor pylon. All AH-1Js were delivered to the Marine Corps painted flat Field Green. (Bell Helicopter)

This AH-1J's squadron code and aircraft number dictated the pilot's call sign, Scarface Two-Six. Seen at Marble Mountain Air Facility (MMAF), this Sea Cobra of HML-367 carries four LAU-68 rocket launchers. (Col James Sexton, USMC (Ret.)/Mike Wilson)

This weather-beaten Sea Cobra wearing a toothy grin comes aboard ship during the 1970s. A salt-water environment was not kind to aircraft components and winds across decks often made it difficult to bring helicopters aboard. (Author's Collection)

In a hasty attempt to tone down their Sea Cobra's high visibility markings for operations over North Vietnam in 1972, members of HMA-369 painted over the white of the national insignia and applied black hash marks to the white rocket launchers. Only two 5-inch Zuni rockets were carried in each launcher. (Rob Mignard)

Mounted to the wing of this AH-1J is a General Dynamics FIM-43 Redeye missile. The direct predecessor of the Stinger missile, the Redeye was test-fired from the Sea Cobra for the air-to-air role, but not qualified for operational use. Originally a shoulder-fired weapon, the heat-seeking Redeye was introduced during the mid 1960s. Seen to good advantage is the AH-1J's TwinPac engine installation. Grilles below the twin exhausts are for oil cooler radiators. (Bell Helicopter)

Cobra with two engines. The argument for the latter obviously was derived from the Marine mission being based on amphibious operations. Simply put, two engines were safer over water. Secondary reasons pointed to increases in performance and growth potential. Supporting the Marine argument were Navy safety records dating back to the Huey's arrival showing eight fatalities and three times that number injured from UH-1 engine related crashes.

The road to acquiring what would be called the AH-1J proved to be long and arduous. Marine officials were up against the Secretary of the Navy, Congress, and Secretary of Defense McNamara. Since McNamara could not fathom that fixed and rotary-wing aircraft worked hand-in-hand in the Marines, he insisted that for every helicopter acquired, a fixed-wing aircraft be relinquished. The practice of such trade-offs thrived throughout much of U.S. military history. Limited numbers of a single-engine

AH-1J were approved, but it wasn't until the North Vietnamese launched the 1968 Tet Offensive that the odds swung in favor of the twin-engine gunship. A number of UH-1Es lost or destroyed in the fighting had to be replaced, and it so happened that a twin-engine pack had become available from Pratt & Whitney of Canada. McNamara relented and diverted funds for the acquisition of 49 AH-1Js, which had been given the name Sea Cobra.

The expected controversy over the use of Canadian-built engines prompted an announcement of competition to engine manufacturers in the United States and Canada. Only two engine manufacturers—Pratt & Whitney's parent company United Aircraft of Canada and Continental Aviation and Engineering Corporation—submitted proposals for consideration. Since United Aircraft's entry was already in production, in August 1968 it was selected to power the Sea Cobra. When the first AH-1J was rolled out at Bell's plant on 14 October 1969, it proved to be nearly everything the Marines wanted, right down to its chin turret with three-barrel 20mm cannon. The aircraft made its first flight the following month.

Like its single-engine cousin, the larger Sea Cobra had commonality with the Huey line, and both crew positions were fit with flight and weapon controls. Maximum take-off weight was 10,000 pounds, and with the T400-CP-400 Twin-Pac rated at 1,800 shp, the Sea Cobra cruised at 155 mph and could dive at 190 mph. The AH-1J introduced the 20mm XM-197 cannon turret, which used a 750-round ammunition supply. For the wing stores stations, the Marines specified three basic armament loads for its Sea Cobra, depending upon the type of targets expected. The basic load comprised a pair of LAU-68 7-tube rocket launchers; the medium load had two SUU-11A minigun pods added inboard of the LAU-68s, and the heavy load consisted of four LAU-61A 19-tube rocket launchers. Attack squadrons would not be limited to these configurations. As more AH-1Js became available, the type became a fixture, along with the Army AH-1G, at Naval Ordnance Test Station (NOTS) China Lake, California, for testing a variety of weapons.

The first four Sea Cobras arrived at Naval Air Station (NAS) Patuxent River, Maryland, in July 1970 for Board of Inspection and Survey (BIS) trials, and the next seven arrived at VMO-1 at Marine Corps Air Facility (MCAF) New River, North Carolina, in September for crew and maintenance training. Four AH-1Js were offloaded from Air Force transports at Vietnam's Marble Mountain Air Facility on 18 February 1971.

For the next two months, the four aircraft underwent combat evaluation while assigned to HML-367. The aircraft were then shipped back to the United States and in July, the first of three attack squadrons, HMA-269, was formed with Sea Cobras at New River. Activation of the next Marine Helicopter Attack Squadron would find the Sea Cobra on its way back to the combat zone. In May 1972, soon after HMA-369 had been established on 1 April at MCAS Futenma, Okinawa, the squadron reported aboard amphibious transport USS *Denver* (LPD 9).

When all hands were aboard, the squadron commander played the song "Never Promised You a Rose Garden" over the loud speaker, and then announced that they were heading to a position off North Vietnam's coast near Tiger Island. Their mission, which was affiliated with *Operation Linebacker II* and code named *Operation MARHUK* (for "Marine Hunter Killer") would be to interdict supplies offloaded from Chinese and Soviet merchant ships, and attack anti-aircraft batteries and convoys.

Until January 1973, HMA-369 would fly seven AH-1Js, first from the *Denver* (LPD 9), and then from LPDs USS *Cleveland* (LPD 7) and USS *Dubuque* (LPD 8). The squadron, called *Pistol Pete* and later *Gunfighters*, also flew cover for downed aircrew and served as Forward Air Control for carrier aircraft. Missions ranged from 80

miles north of the Demilitarized Zone (DMZ) to 80 miles south of Hanoi. A two-ship formation flew during daylight, with the cannon used at low level, covered by a rocket-armed Sea Cobra flying as high bird; the two then reversed roles as they expended ammunition. Since night missions were flown blacked out, aircraft flew single-ship to avoid mid-air collisions.

Typical MARHUK armament loads were LAU-68 7-tube rocket launchers inboard with a mix of white phosphorous and high explosive rockets, while 4-tube LAU-10 5-inch Zuni rocket launchers occupied outboard stations. Each launcher, however, carried only two rockets to maintain balance and stay within weight limitations; depending upon rocket type, the 6-foot-long rocket weighed between 80 and 140 pounds.

After successful operations over the North, the squadron relocated to Okinawa, but remained active in the conflict, flying in support of the evacuation of Saigon.

A second contract brought the number of Marine Corps AH-1Js up to 69, the last of which left the production line in February 1975. Sea Cobra BuNos were 157757 through 157805 and 159210 through 159229. The Army serial numbers of the 38 AH-1Gs diverted to the Marine Corps are as follows:

67-15850	68-15085	68-15176	68-17066
68-15037	68-15104	68-15190	68-17070
68-15038	68-15105	68-15194	68-17082
68-15039	68-15112	68-15198	68-17086
68-15045	68-15113	68-15213	68-17090
68-15046	68-15114	68-17023	68-17101
68-15072	68-15134	68-17041	68-17105
68-15073	68-15140	68-17045	68-17108
68-15079	68-15165	68-17049	
68-15080	68-15170	68-17062	

Aeroscouts

Armament tests with scout helicopters during the late 1950s foreshadowed what would become a major element of Army airmobility in Vietnam. During the early tests, the Army's Research and Development office initiated a study called the Aircraft Development Plan, which outlined Army aviation doctrine and objectives for the next decade. One portion of the study was aimed at replacing the Cessna L-19 Bird Dog observation plane and piston-powered light observation helicopters with a small high performance, turbine-powered helicopter. The requirements for the Light Observation Helicopter (LOH) were rigid, and the industry-wide competition became embroiled in controversy.

Fourteen design proposals were eliminated, leaving Bell's OH-4A (Model D-250), Hiller's OH-5A, and Hughes' OH-6A (Model 369). Hughes' OH-6A was selected, having made its first flight on 27 February 1963. Each manufacturer was required to include in its design two armament kits for mounting dual 7.62mm machine guns or one 40mm grenade launcher. The Army supplied

Aircraft companies that competed in the Army's LOH competition were required to arm them with two weapon systems. Bell's entry was the OH-4A armed with a dual 7.62mm machine gun, which was balanced by a 40mm grenade launcher on the aircraft's right side. The OH-4A served as the basis for Bell's successful Model 206, the military version of which was the OH-58A. (Bell Helicopter)

The Hughes OH-6A prototype LOH initially was armed with the XM-7 system, which used two 7.62mm M-60C machine guns rated at 1,200 spm. (Hughes Aircraft Company)

To augment the firepower of the observer's M-60, a member of the Headquarters Company of the 1st Cav's 1st Brigade added this 3-tube rocket launcher to an OH-13S. It was used successfully for two weeks before it was spotted by a command officer and subsequently banned. Scout pilot Frank Vanatta poses with the rocket-armed Sioux at LZ Betty, Quang Tri in 1968. (Frank Vanatta Collection)

Hughes had both helicopter and armament expertise, which came together for the first time in Vietnam, when the OH-6A carried the XM27E1 minigun. This view of the weapon mounted on S/N 67-16326 of C/7/17 at Camp Holloway in 1972 illustrates how the system fully occupied the cabin area. During the war, Hughes built more than 1,000 minigun kits. The company's work with a lighter, simpler weapon led to the single-barrel chain gun, which was first fired in April 1973. (Steve Shepard/VHPA)

Getting a feel for a makeshift M134 minigun is Lt. Col. Kenneth P. Burton, commander of the 25th Aviation Battalion, 25th Infantry Division in 1968 and 1969. Col. Burton was known for his intense interest in improving tactics and aircraft systems. The minigun gave Loach crewmen of B Company Diamondheads tremendous firepower. Besides the unusual minigun, the 25th Avn Bn was involved with the Mortar Air Delivery system and dropping foo gas from Hueys. Troop D of Three-Quarter Cav, which was near the 25th at Cu Chi used a similar Loach minigun arrangement, suggesting that the units worked together to develop the weapon. (George Reese, Jr.)

the actual weapons, which were the XM-7 and XM-8, respectively. Neither would see operational use, however; tests with both led to development of the XM-27 minigun system tailored to the OH-6A. The gun, which fired at a rate of 2,000 or 4,000 spm, was mounted on the left side of the aircraft. Its 2,000-round ammunition container occupied the rear cabin area, and an XM-70 reflex sight was mounted above the right pilot's seat.

The nimble OH-6A, which was better known as the Loach, quickly earned a reputation as the hot rod of Army aviation. Pilots were in awe of its cruise speed of 145 mph and its responsiveness to control input. In addition, the Loach boasted an impressive power-to-weight ratio, it was built to survive, and its simple design required the least maintenance of any helicopter in the inventory. Less than six months before Loaches began rolling off the production line, one of nine YOH-6A prototypes during March and April 1966 broke 23 world records for speed, distance, and sustained altitude. The Loach proved to be the best helicopter that could be designed around a 250-hp engine. It earned high marks as a key participant in tests of the 11th Air Assault Division during early 1965, and in combat it would enhance its reputation far beyond expectations.

Although labeled an observation aircraft, the OH-6A, when armed with the XM-27 minigun system and a crewman's M-60 machine gun, easily qualified as a gunship. The Loach and its volunteer crew came to be known as "Aeroscouts," a fierce and bawdy lot, which the enemy came to fear and respect. Prior to the Loach's arrival in Vietnam, piston-powered Bell OH-13S Sioux and Hiller OH-23G Ravens pioneered aerial reconnaissance. The first OH-6As arrived in Vietnam during early 1967, and by year's end, nearly 90 were in Vietnam, falling far short of the nearly 400 the Army had hoped to have in country.

Aeroscouts served as the aerial reconnaissance elements of frontline units, finding a home in the air cavalry.

Although tactics varied according to terrain and unit policy, some basic concepts that centered on visual reconnaissance and recon-by-fire missions were standardized. A widely accepted tactic had OH-6As working as a two-ship unit, with a low bird prowling at extremely low level as the high bird provided navigation and relayed radio transmissions. When the low bird made contact, usually by being fired upon, orbiting gunships rolled in on the target. Especially effective was the Hunter-Killer or Pink team, which had a Loach at low level, while one or two gunships flew orbiting patterns that allowed them to instantly roll in on targets.

Loach crews were highly adept at reading sign, working their craft not only just above the treetops, but also often below them. Although it was not originally intended that scout crews trade blows with the enemy in his own backyard, to operate and survive in such high-risk environs, they needed all the firepower they could get. Whether a Loach crew consisted of two or three depended mainly upon use of the minigun system, which weighed 234 pounds when fully loaded. The line for and against arming scouts was clearly drawn, with some commanders, adamant about observing only and not taking aggressive action, while others felt that scout crews should slug it out with the enemy. The weight of the minigun system limited the crew to two; a pilot in the right seat and an observer opposite armed with an M-60, among other weapons. When the minigun was not used, a third crewman perched in the cabin with an M-60. Although the minigun could elevate 10 degrees and depress 24 degrees, gunners with hand-held M-60s not only had greater firing latitude, they could take the weapon with them if the aircraft was downed.

Some units experimentally mounted clusters of tubes taken from rocket launchers, while others went so far as to devise mounts for crew-operated miniguns in the small cabin doorway. Both D Troop, 3rd Squadron, 4th Cavalry and the 25th Aviation Battalion at Cu Chi flew Loaches with makeshift minigun systems. Mounts were designed with quick-release devices, making the gun interchangeable with various special mission aircraft within the unit. Since the units were in proximity, it's likely they worked together to develop the weapon. Grenades of all types were in abundance on the aircraft, along with infantry weapons such as M-79 grenade launchers, rifles, submachine guns, and pistols. Many crewmen fashioned powerful bombs that consisted of grenades encased in plastic explosive, around which shrapnel, such as nails, was taped.

Hunting in the enemy's backyard proved to be a perilous existence; Aeroscouts paid a heavy price for engaging in some of the most dangerous flying of the war. Losses were extremely high. When heat-seeking SAMs appeared in early 1972, some OH-6As were fit with exhaust diffuser systems to reduce infrared emissions.

Loaches were constantly in short supply, and its replacement, Bell's OH-58A Kiowa, arrived in early 1970. Although the Kiowa had many positive features, being 700 pounds heavier and having a less responsive rotor system barred it from matching the OH-6A's speed and agility. And Aeroscout crews knew that made the difference in surviving close-quarter combat. The Vietnam-era Loach and her crews became legend, and both the OH-6A and the Kiowa were progressively improved to prolong their Army careers.

Air Commandos

Although relatively few in number when compared to the massive infusion of helicopters in Southeast Asia, helicopters of the U.S. Air Force Air Commandos participated in some of the most intense combat operations of the war.

After being officially established in 1947, the U.S. Air Force concerned itself with fleets of Cold War bombers and fighter interceptors, venturing ever slowly into the world of helicopters. It took the Korean War to prove the value of helicopters in the Air Force, mainly for utility work and search and rescue (SAR). But those roles would change dramatically with President Kennedy's call to prepare for COIN warfare.

As the situation in Southeast Asia worsened, Sikorsky's CH-3 was relatively new to the Air Force, whose leadership found it ideal for SAR and the rapidly developing COIN role. In conjunction with a 1965 request by Air Force leaders in South Vietnam for nearly 30 CH-3s, the 20th Helicopter Squadron was resurrected on 8 October. In February 1967, the CH-3Cs, called Big Charlies, were joined by the Air Force version of Bell's Huey, the UH-1F.

Based on the short-fuselage Model 204, the UH-1F featured an unusual engine configuration to take advantage of a large supply of General Electric T58 turbine engines used to power the CH-3. The unique design incorporated a gearbox that reduced RPM and changed the direction of drive, which resulted in the exhaust being directed to the aircraft's right side. This arrangement used the larger main rotor and tail boom of the stretched Model 205. The F Model's 1,325-shp engine gave the powerful lifter a top speed of 120 mph. The first of 119 examples were delivered to the Air Force beginning in September 1963. Although intended for missile site support across the United States, the UH-1F, along with the CH-3, found a home in the shadowy world of special operations as the "Green Hornets."

After relocating from Thailand in 1967, the Green Hornets set up shop at Nha Trang Air Base (AB), Vietnam, leaving 10 CH-3Cs and four UH-1Fs in Thailand. The CH-3C element upgraded to CH-3Es and became known as *Pony Express*. The unit was absorbed into the 21st Special Operations Squadron (SOS) "Dustdevil" to consolidate all CH-3 assets in Thailand. The merge left the 20th SOS an all-Huey squadron, which operated from various locations throughout Vietnam. Squadron strength grew to more than 20 UH-1Fs, which were armed with M-60 machine guns on Sagami mounts, and as hand-held Free 60s. Replacement Hueys arrived from the States after being converted into gunships with crew-operated XM-93 minigun systems, and provisions for mounting two LAU-59/A 2.75-inch rocket launchers. Other modifications, which included secure radios, armor pilot seats, and self-sealing fuel tanks, resulted in the designation UH-1P. The Green Hornets then adopted the Army term "Slick" to identify lighter armed UH-1Fs.

In early 1968, the M-60 door guns of some CH-3s were augmented with heavy firepower in the form of General Electric TAT-102 turrets. Containing a 7.62mm minigun and fed by 8,000 rounds of ammunition, turrets occupied the ends of sponsons where auxiliary fuel tanks were carried. Designers of the system took advantage of the hydraulic and electrical lines, control panels, and mount strengtheners that had been permanently installed for the tanks as part of the CH-3E configuration. Each gun traversed through 180 degrees, ensuring a complete field of fire. The gun's adjustable rate of fire was 1,300 or 4,000 spm. Sighting stations were located in the right side forward doorway and left forward window. The weight of the system ruled out long-range missions, and the inability to repair the system in flight spelled the end of its use by 1971.

During 1968, when the squadron was re-designated the 20th SOS, both CH-3s and UH-1s exploited their gunship status to perform their primary mission of supporting secret cross-border missions by commando teams of the Studies and Observation Group, better known as SOG. Green Hornet crews worked closely with SOG teams, becoming adept at inserting, supporting, and extracting the commandos. A typical mission involved one or two slicks, protected by two to four gunships, with an additional slick and, sometimes, two gunships nearby as backup. The high-risk missions guaranteed high drama, especially when the enemy discovered a team in its backyard. The *hot* extraction that ensued often brought a rescue force that consisted not only of Green Hornet choppers, but many types of support aircraft. Teamwork on missions was vital, and although acts of heroism were routine, 20th SOS pilot James Fleming was awarded the Medal of Honor for his daring rescue of a SOG team in November 1968.

In 1970, the Green Hornets began exchanging its UH-1Fs and Ps for twin-engine UH-1Ns. Deliveries to the Air Force totaled 79 UH-1Ns, with the 20th's fleet completely converted by March 1971. Armament systems

As part of its development of a special operations air wing, the Air Force Tactical Air Command experimentally armed this UH-1F (S/N 63-13145). Attached to the Huey's universal mount is the XM-6 quad gun unit that used four M-60C machine guns. Like all USAF UH-1Fs, this aircraft was delivered painted dark blue. (Bell Helicopter)

of the UH-1N were the same as those of UH-1Ps, with a 40mm XM-94 grenade launcher often added.

By the time that the 20th SOS received orders to stand down in March 1972, it had lost half of the nearly 40 UH-1F/P Hueys assigned, as well as half of its nearly two dozen CH-3s.

As larger, more powerful CH-53C helicopters began replacing the CH-3 in mid 1970, the 21st SOS armed them with crew-operated miniguns for large assault missions. After missions in Laos ended in early 1973, the Dustdevils remained in Thailand and participated in the U.S. withdrawal from South Vietnam. The following month, the 21st suffered its greatest losses during the attempt to rescue the crew of the SS *Mayaguez*, when Cambodian communists off Koh Tang Island captured it. In what is called the last battle of the Vietnam War, the bloody assault led to the loss

When the Air Force converted most of its special operations UH-1Fs to UH-1P gunships, the common weapons load comprised 7-tube LAU-68 rocket pods and crew-operated XM-93 miniguns. Markings of 20th SOS Hueys were limited to a serial number on the tail and the unit "Green Hornet" on the tail boom. Like all 20th SOS Hueys, S/N 63-13163 wears the USAF Southeast Asia camouflage. (Tom Hansen)

The UH-1P's XM-93 minigun installation made for a crowded cabin. Ammunition containers were fastened against the rear cabin wall and a long flexible chute kept spent cartridges and links from striking the tail rotor. The Air Force preferred this simpler hard point mount to the Army's XM-156 universal mount, since only rocket launchers were carried. (James Pedriana)

The TAT-102 minigun prototype turret is seen here on CH-3E (S/N 66-13292) at Warner Robins AFB in October 1967. The unit, called a barbette, easily fit the sponson position since an auxiliary fuel tank normally occupied the space. The gun's ammunition bay is similar to that of the Cobra. (Igor I. Sikorsky Historical Archives, Inc.)

This CH-3E (S/N 66-13295) of the 21st Special Operations Squadron in Southeast Asia mounts the TAT-102. Systems on each side of the aircraft provided all-around coverage since each gun traversed 180 degrees. Unfortunately, the gun could not be maintained in flight. This aircraft was the 21st SOS's first combat loss of the war. (U.S. Air Force)

of two crewmen, six wounded, and three CH-53s destroyed. Another 23 USAF personnel on the mission were killed when a 21st SOS CH-53C crashed following takeoff from Nakhon Phanom RTAFB.

Tactics

Helicopter gunship tactics in Southeast Asia remained in a state of flux, due largely to the changing tactical situation and technological advances in aircraft and weaponry. Early helicopter operations in Vietnam proved successful, thanks to helicopter gunship escorts, and the Eagle Flight. The ability of this highly mobile force enabled the South Vietnamese Army to connect with the enemy before large forces could be mobilized. These demonstrations of the feasibility of the airmobile concept were closely monitored and the lessons learned infused into training curriculum. The variety of weapons systems was second only to the sheer variety of aircraft in allowing utmost flexibility to meet mission requirements.

From an ordnance standpoint, dominating the field of aerial weapons was, unquestionably, the 2.75-inch Folding Fin Aerial Rocket (FFAR). During the war, it was the most-fired non-bullet ordnance. Developed during the late 1940s as an air-to-air weapon, its potential effectiveness against Cold War bomber formations remained doubtful, leading to its more practical application for helicopters. The tube-launched, electrically fired FFAR consisted of a motor, warhead, and fuse. Rockets varied in length, weight, and warhead types; weights ranged from 17.9 to 22.2 pounds, and lengths spanned from 47.9 inches to 52.9 inches. The most common warhead was HE,

followed by white phosphorous (called "Willie Pete"), high explosive anti-tank (HEAT), fragmentation, and flechette, which released 2,200 steel darts during flight. Illumination and smoke marker rockets were also available, although not widely used.

Nomenclature of rocket launchers varied between the services, but since model differences were slight, they were more easily identified as 7-tube or 19-tube types. Cylindrical launchers were not repairable, while those of the XM-158 variety, having exposed tubes, could be repaired. Since the rocket's Mk40 motor burned out long before impact, and the projectile tended to weathervane into relative wind, its imprecise non-powered flight made it an area weapon, versus a more accurate point weapon. Fuses were basically of proximity (airburst) and point detonating types, with the latter's deeper penetration more effective against hard targets.

Among the vast array of common-use helicopter weapons were those considered unit and task specific. Most lethal among them were munitions dropped from heavy-lift helicopters. The CH-47 Chinook, for example, periodically served as a bomber when loaded with 30 55-gallon drums containing 80 pounds of dry tear gas (CS) agent. Known as the XM920 burst weapon, the powder saturated fortified positions and denied the enemy infiltration routes. Drums of flammable liquids, or flame fougasse, popularly called "foo gas," were also used to rout large enemy forces or those entrenched in fortified positions. The term fougasse was first used in eighteenth-century Malta, where it was used as a shaped mine for coastal defense.

Britain's Petroleum Warfare Department reconfigured its gunpowder charge into a gasoline-oil mix for use against coastal invasion in 1940. Flammable gel compounds such as tar were later added to give the mixture sticking qualities and to increase burn time. During the Vietnam War, it became basically a nasty concoction of napalm, or fuel mixed with dry laundry soap compound, which made the substance adhere. Used mainly for perimeter defense in Vietnam, the mix was placed in artillery tube containers or interlocking 55-gallon drums and usually ignited with electrically fired Composition 4 (C4) explosives. The Chinook could carry 5,000 pounds of chemical-filled drums, the fuses of which often were set by static lines.

Another heavy-lift helicopter-turned-bomber was the Sikorsky CH-54 Tarhe, better known as the Skycrane. Thanks to its lifting ability, the Skycrane could carry on its cargo hook the largest munitions ever carried by a helicopter: the 10,000-pound M-121 bomb and the 15,000-pound BLU-82 bomb. Developed during the 1950s for the B-36 bomber, the M-121 was fitted with an extended fuse for airburst in a forested area to be cleared. Its detonation produced an instant helicopter landing zone 120 feet in diameter. The BLU-82 saw less use with the Skycrane when it was found to be better suited to the USAF C-130 Hercules cargo aircraft, which became known as *Operation Commando Vault.*

On a smaller scale, other systems were developed to meet specific mission requirements. With a reputation for leading the field in improvising weaponry, the 25th Aviation Battalion came up with a method of air dropping mortar rounds. Personnel fashioned a simple tray that was perched at an angle in a Slick's doorway to allow either 60mm or 81mm mortar rounds to be dropped onto a target.

Another widely used tactic combined science at its best with armed helicopters. In 1965, General Electric and the Army's Limited War Laboratory came up with the "People Sniffer," the principle of which was based on an airborne device used by the Navy during World War II to detect enemy submarine exhaust. Officially labeled the XM3 Airborne Personnel Detector and mounted in helicopters, the unit, along with its backpack derivative, was used to locate the enemy by detecting chemical compounds given off by humans.

The People Sniffer was first carried by Hueys, which flew at treetop level, perpendicular to the wind. Flying behind and at higher altitudes were two helicopter gunships. When not affected by its sensitivity to terrain, climate conditions, and other emissions, such as smoke, the People Sniffer was considered the second most reliable means of finding the enemy, next to visual sighting. A refined version, the M3, began appearing on scout helicopters in 1970. Tactics were revised to include a command and control helicopter flying 1,000 feet above the sniffer aircraft. Often, if the enemy was detected, the gunship dropped smoke grenades to check wind direction prior to dropping E158 tear gas units. True to his endeavors to avoid detection from the air, the enemy went to the ground instead of firing at what appeared to be Sniffer helicopters. Since herbicide spray missions drew fire, some

Sniffer helicopter crews attached fake spray bars to the aircraft to draw the enemy out of cover.

George G. Reese, Jr., a Huey pilot of Company B "Diamondheads" of the 25th Aviation Battalion at Cu Chi, reflects:

"When I was with the Diamondheads, we had a special mission ship used for Sniffer, firefly, and smoke missions. We had a minigun out the left door, mounted on a tripod. That was in addition to an M-60 at the crew chief station, and two M-60s out the right door. I did so many sniffer missions that my unofficial call sign became 'Sniffer 6.' When I did the sniffer mission and we took fire, our minigun was always cleared to fire, and when it did, the bad guys ducked.

"We had a Sniffer mission north of Tay Ninh, and after the mission, we were heading to Tay Ninh for refuel, and then back to Cu Chi. We were a flight of three—my Huey Sniffer and two guns. This was during the Tet Offensive of 1967-68, so things were pretty hot and we were finding bad guys everywhere. As we approached Tay Ninh, we saw a group of civilians coming from an area close to the Cambodian border. These guys may have been cutting trees, or may have been the enemy, having come from an area where we had seen a lot of bad guys. They were on a road heading for Tay Ninh. From the air, they were suspect.

"We attempted to contact U.S. military and have them send South Vietnamese police to check the guys out, but we were not having any luck. So I decided to land on the road in front of the group of about 20. The dirt road was narrow, barely one lane. When I came to a hover, I was facing the group. All they could see were us two pilots. We waved for them to stop, but they tried to go off the edge of the road to get by us. I still had my gunships keeping an eye on us. I finally had enough of these guys ignoring me and trying to get by. I did a right pedal turn, and around comes the minigun and M-60. My gunner on the minigun wore a bright red helmet. When the Viets got a look at the red-helmeted gunner swiveling the minigun around as if to threaten them, they froze, and started to back up. We held them for about 15 minutes and finally got word not to shoot them. So off we went.

"When the minigun was installed, an overhead circuit breaker was put in, which we had drilled, placed wire through, and attached a grenade pin hanging from it. The thinking was that the pilots then had control of the minigun in case the gunner decided on his own to waste people, cattle, etc."

During the final months of the war, as U.S. helicopter units were withdrawn, a greater effort was made to train and equip South Vietnamese forces. But the glut of aircraft, little time, and lack of political will did little to stem the enemy's advance. Compared to the large number of aircraft captured during the 1975 takeover, few helicopter gunships fell into enemy hands. Some were flown to safe haven across borders or aboard ships, while those in North Vietnamese possession fell into disuse, or became museum displays.

CHAPTER FOUR

THE MARINE GUNSHIP EXPERIENCE

BuNo 151267 was the second of 34 UH-1Es built based on the Army UH-1B. All were painted Marine Field Green. The roof-mounted rescue hoist and HF antenna strung along the tail boom were Marine specifications. In Vietnam, some UH-1Es would have their rescue hoists removed, and all would have armored pilot seats. The bell-mouth engine air intakes of some later model Echoes were replaced with screened particle separators. (Bell Helicopter)

The Marines called it "vertical envelopment." While the term defined the development of the helicopter within the Marine Corps, it did not include armed helicopters, despite the Corps' reputation as an aggressive fighting force. The efforts of the Marine officers who had the vision and imagination to integrate the helicopter into the Corps were stymied by the slowness of technology and budget constraints following World War II and Korea. The Korean conflict did, however, boost interest in expanding the Marine helicopter force.

Although the establishment of Marine Experimental Helicopter Squadron One (HMX-1) in 1947 at Quantico, Virginia, is commonly referred to as the beginning of the Marine Corps helicopter experience, Marine interest in rotorcraft actually began during the early 1930s when the Navy evaluated the Pitcairn autogiro. Tested by the Navy in 1931, a Pitcairn XOP-1 received high marks but was deemed a poor performer when payload tested by the Marines. A Kellett XOP-2 tested three years later met with similar results. Marine interest in the helicopter fizzled and did not regenerate until 1946 when 20 Sikorsky helicopters were on the Navy inventory.

During the 1940s, the Navy, on behalf of the Marine Corps, began procuring Piasecki tandem-rotor helicopters for troop lift. Orders were also placed for Sikorsky R-5s and R-6s. When the Navy established Helicopter Development Squadron Three (VX-3) in May 1946 at Floyd Bennett Field, Long Island, New York, it was there that the first Marine helicopter pilots earned their wings.

Since the Marines were in the business of amphibious assault, Marine officials agreed that the dawning of the atomic age and the vulnerability of a massed amphibious landing made dispersion of the landing zone vital. That meant that a new mode of assault was needed to augment amphibious landing craft. Fortunately, the discouraging performance of the helicopter at that time did not dampen enthusiasm for its use in the assault role.

With the formation of HMX-1, the Marines developed a doctrine governing helicopter tactics pending the arrival of Piasecki transports and Sikorsky HO3S-1s. The squadron's secondary mission was to evaluate a small helicopter to replace the OY observation airplane. The Marines' first exposure to Bell helicopters came in April 1948 when Bell Aircraft representatives demonstrated to HMX-1 personnel the firm's Model 47D. As HMX-1 began writing the book on amphibious assault using helicopters, the development and acquisition of the three aircraft types was slow. Despite delays, until 1950 the Marine Corps took the lead among the services in adapting the helicopter to fit its needs.

War in Korea abruptly altered the Marine Corps plan that called for multiple assault transport helicopter squadrons. The war's onset also meant that a helicopter would have to be chosen and be made available in large quantities within a short period of time. The obvious choice was Sikorsky's Model S-55, which the Navy had labeled HO4S-1 when it first flew in November 1949.

Piasecki claimed that his firm was capable of producing a 20-passenger assault version of its H-21; however, timing was critical to the Marine Corps so the HO4S-1 (Marine HRS-1) entering production was chosen. In 1949, the Kaman Aircraft Corporation showed off its K-190, which was turned over to HMX-1 in December. Its success guaranteed Kaman a place in Marine aviation.

Shortly after entering the world of rotary-wing aircraft, the Marines experimented with every aspect of the helicopter including arming them. Studies of using the helicopter for attack, which began as early as 1949, included testing its effectiveness against armored vehicles. It was envisioned that artillery fire would neutralize anti-aircraft weapons and smoke screens laid by helicopters would allow anti-tank helicopters to operate. In 1951, HMX-1 evaluated the Bell HTL-4 with machine guns and 2.75-inch rockets, but the leadership majority within the Corps remained resistive to using the helicopter for close air support, for a number of reasons. Pilots with Korean combat experience were against the concept, and the ceiling on the allowed number of aircraft ruled out the helicopter if it meant that fixed-wing aircraft had to be deleted from the inventory. In addition, altering in any way Marine Corps doctrine, which held that fixed-wing aircraft protect helicopter transports, would not come easy.

During 1952, the Navy awarded Kaman a contract for the HOK-1 to replace the underpowered Sikorsky HO5S-1. In February of that year, when the Chief of Naval Operations had become convinced that Bell's large tandem-rotor HSL would not meet Anti-Submarine Warfare (ASW) specifications or be ready for delivery, Sikorsky was given the go-ahead to proceed with development of its HUS-1, better known in the Marine Corps as the Seahorse. Since the type originally had been

After a fact-finding trip to Algeria in 1957 to observe French armed helicopters, Marine officials approved tests with French-designed SS-11 wire-guided air-to-surface missiles on a Kaman HOK-1, BuNo 125530. Although test outcomes were favorable, the dilemma of arming Marine helicopters would remain into the 1960s. (U.S. Marine Corps)

An ASM-N-7 (AGM-12) Bullpup missile was successfully fired from an HUS-1, BuNo 145762, in June 1960 by HMX-1 pilot CAPT Samuel J. Fulton. Fulton steered the missile with radio control. The Navy Bureau of Weapons and the Continental Army Command's Material Development Office conducted additional testing from February through April 1961. Large red crosses were film reference marks. (U.S. Navy)

The Seahorse's Bullpup installation consisted of a sturdy extended pipe framework attached to the aircraft's frame. The missile's electrical firing cable was attached to the framework and plugged into the launcher. (U.S. Navy)

designed for ASW with the Navy, Marine use required the removal of ASW equipment, installation of a cargo deck and provisions for 12 combat troops, a 400-pound-capacity rescue hoist, and a 500-pound-capacity external cargo hook. The basic weight of the HUS was 8,000 pounds, with a maximum takeoff weight of 13,300 pounds. The 65-foot-diameter main rotor was driven by a 1,525-hp Wright radial engine. HUS-1 deliveries began in 1955. Leaders in Marine aviation found the ideal transport helicopter in Sikorsky's massive Model S-56, designated the HR2S-1. First delivered in 1956, the type also found favor with the Army as the H-37 Mojave, despite the difficulty in maintaining the large aircraft.

The argument for arming Marine helicopters again arose in 1957, bolstering the position of helicopter gunship proponents. LtCol Victor J. Croizat, an expert on French military matters and the first Marine Corps advisor to the South Vietnamese, along with Maj David Riley, conducted a fact-finding trip to Algeria to observe armed French helicopters in combat. Their lengthy report, which included their detailed observation of French helicopters armed with a wide variety of weapons, piqued the interest of Marine aviation officials. Until early 1959, HMX-1 conducted tests, which included French-designed SS-11 wire-guided air-to-surface missiles mounted on an HOK-1. Concurrent tests found that the 5-inch Zuni rocket was easily adaptable to the HUS-1 Seahorse. Although the tests proved successful, the dilemma of arming Marine helicopters persisted.

Probably the most unusual test during this period was the firing of an ASM-N-7 Bullpup missile from a Seahorse in June 1960. The 11-foot-long, 600-pound missile was fired from an altitude of 1,500 feet; the Bullpup traveled over 10,000 yards and its accuracy was observed to be excellent. Personnel of HMX-1 conducted the tests, and from February through April 1961, the system was given a work-out by the Navy's Bureau of Weapons and Army Material Development, Continental Army Command at Fort Rucker. A single HUS-1 was used, which later was brought up to its maximum gross weight with the addition of a twin 20mm cannon pod opposite the Bullpup mount. During the evaluation, a total of 11 Bullpups were fired successfully.

The Army's 1958 experiments with a heavily armed H-34 had not been lost on Marine aviation officials, who closely monitored the Army's work with armed helicopters. Enthusiasm for helicopter gunships in both services ran equally high; however, the Army had the added motivation of being prohibited from using fixed-wing attack aircraft. Thus, its airborne firepower would have to come from aircraft with rotors.

With their own skilled close air support and helicopters, Marine leaders were confident in their ability to deliver the most powerful assault punch of any fighting force. The winds of war, however, brought with them the uncertainty of change. The HUS, initially intended to revert to the utility role when replaced by the HR2S Deuce, would instead fill the ranks of transport squadrons. Throughout the 1950s and 1960s, three observation squadrons, called VMOs, operated a mix of HOK-1s (later designated OH-43Ds) and Cessna Bird Dog light fixed-wing aircraft. A three-year search for a single replacement for both met with little success until the advent of turbine power.

For Marine and Navy aviation, 1962 was the year of transition from reciprocating to turbine engines. The year marked not only the conversion of the Navy DASH drone to turbine power, but the first deliveries of Kaman's turbine-powered Seasprite. For Marine aviation, that year marked the first flight of Boeing Vertol's HRB-1 (later CH-46A) Sea Knight and the selection of Sikorsky's large CH-53A transport, along with Bell's UH-1 Huey to fill the Assault Support Helicopter (ASH) role. Based on the Army's UH-1B, the Marine UH-1E was the smallest and the lightest helicopter in the new Marine helicopter fleet, having met all the ASH performance requirements. By the time the UH-1E joined the fleet in 1964, more than 400 UH-1Bs were in Army service.

After number 762 successfully fired the Bullpup missile, a massive dual 20mm cannon pod was installed on the opposite side. The use of both systems brought the Seahorse up to its maximum takeoff weight and required strengthening of its airframe. Visible on the aircraft's nose and fuselage are areas where photo reference marks were painted for initial Bullpup firings. (U.S. Marine Corps)

While preparation had been under way for the Marines' transition to an all-turbine helicopter fleet, major changes had taken place in the Navy shipbuilding program to convert and build a fleet of 12 amphibious assault ships (LPHs). In 1962 the Marines possessed 341 helicopters of all types, 225 of which were HUS-1s, then designated UH-34Ds. All contributed in some way to the amphibious assault mission. Since the design and production of large assault helicopters proved technically vexing, the Marine Corps became more reliant on the UH-34, even ordering more. By the time the last UH-34 had been delivered to the Marine Corps, more than 540 of them had worn Marine Field Green.

SHUFLY

As the military situation in South Vietnam deteriorated during 1961, Marine involvement was limited to advisory and communication elements. During early 1962, Marine aviation leaders pushed for a squadron of 24 UH-34Ds to augment three Army H-21 units already in country. This, they reasoned, would increase the much-needed lift capability and the Seahorse could carry more and be less affected by altitude and heat than the H-21s. Since Marine Squadron HMM-362 was one of two in the Philippines and had been aboard the LPH USS *Princeton* (CVL-23) patrolling the South China Sea, it became the first participant in *Operation SHUFLY*.

Led by LtCol Archie J. Clapp, HMM-362 set up shop at Soc Trang Airfield in the Delta during April 1962. Nine days after the squadron's arrival, a UH-34D was shot down and the Marines began learning the hard lessons of helicopter operations in Vietnam.

Initially, protection for UH-34D crews consisted of submachine guns for the crew chief and copilot. Body

Stinger pilot Capt George Boemermann and crew of HMM-365 at Da Nang inspect the TK-1 system of a squadron UH-34D. Eighteen of the rocket launcher's 19 tubes were used since one contained an intervalometer for firing in pairs. The twin M-60C machine guns were mounted on the right side only as spent cartridges of a left side gun would damage the tail rotor. (George Boemermann, LtCol USMC Ret.)

armor and armor for the aircraft went to the top of the priority list. As armor became available for the crew and to protect engine components, its weight reduced lift capability. As "Archie's Angels" of HMM-362 wrote the book on helicopter combat operations, other Marine helicopter squadrons were tested, flying mainly UH-34Ds from LPHs in amphibious exercises *Steel Pike* and *Silver Lance*. Remembering the lessons of fighting in jungles during World War II and in the frigid mountains of Korea, Marine leadership, realizing that Vietnam was unique, also knew the pitfalls of focusing on a specific theater or form of warfare. While helicopter gunships were being considered for SHUFLY, the potential existed for deployment to a number of world trouble spots, pointing to the need for a new generation of helicopter to replace the radial engine workhorses.

The fixed-wing air support available for SHUFLY squadrons often was insufficient, and Marine attack aircraft were barred politically from Vietnam until April 1965. The most reliable support came from UH-1Bs of the Army's UTTHCO. Col Clapp's decision not to install machine guns on the aircraft, since they impeded troop movement through the aircraft's doorway, was overruled as attacks against helicopters increased. Eight UH-34Ds were shot down during 1963 and four in 1964. Even with two M-60s installed on the UH-34D, aircrew often were outgunned, prompting a harder look at ways to counter enemy fire. The immediate need for responsive fire suppression overrode the importance of pinpoint accuracy of heavy weapons. Accuracy was important, however, in populated areas, especially where the enemy used civilians as shields. A load of 500-pound bombs dropped from a jet would obliterate the enemy, but it would not win the hearts and minds of the people, the very rallying cry of the war.

In August 1964, Marine Commandant LtGen Wallace M. Greene, Jr., directed the Landing Force Development Center and HMX-1 to devise an armament package for the UH-34. Resourceful metalsmiths at Quantico went to work and in less than two weeks, Temporary Kit One (TK-1), consisting of two 19-tube rocket launchers on standard Aero 65A bomb racks and two M-60C machine guns, was test-fired. After one month of rigorous testing, the Bureau of Weapons gave the go-ahead for the fabrication of 24 kits. Weighing just over 1,000 pounds, the system had a rocket launcher on each side of the UH-34, with the guns mounted above the right side launcher.

Two of the kits were sent to Okinawa for pilot orientation. In November, the first TK-1s arrived in Vietnam, where they were found useful only at short range and accurate only in balanced flight. The fixed weapons fired forward only, meaning that the aircraft had to be pointed at the target. Fired by either the pilot or copilot, the weapons were sighted simply with a makeshift cross-hair ring mounted to the instrument panel lined up with a grease-pencil mark on the windshield. An intervalometer allowed 36 rockets to be fired in pairs. Although gunship pilots lived up to the Marine creed to adapt, it was concluded that the

UH-34 fared poorly as a gunship in view of its slow speed due to increased weight. Since attacks were made in a dive, the heavy aircraft was at the very edge of blade stall.

Shortly after HMM-365 arrived at Da Nang in October 1964 to become part of SHUFLY, squadron personnel modified three UH-34Ds into Stinger gunships by installing TK-1 systems. The squadron's first gunship mission had a pair of Stingers firing 90 rockets and 500 rounds of ammunition on enemy positions during pre-landing strikes. George Boemermann adds:

"I served in HMM-365 from 1963 to 1965, 'Koler's Klowns,' so named for our skipper, Lt. Col. Joe Koler. We

During development of the TK-2 weapon system, HMX-1 experimented with a variety of weapons on the system's Aero bomb rack. This early UH-1E at MCAS Quantico mounts an XM-18 system, which used a 7.62mm GAU-2B/A minigun. The 1,500 rounds carried in the pod and a firing rate of 2,000 or 4,000 spm allowed little time over the target. (Bell Helicopter)

After members of VMO-1, MAG-26 received their UH-1Es, they designed this door gun mount, which became the standard for Marine Hueys. Mounting the aviation-type M-60D machine gun, the unit featured a brass and link bag, a 200-round ammunition can, and cams that prevented overzealous gunners from hitting the aircraft. An aluminum swivel base allowed the gun to be stowed far enough inside the cabin so the doors could be closed. (U.S. Marine Corps)

had 24 H-34s for support of SHUFLY plus six more for training South Vietnamese pilots. In early winter things really started heating up. Headquarters sent kits to convert six of our helos to gunships. A small metal sight was affixed above the right instrument panel and the reticle was a black grease pencil dot on the inside of the front canopy; high-tech stuff; surprisingly, it worked. To complete the arsenal of our gunships, the crew chief manned the starboard door with an M-60, the assistant crew chief had another M-60 in the port hatch, and we later added another crewmember to fire an M-79 grenade launcher from the starboard door. Quite a formidable arsenal for the H-34. The aircraft commanders chosen to fly the Stingers were all transitioned former fixed-wing fighter and attack pilots. Our boresight expert took each bird out to a range where we were able to establish and adjust the grease mark on the windscreen to enable the guns to hit reasonably close to a target.

"We worked in conjunction with an Army Eagle Flight of armed Hueys. They enjoyed our added firepower, especially when we carried 36 rockets, whereas they carried only 14. Our armorer sergeant who installed and maintained the kits provided a valuable asset to the squadron. In his spare time he volunteered his services to the Air Force and the Army Special Forces units on the base. We were able to gain their support in some critical areas in return. The Army helo unit could not draw C rations, which they preferred for all day long missions. We had trouble being supplied with rockets. We had no problem drawing C rations, and they had no trouble being supplied with rockets. Those problems were solved quite easily. We traded a pallet of C rations for a pallet of rockets."

During 1965, HMM-365 flew two Stingers mounting four M-60s, two on each side, despite initial concern of tail rotor damage from brass ejected on the left side. Other squadrons, including HMM-162 and HMM-163, mounted

In 1967, the Naval Weapons Laboratory, Dahlgren, Virginia, fabricated the gun mount, which swiveled on firing safety contour cams. The proximity of the gun makes obvious the need for limiting the gunner's firing latitude. (U.S. Marine Corps)

Sgt. John Rogers (left) and 1Lt David Geaslin of HML-167 pose with a squadron gunship in 1970. The M-60C machine guns are pointing in different directions, the result of aircraft vibration. This was quickly remedied by severing the ammunition belt to stop the gun from firing. Rogers was later killed in action. (Pop-A-Smoke)

The early version of the Emerson Electric TAT-101 turret containing two 7.62mm machine guns. VMO-3 was the first to use the gun in combat. The turret's ammunition feed chute extended to the cabin where ammunition was stored. (U.S. Navy)

Although the Marine Huey was built in two separate versions, both were labeled UH-1E. This later version was based on the Army UH-1C, which is distinguished by its asymmetrical elevators, wide-chord tail fin, 540 rotor head, roof-mounted pitot tube, and left side fuel filler. Beginning in 1966, green flight suits replaced tan, and white rocket launchers were painted green. Crewmen were quick to spray over most high visibility markings. (Bell Helicopter)

TK-1s as well. As the Marines moved closer to turbine power and the Army provided more UH-1B gunships for support, the Stingers were returned to transport mode.

It had become obvious that arming transport helicopters with heavy weapons resulted in payload degradation; every gunship component added meant lesser troops carried until the aircraft was no longer a transport. In the realm of armed helicopters, the line between defense and offense was never more indistinct. The Huey brought to the Marines not only excellent payload characteristics, but exceptional maneuverability. The Huey's turbine power diminished the tradeoff of firepower for excessive weight and subsequent performance loss. It was envisioned that Marine gunship Hueys would become part of a transport formation, guaranteeing available and immediate fire suppression, while retaining transport capability. And since Marine air support and the infantry were inseparable, Marine pilots had the same boss as infantry battalions, ensuring that in the heat of battle, everyone was *on the same page.*

The Corps accepted its first UH-1E at Bell's plant on 21 February 1964, with the first examples being assigned to Marine Aircraft Group-26. The first 34 Echo models to leave the production line were patterned after the UH-1B, although with Marine specified changes. To protect them in salt-water environments, they were of all-aluminum construction, versus the lighter, but highly corrosive, magnesium normally used. Rotor brakes were added to counter winds over a ship's deck, since fast-paced carrier operations required that decks be quickly cleared. To prevent the rotor head from bumping against the mast at low RPM on a windy deck, which caused the blades to strike the tail boom, an improved anti-mast bumping system was used.

Also unique to the Marine Huey was additional avionics, a roof-mounted rescue hoist, and an HF radio antenna mounted on stand-offs along the tail boom. The Marines used TACAN, while the Army used VOR. When Bell opened its UH-1C production line, the balance of UH-1Es was based on that model. A total of 192 Echo models were built by the end of 1964, with some early models retrofit with C Model tail booms, engines, and rotor systems. As with Army B and C models, it became difficult to distinguish between the two.

While the exact role of Marine Hueys remained uncertain, they were assigned to Marine Observation Squadrons (VMOs), which flew both fixed- and rotary-wing aircraft. Despite the Army's satisfaction with the UH-1B as a gunship, and ensuing recommendation by the Marine Deputy Chief of Staff/Air that a dozen UH-1Es in each squadron serve as gunships, controversy among Marine leaders about the Huey's combat role stymied a decision. Enough reports came in from SHUFLY pilots in Vietnam decrying fixed-wing air support that the Commandant of the Marine Corps, on 13 October 1964, directed that high priority be given to the development of UH-1E weapons kits. The system selected among three that were tested was labeled TK-2, which was similar to the H-34's TK-1.

Since UH-1Es were copies of the Army's UH-1B and C models, they featured the same hard points for attaching weapons. Under "Air Frame Change No. 7," an assembly that incorporated two M-60C machine guns and an Aero 65A bomb rack was mounted on both sides of the aircraft. In January 1965, most of the initial batch of 15 kits was installed on UH-1Es of VMO-6 at Camp Pendleton, California. The TK-2 received high marks, prompting the Chief of Naval Operations to request kits for 33 more UH-1Es.

During this period, HMX-1 experimented with other armament packages for the Huey, including machine gun pods, minigun pods, various rocket launchers, and chin turrets. The latter proved successful enough to warrant further tests, with the decision made to purchase 94 units for installation beginning in spring 1967. The turret, which was designated TAT-101 and built by Emerson Electric, housed a pair of M-60 machine guns that were controlled by the pilot. For additional suppressive fire, crewmen fabricated flexible M-60 machine gun mounts in both doorways. Since these were deemed unsafe and often were not interchangeable, a door gun mount built by VMO-1 members in 1966 was found to be the most effective, and subsequently was tested for use as the standard for UH-1Es.

The first six UH-1E gunships arrived at Da Nang, South Vietnam, in early May 1965 to equip VMO-2. Marine assault troop helicopters now had their own armed escorts and began writing a new chapter in Marine aviation history. As the buildup of Marine helicopters in Vietnam continued, the UH-1E force was plagued with maintenance problems; expended cartridges from machine guns were hitting tail rotors, which was solved by fashioning an ejection chute that fit over rocket launchers.

The white rocket launchers of this later model UH-1E of HML-367 at Phu Bai in 1968 were rare. Its forward engine cowling lies beneath the launcher. The aircraft number was worn on the nose and tail fin, and in Roman numerals on the doorpost. Wording beneath the buzzards on the pilot's door reads, "Patience Hell." Rescue hoists and cabin doors were often removed to lighten the aircraft. (Gary Zimmerman)

A more vexing problem was the erosion of rotor blades in Vietnam's sandy conditions. Bell made replacement blades available, but the firm was hard pressed to make up for the most serious setback, which occurred on 27 October 1965 when the enemy attacked the Marble Mountain Air Facility, destroying 13 UH-1Es and severely damaging two. Especially disturbing to Bell engineers were complaints by the Marines that the engine cowlings of their Hueys did not fit snugly; often there were inch-wide gaps between the cowling and the fuselage. Knowing that the Hueys left the factory without flaws, Bell sent a senior test pilot to Vietnam to look for the cause of the Marines' complaints. He found nothing until he flew along on a mission in which the Huey made a gun run on a target.

The pilot attacked at 165 knots, exceeding the 140-knot redline limit, and then made a steep and hard pull-out. Back at the base, the test pilot knew exactly where to look; he discovered that the Marine pilots were pulling so many gs in combat that they were bending structural beams, which distorted engine cowling fits. Knowing it was pointless to tell the Marine flyers to slow down, they were told simply to firmly secure the cowlings.

Although the Marine Corps planned to equip its three observation squadrons, VMO-1, -2, and -6 with 24 UH-1Es for both observation and support, Marine leadership remained indecisive over the Huey's combined role, or acquiring a new fixed-wing aircraft to share the role. North American's OV-10A Bronco was under study for close-in support; however, it would not be available until

1968. To make matters worse, the 58 UH-1Es in the inventory fell short of the authorized 76 aircraft. While Bell struggled to meet demands for the war effort, 20 UH-1Bs were loaned from the Army, thereby freeing stateside UH-1Es for war duty.

In December 1966, VMO-5 was established at camp Pendleton as a training squadron under the first helicopter training group, MHTG-30. Earlier that year, VMO-3 had been commissioned, and by mid 1967, VMO-2, -3, and -6 were flying a total of 68 UH-1Es in Vietnam. Statistics showed that the majority of missions flown by UH-1Es in Vietnam were armed attack. Although such figures spoke well for the Huey, it was labeled misuse, since the type was not intended for the armed role. Despite the report, four American soldiers were especially grateful for the Huey's weapons.

When stranded on a beach and under attack by a large enemy force on 21 June 1967, gunship pilot Maj Stephen W. Pless of VMO-6 rescued them. Exemplifying the skill and tenacity of Marine gunship pilots, Pless repeatedly attacked the enemy at close range, placing his aircraft between the soldiers and the enemy so that his crew could pull them aboard. As Pless headed out to sea, his overloaded Huey settled into the water four times before it became airborne. For his actions, Pless became the only Marine aviator of the war to receive the Medal of Honor.

Until the arrival of the Bronco for observation and helicopter escort, the Marines bolstered its O-1 Bird Dog inventory. Upon the Bronco's arrival to VMOs, they replaced 12 squadron UH-1Es, which were used to form

The UH-1E's armament system was a simple pipe frame attached to the Huey's hard points. The right-side fuel filler and rotor head identify this Huey as an early model based on the UH-1B. The right door gun is swiveled inward against the cabin wall. BuNo 151292 stands alert at Da Nang in May 1966. (U.S. Marine Corps)

a Huey-equipped light helicopter squadron for each wing. Called HMLs, for Helicopter, Marine, Light, HML-267 was formed at Camp Pendleton in March 1968, followed by HML-367 at Phu Bai, South Vietnam, and HML-167 at Marble Mountain in April. Under the reorganization, VMO-3 and -5 were redesignated HML-367 and HML-267, respectively.

Typical of the squadrons was VMO-3 whose assets formed HML-367. Called "Scarface," the squadron flew mostly gunships for armed escort, re-supply, medevac, support of reconnaissance teams, and SOG support. Its inventory of 18 UH-1Es peaked at 25 Hueys as new aircraft left Bell's production line. Squadron Slicks flew as command and control, visual reconnaissance, and utility platforms. Some squadrons flew night missions called *Firefly* or *Back Hammer*, which had a low bird trolling for fire with a searchlight and night vision device, while a high bird flew blacked out 300 feet above and behind. If the low bird was fired upon, the high bird dropped down to deliver punishing blows.

K. C. Carlon, who flew Huey gunships of VMO-6 at Quang Tri in 1968 and 1969, notes: "The role of the gunship pilot was unique. The concept was routinely to fly as a section of two. What made these missions unique was that the gunship section leader normally was a Tactical Air Controller, which included the navigation responsibilities for the mission, being a Forward Air Controller, and controlling artillery as the mission demanded. All this while providing suppressive fire for the transport helos or for ground units."

With a full ammunition load, and a crew of four—pilot, copilot, crew chief, and gunner—UH-1Es were usually flown at maximum gross weight. Not surprisingly, combat casualties among Marine helicopter pilots and crew were high. It was concluded that helicopter crews averaged a 14-hour workday; crew chiefs flew with their Hueys on missions, manned guns, and maintained the aircraft when not flying. Marine training groups were hard pressed to maintain the air crew pipeline, until relief came in 1968 when Marine helicopter student pilots reported to the Army for training, a practice that continued until 1971. By that time, a total of 205 UH-1Es had been delivered to the Marine Corps.

By 1969, when the Marines took on the AH-1G Cobra, squadrons were doing their best to operate four different types of rotary-wing and fixed-wing aircraft. The formation of HMLs had helped to alleviate the problem, but commonality was achieved only by giving the O-1s to the South Koreans, VMO-2 ended up with all of the Broncos, HML-167 absorbed all of the UH-1Es, and HML-367 owned all of the Cobras; VMO-6, which had been flying O-1s and UH-1Es, was transferred to Okinawa. The Huey gunship configuration remained unchanged, with few exceptions. The TAT-101 turret had proven troublesome to the extent that they were removed by June 1970. On 21 June 1969, HML-167 had the distinction of dropping the first bomb-type weapon from

a UH-1E in combat when the squadron commander released a Helicopter Trap Weapon.

For some time, Marine Huey crews used both 7-tube and 19-tube rocket launchers. An event that could have proven disastrous brought that to an abrupt halt. David Geaslin, who flew Marine gunships of HML-167 during 1969 and 1970, explains:

"Only the 7-shot rocket pods were authorized by Naval Air Systems Command. We found out later why. The authorized 7-shot pods were shielded against Radiation Hazard (RADHAZ) for operations aboard ships where high-power radars and communications gear were in proximity to the helicopter. We didn't know this and 'borrowed' some 19-shot rocket pods from the Air Force at Da Nang. We used them for about a month until one of the birds came in for a calendar check. One of the checks was to test the HF radio. When the pilot keyed the mic and said, 'Any ship at sea...' 36 rockets left the bird at one time! Fortunately, all landed in bad guy country out in Mortar Valley. It seemed that the Air Force pods were not RADHAZ shielded and the electromagnetic pulse from the HF antenna ignited all of the rockets simultaneously, even though the cannon plugs were removed from the pods and the master arm switch was in the off position! We switched all rocket pods back to 7-shot pods."

As a gunnery sergeant and UH-1E gunner, William H. Cox flew 200 missions with VMO-2 during 1968 and 1969. He describes a mission that not only illustrates the challenge of facing the well-fortified North Vietnamese Army with the UH-1E gunship, but the coordination of Marine tactical-air.

"Our mission started out as medevac but later became an anti-personnel detection (APD) mission. We had flown several routine medevac escort missions for CH-46s out of An Hoa. We had returned there and were on standby when we were diverted to check out enemy activity that a recon team had reported up in the Que Son Mountains. They had reported a large force of NVA that were in heavy fortifications (bunkers). We launched, leaving one of the gunships with the '46 in case they had a medevac.

"When we arrived at the grid coordinates, it was mostly heavy jungle. However, it did not take us long to spot the fortifications that the recon team had reported. At first it looked like several large bunkers in an open spot in the jungle. We had two 19-round rocket pods with HE warheads strapped on and a full load of ammunition. We had the 'stuff' on board to take on the bunkers.

"On our first pass, the pilot chose rockets and the gunner and I would provide covering fire while pulling off of the target. This was a standard tactic that we used on this type of target. The pilot fired two pairs of rockets that hit just short of the bunker entrance, with little or no damage to the bunker. Gunner and I sprayed the bunker with our door guns to keep the troops pinned down. We didn't take any ground fire on the first pass.

"On our second pass we were greeted with heavy machine gun fire. This time the pilot fired eight rockets that bracketed the bunker and scored several direct hits. As we pulled off, the whole mountaintop opened up on us. We also realized that there were more than just two fortifications. We had stumbled into a large NVA buildup! How many were down there, we had no idea. We did know that we were no match for the target.

"We backed off to a safe distance and the pilot called for fixed-wing support. We got lucky, as there were two Marine F-4 Phantoms nearby that were loaded for bear. One was loaded with napalm bombs and an Mk4 20mm gun pod, and the other had 16 250-pound 'Snakeye' bombs. These boys had the right stuff strapped on and were looking for a place to unload it!

"In about ten minutes, the F-4s arrived on target. We were asked to spot the target for them with our rockets. We rolled in and the pilot fired two rockets at about the

The development of fuel-air explosives included tests with a mass air delivered system. A Marine CH-53 was one of the helicopter types tested in 1972 by suspending a large FAE container from its cargo hook. (U.S. Navy via Gary Verver)

VMO-5, which formed in 1966, tested the CBU-55A/B fuel-air explosive on the UH-1E at Camp Pendleton in 1967. The tail code for the squadron, which became HML-267 in 1968, was UV, seen here with the aircraft number 5 on the cabin door. (U.S. Navy)

maximum range. The first F-4 laid down two napes dead center of the target and the second one dropped two snakes. We stood off to the side and called out hits and additional targets. The F-4s put on a good show and used up all of their ordnance. The F-4 with the gun pod made several runs and probably used up all of his ammo. We thanked them for their work and they returned to Da Nang. We circled the area several times, at a distance, to make a damage assessment. The F-4s made a hell of a mess in the area.

"The next day, several A-4s and F-4s made repeated strikes into that area."

David Geaslin provides more interesting details about the weapon systems:

"The Marine Corps gunship package was nothing more than welded pipe bolted to the airframe. These racks were not very rigid and were often bent from people stepping on them to climb up to work on the engine deck. The vibration of the rotor system constantly shook these pipe racks into new configurations. You could boresight the guns before a mission and in an hour or so the vibration would have them shooting in different grid squares, as we used to say. Each crew chief carried a Phillips-head screwdriver and if they saw a gun shooting too far off boresight, they would stab the screwdriver through the feed chute to break the link ammo belt and the gun would stop firing.

"If you were not flying the airplane in a gun run, you could not rest your elbow on the window ledge. You had to keep your elbow inside because if the fixed M-60 gun barrels got too hot, they would begin to sag. When they sagged, the flash suppressor would start shaving the brass off each round and deposit it in the back of your arm.

"We also tested a Fuel-Air Explosive (FAE) bomb delivered by a Huey. Each weapon had three one-gallon sub-bombs containing one gallon of fuel each. Upon dropping, the three bombs separated and a small drag chute deployed from each to ensure a vertical impact. Then a telescoping fuse dropped down about three feet from each. When the fuse impacted, fuel was forced through small holes, atomizing it into a white cloud. Then three pyrotechnic heat sources popped out and detonated the cloud. Each cloud had the overpressure of a 500-pound bomb. However, any wind and the thing would not work."

Tests with FAEs were conducted by the Navy at China Lake beginning in 1960. Typically, anything associated with naval weaponry passed through the NOTS at China Lake, California. When the bomb's liquefied petroleum gas (LPG), and later ethylene oxide, were released from a pressurized casing, it rapidly expanded into a heavier-than-air cloud that filled caves, tunnels, and bunkers. When the cloud was ignited, it not only had a devastating blast and overpressure effect far beyond that of conventional weapons, it consumed the oxygen in the area, causing suffocation.

The first FAE was the CBU-55A/B 550-pound bomb developed for use by helicopters and slow-speed aircraft. Although tested by Marine UH-1Es in Vietnam, no record has been found indicating such use in combat. It was, however, used successfully by OV-10As. The development of FAEs led to further helicopter testing by the Navy, which included a massive system suspended by a Sikorsky CH-53. This Mass Air Delivered (MAD) system had FAEs released from a large container suspended from the aircraft's cargo hook. Although it proved effective in breaching minefields and covering vast target areas, it is not known to have been used operationally.

By the end of 1971, Marine Huey gunship squadrons had left the war zone, having lost numerous aircrew, along with 69 UH-1Es; 53 on missions and 16 during ground attacks. The transfer of HML-167 from Vietnam to MCAS New River, North Carolina, in June 1971 marked the beginning of a new era in Marine Huey helicopters by becoming the first light helicopter squadron equipped with the new twin-engine UH-1N.

During the late 1980s and early 1990s, the Marine Corps evaluated the feasibility of arming Sikorsky CH-53Es with AIM-9 Sidewinder missiles. A CH-53D was used to test a rocket launcher and Sidewinder, while this CH-53E, BuNo 161181, served as the test firing vehicle for the Naval Air Test Center. (U.S. Navy)

The UH-1N twin-engine Huey was introduced to the Marine Corps in 1971, eventually replacing the UH-1E. Gunship versions of the N model, such as this example of HMLA-367, were teamed with Cobra gunships to form light attack squadrons. (U.S. Navy)

The CH-53 Sea Stallion's massive size easily accommodated the AIM-9 missile installation alongside the fuselage, atop the sponson. (U.S. Navy)

CHAPTER FIVE

GUNSHIP SAILORS

This Seasprite, which carried both HH-2D and YSH-2E designations during tests, is seen with AN/APS-115 radar at NADC Warminster in June 1972. (Stephen Miller)

Equally important in the realm of U.S. attack helicopters is the Navy's use of armed rotary-wing aircraft. Having committed helicopters to anti-submarine and rescue duty, the Navy, during the Vietnam War, would venture beyond that commitment with heavily armed helicopters for riverine operations, as well as for combat search and rescue. Although deck space aboard ships was, and remains, prime real estate, armed helicopters would become vital components of the surface fleet. The development of the helicopter force that is integral to today's U.S. Navy did not come easy.

Despite the emerging promise of rotorcraft during World War II, the U.S. Navy had little interest in the helicopter. Those in naval aviation viewed the fragile, underpowered craft as impractical and having little to offer the fleet. Their focus on fixed-wing operations was steadfast. But Sikorsky's success with the VS-300 had not gone unnoticed by ADM Ernest King, the Navy's Chief of the Bureau of Aeronautics (BuAer). On 24 July 1942, seven months after the first Army Sikorsky R-4 helicopter took to the air, he directed that four of the aircraft be procured for evaluation. Sidestepping the skepticism surrounding the helicopter in its aviation community, the Navy was content to assign the helicopter program to the Coast Guard. "Coastie" seaplane crews were not amused by the intrusion into their territory.

After LCDR Frank A. Erickson—the Coast Guard's first helicopter pilot—accepted the Navy's HNS-1 (identical to the R-4) during October 1943, he implored Navy officials to consider the helicopter for anti-submarine and search and rescue work. Merchant ships were being sunk in the Atlantic, forcing even the skeptics to admit that the helicopter might have a place in ASW. Tests had already proven that the HNS-1 could carry a 200-pound MK IX depth charge. And, beginning in April 1944, they were equipped with dipping sonar similar to that used by blimp crews.

The Coast Guard managed most of the Navy's helicopter operations and evaluations during wartime. The Navy showed its confidence in the results by establishing in 1946 its first helicopter unit: Helicopter Development Squadron Three (VX-3) at Floyd Bennett Field, Long

Sikorsky's HSS-1 Huss, officially named Seabat, was considered the Navy's first effective sub hunter. Armed with an Mk 43 torpedo, the Seabat was the killer half of a hunter-killer team. The HSS-1 is seen at NAS North Island in May 1956. (Lennart Lundh Collection)

Island, New York. Its mission was to study the helicopter for fleet and land-based use. Two years later, on 1 April, VX-3's assets were divided to form Helicopter Utility Squadrons One and Two; HU-1 stayed at NAS Lakehurst, New Jersey, and HU-2 went to NAAS Miramar, California. Finally convinced of the helicopter's ability to counter the submarine threat with dipping sonar and air-dropped torpedoes, the Navy on 3 October 1951 established Helicopter Anti-Submarine Squadron One (HS-1) at NAS Key West, Florida.

The Korean conflict provided Navy leaders the opportunity to explore the helicopter's role in combat support. With direct helicopter combat support left largely to the Marines, Navy helicopters successfully filled the roles of plane-guard duty aboard carriers, medical evacuation, and utility. Although seldom documented, Navy helicopter pilots in Korea performed some of the earliest light attack experiments. When LTJG John W. Thornton and his crew repeatedly attacked North Korean soldiers with small arms fire and hand grenades, little did they realize that their actions foreshadowed the helicopter's use as a weapons platform.

Sikorsky's success with its R Series S-51 helicopter led to development of the S-55, which was first flown in 1949. Billed as the first transport helicopter, the S-55 proved its worth in Korea as the H-19 (Navy HO4S and Marine HRS). Since nuclear-powered submarines that appeared after the conflict proved harder to detect, much less destroy, the Navy ordered 10 S-55s—which it labeled HO4S-1s—for high priority evaluation as sub hunter/killers. The HO4S-3 with increased power could carry one torpedo; however, the entire S-55 series proved to be underpowered.

Sikorsky engineers went back to the drawing boards and in 1953 came up with the S-58, known in Navy parlance as the HSS-1 Seabat. The HSS-1 was in competition with Bell's tandem-rotor HSL-1; however, the latter was judged too large for carrier operation and too noisy for sonar operation. Considered the first effective ASW helicopter, the HSS-1 was powered by the proven Wright R-1820-84 Cyclone engine. Despite the powerplant's reputation as a workhorse, the Navy used HSS-1s in hunter/killer pairs, with one aircraft carrying variable depth, dipping sonar and the other an Mk-43 torpedo.

DASH

While HSS-1s detected and tracked submarines, concern over the growing number of Soviet submarines following World War II created a new dimension in naval warfare. Seemingly ahead of their time, unmanned attack helicopters made their debut, meeting only limited success, while manned armed helicopters would become mainstays of the fleet. It is ironic that armed unmanned aircraft became front-line hardware during the twenty-first century when a small obscure company was mass-producing them nearly a half-century ago.

The U.S. Navy ushered in the use of drone helicopters, which, basically, are unmanned craft that can perform missions without endangering the lives of crew, or that

Flowerfield Airfield, New York, was the home of the little known Gyrodyne Company of America. Its founder, Peter Papadakos, perfected the American coaxial helicopter design, which he demonstrated to the military. This is his first aircraft, the Compound Model 2B, which first flew in 1951 and was later converted to Model 2C with side engines removed. (Author's Collection)

require the decision-making ability of a pilot. Although interest in pilotless aircraft began during the days of the autogiro, Navy officials initially were reluctant to approve funding for a drone helicopter. That would change when Aeronautical Engineer Charles Kaman, who had developed a keen interest in anti-submarine warfare, convinced Office of Naval Research (ONR) officials that the drone helicopter was a fresh approach to detecting and attacking submarines. After all, he reasoned, anti-submarine warfare had proven to be a cog in the wheel of national defense, and a simple rotary-wing drone with listening sonar and torpedoes could serve as the eyes and ears of a ship far beyond its horizon.

The Kaman Aircraft Corporation began experimenting with a drone helicopter called the HTK-1. Electronic assisted control systems allowed pilots to fly the aircraft hands-off, a breakthrough that encouraged engineers to develop a pilotless helicopter—an unthinkable feat during the early 1950s.

Kaman's success in proving that an unmanned, remotely controlled helicopter could provide long endurance at low gross weight prompted the Navy to announce an industry-wide competition for a Drone Anti-Submarine Helicopter (DASH). Navy officials focused on the proposals of firms Bell, Kaman, and Gyrodyne, with the latter selected for the DASH program in December 1958.

Bell Helicopter proposed this torpedo-carrying drone during the mid 1950s. Like manned helicopters, drones followed a manufacturer's specific rotor design, with Bell and Sikorsky using the anti-torque tail rotor. (Bell Helicopter)

Although the DASH carried both the Mk-44 or Mk-46 torpedoes, the former saw wider use by the Fleet from 1960 to 1970; the Mk-46 was introduced in 1967. The Mk-44 was an active homing torpedo mounted to the QH-50 with an Mk 8 Mod 4 bomb shackle. The torpedo was dropped from about 100 feet altitude, becoming armed by a saltwater-activated electric battery. (National Museum of Naval Aviation)

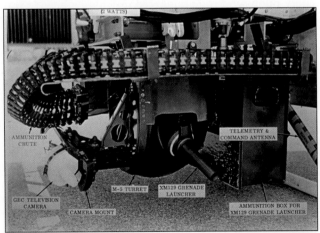

For interdiction missions in Vietnam, which were code-named "Snoopy," the DASH was armed with a remotely-controlled M-5 turret with 40mm grenade launcher. The weapon, like others mounted to DASH, were specific to Army gunships. (Author's Collection)

Using its patented coaxial rotor configuration, Gyrodyne designed its RON Rotocycle, which spawned the unmanned DASH. This Marine YRON is seen in April 1966. (Author's Collection)

The Navy's selection of Gyrodyne's DASH proposal hardly spelled the end of Kaman's work with drone helicopters. Success with the firm's HTK-1 had led to a 1955 joint Army-Navy contract for three drone helicopters. The Marines became interested to the extent that studies were drawn up recommending that drone helicopters be evaluated for atomic weapons delivery, intelligence gathering, battlefield illumination, and cargo transport. Kaman suggested broader applications to include clearing minefields, all-weather navigation, and the all-important ASW. So impressed were Marine officials with the results of their 1959 evaluation of an HTK-1 that they considered forming three cargo helicopter drone squadrons during 1963 and 1964. Although Marine interest dwindled in view of the helicopter's cost and then-questionable reliability, the Navy, in its perpetual quest of ASW hardware, remained active in the drone helicopter program.

The advent of the turbine-powered helicopter brought about Kaman's QH-43G, which, while secretly testing communication with submarines at sea, proved that a homing weapon could be positioned directly over a sub, dramatically increasing the kill probability. Certain that drone helicopters could provide a destroyer-based capability, the Navy began trials in May 1957 aboard the USS *Wright* (CVL-49) and USS *Mitscher* (DL-2). Secret tests continued into the 1960s not only proving the feasibility of assigning torpedo-carrying drone helicopters to destroyers, but giving rise to the DASH concept.

The DASH became a vital element in helping the U.S. Navy address the Soviet submarine threat during the Cold War. Chief of Naval Operations ADM Arleigh Burke is credited with implementation of the dual stand-off weapon system, which comprised DASH and an anti-submarine rocket (ASROC), both of which used the Mk-44 torpedo. The DASH initially was favored over the ASROC since it could be re-used after being recalled, whereas the ship-launched ASROC could not. The ASROC's limited range of five miles with the convergence zone sonars of the 1950s highlighted the need for an attack helicopter.

Both systems focused on extending the life of World War II–era destroyers under a Fleet Rehabilitation and Modernization (FRAM) program. Although the Eisenhower Administration sought major cuts in defense spending, U.S. Navy destroyers had to be updated to meet the threat of more than 300 Soviet fast-attack submarines plying the world's oceans during the late 1950s. To give destroyers longer-range standoff weapons delivery capability with aircraft, the Navy sought refinement of a remotely controlled helicopter then being tested by the U.S. Marine Corps. The machine had been built by the little known Gyrodyne Company of America, whose founder, Peter Papadakos, perfected America's coaxial helicopter design. Papadakos, an engineer, was in the right place at the right time, having purchased in 1946 the assets of the Bendix Helicopter Company, which included the unfinished design of a rotorcycle with coaxial rotors.

Intrigued by the small machine's contra-rotating rotors, which ruled out the need for an anti-torque tail rotor, Papadakos improved the design, which evolved into the Gyrodyne Model 2B.

In June 1951, Gyrodyne received from the Navy Bureau of Aeronautics a contract to study the coaxial rotor configuration. Recognizing Papadakos' design as an important element in bolstering its helicopter force, the Marines, under Navy contract, in 1958 acquired the small one-man helicopter for use as a reconnaissance vehicle. Called the XRON Rotorcycle, the craft was powered by a specially made Porsche engine, which drove two two-blade coaxial wooden rotors. Success with the Rotorcycle led to Gyrodyne's selection as the prime contractor for the production of a long line of armed drone helicopters.

At the Navy's behest, Papadakos drew up a proposal for a torpedo-carrying remote control version of his Rotorcycle to meet the convergence zone attack requirement. Gyrodyne's drone would be guided far beyond a destroyer's intended course to detect subs, and, if necessary, destroy them with torpedoes. Being pilotless and low cost gave the machine a degree of expendability, which was evidenced by its lack of redundant and fail-safe systems.

To fill the DASH requirement, Gyrodyne designed a 1,000-pound machine. It was powered by a Volkswagen automobile engine and mounted on elongated skid gear to accommodate two torpedoes. Its "stacked" coaxial rotors only added to its ungainly appearance. The DASH was originally built for one-time use to deliver a single nuclear depth bomb. The drone was to drop the weapon in the kill radius of Soviet fast-attack submarines, and, therefore, would not survive the blast. However, safety measures necessary for storing the weapon aboard ships ruled out its use, resulting in the dual torpedo package.

The Navy contract called for nine DSN-1s (QH-50A) and three DSN-2s (QH-50B). Two DASH models flew trials from NAS Patuxent River with one torpedo and a safety pilot, who rode hunkered down on a bicycle seat immediately behind the rotors. The pilot was required for flights over residential areas of Long Island, while shipboard operations did not require a pilot. The first shipboard landing was made aboard the *Mitscher* on 1 July 1960, and the first unmanned DASH landed aboard the USS *Hazelwood* (DD-531) on 7 December.

The switch to turbine power occurred in 1962 with Boeing's 270-hp T50-BO-4 engine (later T50-BO-8A), resulting in a change in designation to DSN-3 (QH-50C). At a gross weight of 2,300 pounds, the -3 could carry two 500-pound torpedoes at 90 mph. DASH aircraft updated with the 330-hp T50-BO-12 engine were labeled QH-50Ds. The final version, the Allison-powered QH-50E, could carry two Mk-44 torpedoes, one Mk-46, or a special weapons payload of 1,500 pounds. The shipboard DASH weapon system in its entirety consisted of the aircraft, flight deck hangar, deck control system, Combat Information Center (CIC) station, and transmitter with associated antennas. During trials at NAS Patuxent

River, and aboard frigates and destroyers, several QH-50s were lost to severe vibration problems.

In 1966, the Navy reduced procurement of the QH-50, and the following year, Secretary of Defense McNamara stated, ". . . the DASH ASW drone helicopter was encountering higher-than-expected peacetime attrition and lower-than-expected performance . . ." It was no secret that the war in Southeast Asia created budget constraints and, subsequently, realignment of military priorities. Besides, the Vietnam War was not a submarine war. It didn't help that an errant DASH had crashed into the bridge of a Pacific Fleet destroyer.

What McNamara didn't mention in his January 1967 report to Congress was that he had authorized the Navy to bypass the QH-50's ASW mission and fly surveillance and gun-spotting missions in Southeast Asia. Under code-name *Snoopy*, QH-50s were modified with real-time television cameras, telemetry systems, and radar transponders. Even lesser known is the fact that QH-50s flew surveillance missions armed with bombs hanging from torpedo shackles to attack vehicle traffic. Some were armed with the XM-5 turret incorporating the XM-129 40mm grenade launcher, which was a standard fixture on Army helicopter gunships. Given the U.S. military's penchant for weapon experimentation, many other weapons were tried as well. Later, the Advanced Research Projects Agency stepped in to refine three DASH systems for armed and armored programs named *Blow Low, Night Panther,* and *Night Gazelle.* All three were lost in Vietnam waters.

DASH aircraft also could be equipped with a quick-release cargo hook for resupply in hostile territory, and 10-minute duration smoke generators. Such capabilities, along with its expendability, enhanced the machine's appeal for rescue of aircrew downed in hostile areas; it is not known if use of the DASH as a combat rescue vehicle was pursued. Despite the unavailability of official records relating to DASH operations in Southeast Asia, it is known that both armed and unarmed QH-50s flew in extremely hostile areas, with their success measured in lives saved. The Navy acknowledges the loss of 411 QH-50C/Ds among 746 produced. Five percent of these losses are attributed to enemy action, while 80 percent were the result of failed electronic systems.

The last QH-50D was delivered to the Navy in August 1969; 18 had been delivered to the Japanese Maritime Self Defense Force. The cessation of *Snoopy* missions in 1970 did not spell the end of DASH, but instead gave the unique craft a new life in the U.S. Army as night reconnaissance and target platforms at White Sands Missile Range. Until 1995 the Navy continued use of the DASH at the Naval Air Weapons Station, China Lake, California, for research and as targets for anti-helicopter missiles; those acquired by the Army continued to fly missions, albeit out of the public eye, until May 2006. Gyrodyne proudly claims the first, the last, and the only deployed Vertical Take-Off and Landing (VTOL) Unmanned Aerial Vehicle in history.

LAMPS

Since the DASH proved unreliable and was limited mainly to torpedo attack, in 1965 a follow-on concept was conceived to carry a pilot. That program too had a limited mission capability of ASW only, and was dropped in less time than it took to learn its multiple titles: Light Anti-Submarine Helicopter, Manned Anti-Submarine Helicopter, and Light Aerial Anti-Submarine Vehicle. The Navy then came up with the term Light Airborne Multi-Purpose System (LAMPS) to identify a helicopter capable not only of ASW but of Anti-Ship Missile Defense, Anti-Ship Surveillance and Targeting, while retaining the search and rescue and utility capability.

Regardless of whether Navy leaders considered the DASH a success, they were resigned to the fact that helicopters would be a mainstay of the Fleet; it was envisioned that ships of all sizes would operate helicopters from their decks, a practice that already had become standard in the Canadian Navy. As the number of surface ships decreased, their size increased, with their flight decks made as large as possible to accommodate helicopters. Operating helicopter anti-submarine detachments aboard carriers was ideal for close-in protection, but destroyers and frigates also needed the capabilities that only helicopters could provide. But they had to be small helicopters and that set the parameters for the ideal ship-borne multi-purpose helicopter. Mindful of the sinking of the Israeli destroyer *Eliat* by an Egyptian Styx missile during the six-day Arab-Israeli War in October 1967, Navy planners began drawing up requirements for LAMPS.

Based on experience with the DASH, the Navy had imposed a 4,000-pound maximum gross aircraft weight due to perceived structural limitations of destroyer escort decks. The limit was raised to 6,000 pounds in 1969, and, ultimately, deck strength analyses and tests conducted by Kaman Aerospace engineers proved that much higher

This Model 608 was Bell Helicopter's proposal for the Navy's LAMPS III in 1970. Painted gray and white, the aircraft featured folding main rotors, float-type skids, an MAD, and torpedo. (Bell Helicopter)

gross weights were tolerable. Kaman's impetus for conducting such research stemmed from the Navy's selection of the company's H-2 Seasprite helicopter as the LAMPS platform. The Navy had selected the Seasprite in 1956 for plane-guard, gun spotting, search and rescue, and utility work. The H-2—originally designated HU2K—first flew in 1959, with deliveries beginning in 1962. Kaman built 190 UH-2A and UH-2B single-engine Seasprites. The twin-engine UH-2C Seasprite, which first flew in 1966, ranked high on the list of proposals submitted by manufacturers for the LAMPS package. This version's two General Electric T58-GE-8B turboshaft engines added power to and broadened the safety margin of a proven durable and reliable airframe.

In October 1970, the HH-2D SAR Seasprite was selected as an interim LAMPS platform, becoming the SH-2D. The Naval Air Development Center (NADC) then contracted with IBM Electronics to come up with the avionics-helicopter integration package. The event most responsible for creating the LAMPS system, and for quickening the pace of Navy helicopter research and development, was the arrival in 1971 of ADM Elmo R. Zumwalt as Chief of Naval Operations (CNO). Citing the importance of helicopters aboard escort ships, the LAMPS project became Zumwalt's highest priority immediately after taking the helm.

What had been considered long inconceivable had happened: A CNO wanted helicopters, and lots of them. The Naval Material Command took charge and the NADC began the at-sea "Development and Validation-98 Program (DV-98)" with four Seasprites. The initial phases of DV-98 were aimed at evaluating the Magnetic Anomaly Detector (MAD) on a helicopter. In 1970, the Seasprite MAD test beds were sent to Vietnam for *Project Iron Barnacle*, which was an attempt to use MAD to locate enemy equipment in dense jungle. The project, which was carried out with heavily armed Army helicopters, met with dismal, yet interesting, results.

Shortly after Kaman received a contract to convert 10 HH-2Ds into SH-2Ds, the term interim was replaced in favor of the designation LAMPS MK I, and 10 more SH-2Ds were ordered. The conversion introduced an under-nose Litton LN-66 search radar and an ASQ-81 MAD, along with a launcher for 15 SSQ-47 active or SSQ-41 passive sonobuoys, which replaced the time-honored dipping sonars. Offensive armament consisted of two torpedoes.

The first deployment of the SH-2D LAMPS was made in December 1971 by Helicopter Combat Support Squadron Four (HC-4) for three months aboard Guided Missile Cruiser USS *Belknap* (CG-26). During this period, evaluation of the Seasprite was expanded to include arming an NUH-2C (BuNo 147981) with Sidewinder and Sparrow III air-to-air missiles at the Naval Air Test Center (NATC) at NAS Patuxent River.

The LAMPS MK II system was envisioned as a major upgrade for the Seasprite, pending the arrival of the ultimate

MK III. Two HH-2Ds (BuNos 149033 and 150181) were modified with AN/APS-122 radar, becoming YSH-2Es. They began trials for MK II in March 1972 and began sea trials aboard the cruiser USS *Fox* (CG-33) in June. While at sea, their resounding achievement was transmitting a real-time radar picture to the Fox's CIC. The program, however, was canceled later that year to accelerate work on the MK III. Tests with the YSH-2Es, although brief, led to an improved MK I version, the SH-2F, whose main purpose was to extend a ship's surveillance horizon against missiles and torpedoes.

The SH-2F featured 1,350-shp General Electric T58-GE-8F engines and an improved rotor system, increasing the gross weight to 12,500 pounds. The F version's landing gear was strengthened, and the tail wheel

The fifth Messerschmitt-Bolkow-Blohm Bo-105 prototype went to Boeing Vertol for evaluation, and was entered in the LAMPS competition. Its magnetic anomaly detector was mounted on the right side, while a single torpedo was mounted opposite. (Author's Collection)

Three available production airframes were selected for the final LAMPS trials. Their cockpit mockups are seen here. In the foreground is Westland's Lynx, then Bell's UH-1N, and the winner of the competition, Kaman's HH-2D. The cockpits were designed for a pilot and airborne tactical officer (ATO)/copilot, each having flight controls and instruments, with the ATO responsible for weapons launch. (U.S. Navy)

Although only two YSH-2Es are commonly reported as having been built by Kaman, this Seasprite, BuNo 150171, was also recorded as a YSH-2E. It started life as a UH-2B, and then became an HH-2D and YSH-2E. It is seen here at NADC Warminster, Pennsylvania, in 1972, testing a sonobuoy launcher, which had been adorned with a face and the words "The Buoy Boy." (U.S. Navy)

was moved forward 6 feet for deck-edge clearance when operating aboard smaller ships. Canadian Marconi LN 66HP surface search radar enabled pilots to spot surface items as small as submarine periscopes and equipment of downed aviators. The SH-2F was armed with two Mk-46 torpedoes. Installation of a tactical navigation/communication system necessitated a sensor operator in addition to the two pilots. The first SH-2F deployment was aboard the destroyer USS *Bagley* (DE-1069) in 1973. So successful was the LAMPS that not only was every existing H-2 airframe, a total of 104, eventually converted to SH-2F standards, Kaman's SH-2F production line was re-opened in 1982 to produce 60 SH-2Fs; the last six airframes came off the line as SH-2Gs. Eleven squadrons would operate the SH-2F, usually in two-plane detachments dispersed among frigates and cruisers.

Since computers were the heart of the LAMPS III system, the Department of Defense in mid 1973 specified that

a contractor be responsible for its development, replacing Navy laboratories. Equally revolutionary was the Naval Air System Command's classifying the project as a major weapon system that contained an aircraft as a sub-system.

Although Kaman's Seasprite had been a mainstay of the LAMPS program from its inception, Navy planners considered other airframes to meet the LAMPS III requirement of a medium size helicopter with two pilots, tactical sensors, expendable stores, and computers for the ASW and anti-ship missile defense mission. Search and rescue, medical evacuation, vertical replenishment, and gunfire spotting capabilities were retained as secondary missions. Three available production airframes—Kaman's HH-2D, Bell's twin-engine UH-1N Huey, and Westland's WG.13 Lynx—were selected. Compared to the HH-2D, the Huey and Lynx were relatively new, with the UH-1N having first flown in 1969, and the Lynx in 1971. Other competing designs were Bell's Model 608, Hughes' Model

The twin-turbine Kaman Seasprite was originally designated as the HH-2D, but two helicopters were modified and designated as YSH-2Es for developmental testing of new radar systems in early 1972. (Stephen Miller)

Kaman completed two YSH-2Es in March 1972 for trials of the LAMPS II system. The program was canceled later that year to better concentrate on the LAMPS III. The YSH-2Es, BuNos 149033 and 150181, tested the under-nose APS-122 radar seen here. Below the cockpit is a launcher for eight Mk 25 smoke floats. (U.S. Navy)

The first of five YSH-60B prototypes, BuNo 161169, undergoes flight test for LAMPS in 1980. High visibility markings would be replaced by a tactical color scheme comprising three shades of light gray. (Igor I. Sikorsky Historical Archives, Inc.)

500, and MBB's (Messerschmitt-Bolkow-Blohm) Bo-105, all of which were dropped due to their small size.

The Navy, however, watched closely the development of Sikorsky's UH-60 Blackhawk, which first flew in 1974, and in 1976 won the competition for the Army's Utility Tactical Transport Aircraft System (UTTAS) program. Since the LAMPS mission range requirement was extended, and, subsequently, the weight, in 1975 the H-60 was chosen in view of its larger size and lower development costs. IBM was named the prime contractor along with three associate contractors: Sikorsky for the aircraft, General Electric for the engine, and the Canadian firm DAF/INDAL for the aircraft's Recovery, Assist, Securing and Traversing (RAST) system; using a cable lowered from the aircraft, this system can bring a helicopter to the ship's deck in four seconds, even in rough sea states.

Officially labeled the SH-60B Seahawk, the helicopter was powered by GE's T700-401 turbine engine, which allowed an ASW configuration gross weight of 21,700

As a primary Seasprite testbed, BuNo 147981 carried numerous designations. Beginning life as a UH-2A, and then UH-2C after twin-engine conversion, it became an SH-2D LAMPS prototype in 1970. When evaluating Sidewinder and Sparrow missiles, along with fire control radar in 1972 and 1973, it was designated NUH-2C, seen here with NADC Weapons Test Directorate markings. Then it served as an NHH-2D LAMPS testbed at NADC facilities at NAS Lakehurst. Finally, it was brought up to SH-2F standards. (U.S. Navy)

In a role for which it was well suited, an SH-3H, BuNo 154107, of Helicopter Anti-submarine Squadron Two (HS-2) flies an ASW training mission over the Pacific in 1975. During the Jordanian crisis in 1970, when HS-2 deployed to protect the battle group, U.S. flags were hastily applied to the squadron's Sea Kings to distinguish them from Israeli Sea Kings also operating in the area. The squadron retained the flags as a standard marking. (U.S. Navy)

pounds and a top speed of 180 knots. A full stores load comprised 25 sonobuoys and two Mk-46 torpedoes. The crew consisted of pilot, ATO/copilot, and sensor operator. The LAMPS III operated in two modes in which tactical decisions were made by shipboard personnel, or by the Seahawk crew.

Since the SH-60B would not be rolled out until 1979, in 1976 an SH-3 Sea King assigned to the NADC underwent trials with the prototype LAMPS III system. The newly launched, turbine-powered USS *McInerney* (FFG-8) was modified to evaluate LAMPS III, and the first of five YSH-60B prototypes arrived at IBM's Oswego, New York, facility for trials in April 1980. The Navy established its first LAMPS III squadron, HSL-41, at NAS North Island, California, in January 1983.

Although the Seahawk assumed the LAMPS III role, the SH-2F Seasprite continued ASW duty, with the more powerful SH-2G appearing in 1985.

Sea King

Prior to the development of the LAMPS system, the Seasprite was not alone in its vigil over the world's oceans. Changes made by the Navy about 1960, including replacement of the Mk-41 torpedo with the Mk-44, and

assigning manned helicopters to ships, led to the quest for a bigger and better helicopter, the result being Sikorsky's Sea King. Heavily armed versions of both the Seasprite and the Sea King would play major roles in the Vietnam War.

With the advent of the turbine engine, the Navy was quick to request that Sikorsky design a turbine-powered ASW helicopter that combined the HSS-1N's hunter and killer capabilities. Navy specifications called for dunking sonar, four-hour mission endurance, and a weapon load of 840 pounds, which allowed a 550-pound Mk-46 torpedo or a nuclear depth bomb.

Sikorsky began work on its Model S-61, which was based on its Model S-62; although numerically out of sequence, the S-62 had flown first. Called the Seaguard, the S-62 was powered by a single turbine engine and retained the rotor dynamics of the HSS-1. The S-61 used two 1,050-shp General Electric T58-GE-6 engines, marking the first time that a single-rotor helicopter could approach speeds of 200 mph. The S-62 and S-61 used the same basic airframe with boat-shaped hull and sponsons for landing and flotation gear. In a radical design change, engines were mounted above the cabin. Despite such similarities, the Navy designated the S-61 the HSS-2 to instead imply commonality with the HSS-1, lest a completely new aircraft be denied funding.

Ten prototypes were produced, the first of which made its maiden flight on 17 March 1959. Trials with two prototypes aboard the USS *Lake Champlain* (CV-39) in early 1961 proved the Sea King's ability to fold and spread its main rotor blades, plus take off, in winds of nearly 50 mph. Production HSS-2s, re-designated SH-3As in 1962, eventually were upgraded with more powerful engines, increasing the gross weight to more than 19,000 pounds. The Navy not only had its first all-weather amphibious helicopter, but one that could carry the latest ASW gear. The SH-3A's impressive weapons load included four Mk-46 or Mk-48 torpedoes, or a 510-pound Mk 57 nuclear depth bomb, or a 1,200-pound Lulu nuclear depth bomb.

Its many attributes made the Sea King so popular that it was successively developed in numerous models, both military and civilian. Besides serving the U.S. Navy in a variety of roles, Sea King derivatives performed countless rescues in the U.S. Coast Guard, in Army livery they transported Presidents, and, as the famed "Jolly Green Giant" of the U.S. Air Force, they helped write the book on Air Rescue and Air Commando operations. It served the air arms of many nations, and was built under license in Japan, Canada, Italy, and Great Britain.

Lessons of War

Outside of the ASW community, the most heavily armed U.S. Navy Sea Kings were SH-3As converted to HH-3As for combat search and rescue (CSAR) in Vietnam. Naval aviators would learn much about CSAR before implementing a dedicated combat rescue system.

When air operations over North Vietnam began in 1964, few options existed for the recovery of downed airmen. As the tempo of the air war increased, the need for a major commitment to search and rescue became painfully obvious. Although the U.S. Air Force was largely responsible for the SAR mission, the northernmost regions of North Vietnam and the waters of the Gulf of Tonkin were beyond the reach of land-based helicopters, including those launched from forward locations in Laos. The responsibility for much of the rescue in those regions fell upon Sea Kings aboard four ASW carriers—USS *Bennington* (CVS-20), *Hornet* (CVS-12), *Kearsarge* (CVS-33), and *Yorktown* (CVS-10)—and escort ships in the Gulf, along with Seasprites aboard smaller ships of *Task Force 77*. At the war's onset, plane-guard duty was assigned to UH-2A and UH-2B detachments of Helicopter Utility Squadron One (HU-1) of the Pacific Fleet and HU-2 of the Atlantic Fleet. They were re-designated Helicopter Combat Support Squadrons (HC-1 and HC-2) on 1 July 1965 and combat rescue was added to their multiple roles.

Pilots flying attack aircraft knew that their best chance of being rescued was to eject over the sea. Since this was not always possible, it was only a matter of time before a ship-based helicopter had to make the perilous dash inland to attempt rescue. It occurred on 20 September 1965 when a UH-2B of HC-1, Det. A took off from the cruiser USS *Galveston* (CLG-3), crossed rough terrain, and endured ground fire to rescue a downed A-4E Skyhawk pilot. Since the Sea King had greater range and the safety of two engines to venture into North Vietnam, the SH-3As of HS-4 aboard USS *Yorktown* (CVS-10) became the first to fly rescue sorties overland as well as at sea. Eventually, other ASW helicopter crews were taking their unarmed and unarmored aircraft into North Vietnam. The time had come for the Navy to adopt a CSAR plan for its helicopters.

Since many destroyers retained 7,000-gallon fuel tanks from DASH operations, a technique was developed

The Mk-46 torpedo installation on a Sea King of HS-8 during trials at Naval Torpedo Station, Keyport, Washington, in November 1976. The SH-3's MAD is seen being reeled out on its cable to begin the hunt for submarines. (U.S. Navy)

that enabled Sea Kings to tap the tanks, thereby extending their range. By the time that HS-2 aboard USS *Hornet* (CVA-12) had arrived on Yankee Station in the Gulf of Tonkin in 1965, it had perfected the technique called Hover In-Flight Refueling (HIFR), or High-Drink. While hovering close to a ship, the Sea King used its hoist to pull up a fueling hose from the ship's deck to the fueling receptacle just below the helicopter's cabin doorway. Field-modified Sea Kings carried two 55-gallon drums in the cabin to augment their fuel supply. This practice, however, was found unsafe and the drums were replaced by two A-4 Skyhawk drop tanks held in wooden cradles. As HS-2 crews became expert at the High-Drink technique, two destroyers or cruisers were positioned off the North Vietnamese coast for SAR support.

Not only was HS-2 first to use the HIFR technique at night, during one night in November 1965, one of the squadron's SH-3As performed three HIFRs to remain airborne for more than 11 hours on a CSAR mission over the Gulf. As air attacks over North Vietnam were stepped up, Navy pilots took comfort in the fact that every effort was being made to improve their chance for rescue.

Aboard the *Hornet*, five of HS-2's SH-3As were stripped of ASW gear, armed with M-60 machine guns in both cabin doorways, and had their high visibility markings

painted over to blend with their dark gray finish. Meanwhile, Sikorsky, Kaman, and Navy shops worked on long-term modifications. From more lessons came more improvements. When the *Hornet* was in the Philippines in November 1965, some of HS-2's Sea Kings were given self-sealing fuel tanks. When relieved by HS-4, HS-2 passed along its recommendation that the cable on the rescue hoist be doubled to 200 feet, and that the hoist's capacity be increased from 600 to 1,000 pounds.

When HS-6 aboard the ASW carrier USS *Kearsarge* (CVS-33) arrived in Vietnam in 1966, five of its SH-3As had been modified for combat SAR by the removal of their sonar and the addition of armor plating around the engines, transmission, and crew stations; M-60 machine guns were added for crewmen. Especially useful for rescues was the Sea King's integrated all-weather ASW Doppler radar, radar altimeter, and auto-stabilization system, which transitioned the aircraft from cruise into a low hover, and back to cruise.

Simultaneous efforts to better prepare single-engine Seasprites for CSAR were undertaken. One unit's experience highlighted the problems associated with operating helicopters aboard ships. After Detachment 5 of HC-1 modified a UH-2, the Seasprite was secured to the small deck above the missile launcher of the USS *Coontz*

Squadrons that carried out combat search and rescue (CSAR) in Vietnam not only armed their Sea Kings, they applied camouflage with subdued markings. This SH-3A, BuNo 148985 (tail code NV-70), is seen aboard USS Mahan (DLG-11) on 23 May 1967. Visible in its rear cabin doorway is a shield for an M-60 machine gun. This Sea King and its crew of four were lost at sea two weeks later. (U.S. Navy)

(DLG-9). While en route to Vietnam in January 1966, the launcher was rotated to test the system, tearing the tail section from the Seasprite. A replacement UH-2 was built up from the original aircraft, given an uprated Gold Stripe engine, and painted black overall. The Gold Stripe T58 engine was rated for higher speeds and temperatures, and eventually was installed in CSAR Seasprites and Sea Kings.

During its first three combat cruises aboard the Hornet, HS-2 rescued 15 aviators, flying eight combat SAR missions into North Vietnam. Such successes were not without losses; the "Golden Falcons" of HS-2 lost three aircraft over the North, the first being SH-3A BuNo 148993 shot down on 13 November 1965. Another three were operational losses. Among 20 SH-3s lost during the war, eight were combat losses. The Navy lost two CSAR helicopters for every three aircrew rescued, and one crewman killed or captured for every two aircrew rescued.

Big Mothers

Heavy aircrew and aircraft losses suffered by HS-2 during its 1967 cruise aboard the *Hornet* underscored the dangerous nature of helicopter operations in the Gulf of Tonkin; the overwhelming need for a dedicated combat SAR unit prompted action. Capitalizing on the momentum of the Navy CSAR experience, the Navy on 1 September 1967 commissioned Helicopter Combat Support Squadron Seven (HC-7) at NAS Atsugi, Japan; HC-7's primary job would be CSAR. At the squadron's core was a detachment of HC-1; however, it absorbed other detachments, giving it a mix of aircraft types and duties. Besides UH-2s and SH-3s for CSAR, HC-7 used them for VIP transport and mine countermeasures, along with a pair of UH-46s for vertical replenishment, and an H-34 for survey work in Japan. HC-7 took under its wing the "Clementine" Seasprites operating from SAR ships,

while HC-1's UH-2s continued plane-guard duty. Although a specialized force was now in place, the HS squadrons often were reluctant to give up their combat role, eager to fly SAR missions when the need arose.

Like the Sea Kings, Seasprites were equipped for hover refueling, and by 1968, both types flown by HC-7 were pre-positioned for two to three days aboard destroyers off North Vietnam's coast; others typically cross-decked between carriers for 10 to 15 days. Besides adding M-60 machine guns to their helicopters, HC-7 crews camouflaged their aircraft to give them an edge when flying inland. Despite the Navy's attempt to standardize helicopter schemes with Gunship Gray, crews used whatever paints were available, resulting in a variety of schemes usually comprising dark green and tan. One HC-7 Seasprite pilot, LTJG Clyde Lassen, was certain that camouflage had spared him and his crew from withering gunfire during a daring rescue mission.

Lassen and his crew exemplified the mettle of HC-7's crews on the night of 18-19 January 1968 when they flew inland to rescue the crew of an F-4 Phantom, which had been shot down over Vinh, North Vietnam. After the mission, Lassen commented, ". . . it seemed that the dark paint scheme and Vietnamese gunners trained to lead fast moving targets had spared the Seasprite from most of the ground fire." But it was Lassen's courage that earned him the Medal of Honor.

A unit dedicated to CSAR in an ever-changing tactical environment required special aircraft, and the Navy, along with Sikorsky and Kaman, were prepared to fill that requirement. Drawing upon the experience it gained from testing a Seasprite as a gunship for the U.S. Army, Kaman began work on an armed rescue version. Since the improved performance and safety of twin engines was vital, the UH-2C was chosen. The Navy ordered six HH-2Cs, whose main armament was an under-nose GE TAT-102

BuNo 149773 was one of six Seasprites converted to the armed and armored HH-2C version flown in combat by HC-7's Big Mothers. The offset nose-mounted minigun proved troublesome and was not used operationally. A rescue hoist extends over the right cabin doorway. Dual-wheel main landing gear was necessary to handle the HH-2C's extra weight. (U.S. Navy)

minigun turret rated at 4,000 rounds per minute. Crew-operated M-60 machine guns were added, along with armor around the cockpit, engines, and other critical components. Other improvements included two-wheel main landing gear to handle the 12,800 pound gross weight, a four-bladed tail rotor, UHF radios, and shatterproof acrylic windows.

Typical of the compromise that came with aircraft improvement was the HH-2C's added weight, which doubled fuel consumption; and tapping two external 116-gallon fuel tanks often proved unreliable. To make matters worse, the C model's outboard engine inlets sucked in salt spray during a low hover, increasing the chance for engine stall; the single-engine Seasprite, on the other hand, could hover with its tail wheel in the water.

Phil Poisson, a seasoned Seasprite pilot, commented: "After having flown about 1,500 hours in the UH-2A/B and having been in four major accidents, it was a pleasure to climb into the HH-2C. The A/B was a single engine and quite underpowered. When they added the Gold Stripe engines to the A/B for SAR missions, that was good, but it was still underpowered. We got the first HH-2C without the gun turret as that function was quite dangerous. If you landed too hard, the gun would fire some rounds—not a healthy thing on a small deck.

"After a few flights in the HH-2C, one could figure this baby had a massive amount of power and could haul ass. Though it was rated at 140 knots, it flew 158 knots in a dive, and still was very smooth. The first time I hovered an HH-2C at 2,500 feet in the Philippines, I knew we had a beast that could do it all. We had flown them for two years before they were all taken back to be switched into SH-2s. Damn, what a waste."

Unexpected firing from the jolt of deck landings spelled a quick end to the turrets, and they were removed before they could be used operationally. On 25 June 1970, just 10 days after *Seadevil 20*, the first HH-2C, entered service, all single-engine Seasprites were pulled from SAR duty. During 1971, Sea Kings had replaced all of the

The HH-3A configuration included 175-gallon fuel tanks attached to forward torpedo mounts. The TAT-102 minigun turret is seen in the stowed position on the prototype HH-3A, BuNo 149896. (Igor I. Sikorsky Historical Archives, Inc.)

remaining twin-engine Seasprites, and by the end of that year, HC-7 shed its original missions, becoming solely dedicated to CSAR. The squadron was prepared for the commitment—not only was it seasoned in combat, but the year before, work had begun on the ultimate CSAR Sea King.

Venturing well beyond the Sea Kings that had been hardened for CSAR, Sikorsky, with the blessing of the U.S. Navy, undertook a low-profile program of producing the ultimate rescue Sea King. Designated HH-3A, this variant had all ASW equipment removed and the sonar well faired over. Titanium armor was installed to protect the engines, transmission, cabin floor, and avionic and hydraulic components, with armored seats installed for the pilots. Self-sealing, extended-range fuel tanks were used along with a rapid fuel dump system to help quickly lighten the aircraft. External 175-gallon fuel tanks were added to the sponson torpedo mounts; however, they were not used operationally as the in-flight refueling procedure proved sufficient.

The HH-3A took on a gunship-like quality with Emerson TAT-102 7.62mm minigun turrets on the aft torpedo mounts. The turrets, called "barbettes," each housed a GE GAU-2B/A minigun and 6,000 rounds of ammunition. The guns were rated at 4,000 spm and could be operated by the pilots or the crewmen in the aft cabin. Few "Big Mother" pilots were disappointed that the gun packs were removed when they proved too heavy and created a center-of-gravity shift, ruling out combat evaluation. They were replaced by crew-operated M-60 machine guns in the main cabin doorway and in the forward entry doorway. These, in turn, were replaced in favor of hand-operated miniguns on armored pedestal mounts, which were hinged to swing inward when not in use.

To handle the HH-3A's increased weight, more powerful GE T58-GE-8F engines were installed. Sikorsky converted one SH-3A (BuNo 149896) to an HH-3A and provided the Navy with kits for conversions done at NAS Quonset Point, Rhode Island, and Cubi Point, Philippines. A total of 12 HH-3As were built, which were divided among HC-7 and HS squadrons. Their BuNos are as follows:

148036	149903	149922	151552
149682	149912	149933	151553
149896	149916	151531	151556

Although falling short in performance for the DASH mission, five HH-3As formed the main combat rescue force of HC-7 Big Mothers in the Gulf of Tonkin; the squadron took its name from an air boss aboard the USS *Independence* (CVA-62), who, when broadcasting aircraft deck movements, called the Sea Kings Big Mothers. The squadron's all H-3 afloat Detachment 110 performed shipboard rotation to the extent they became known as Orphans of the Seventh Fleet. With its maintenance section at Cubi Point and its headquarters at Imperial Beach, Det. 110 staged Sea Kings and crews aboard carriers, deploying three HH-3As to destroyers and cruisers along

North Vietnam's coast. One stood alert on the carrier, while the remaining aircraft underwent maintenance.

When large-scale air strikes resumed over North Vietnam in December 1971, the Big Mothers were heavily committed. During 1972, Det. 110 performed 48 rescues, 25 of which were under fire, often at night and in bad weather, yet without suffering losses. When Det. 110 stood down in the Gulf on 25 September 1973, not only had it logged more than 140 rescues, it had established CSAR doctrine that remains in use. Back at Imperial Beach, the Big Mothers kept two HH-3As on alert aboard USAF C-5 transports for rapid global CSAR deployment. Detachments sent to NAS Fallon, Nevada, shared with soon-to-deploy air wing pilots the lessons of CSAR they had learned in Vietnam.

With little need for a CSAR force, HC-7 was disestablished in June 1975 and its 10 HH-3As passed to reserve squadron HC-9; one HH-3A (BuNo 151531) had been lost in the Philippines, and the oldest airframe (BuNo 148036) spent most of its time in test mode at NATC. The "Protectors" of HC-9 performed the CSAR training and test role with HH-3As until they were retired in 1990.

Seawolves

Navy helicopter crewmen who found challenge in the anti-submarine role, but longed for a greater sense of military accomplishment, would find satisfaction in the Navy's association with gunships. As the ultimate proving ground, the expanding conflict in Vietnam would spawn a concept unprecedented in the history of U.S. naval aviation—the Navy's first and only attack helicopter squadron of the war. The unique unit was commissioned, operated, and decommissioned entirely within South Vietnam's Mekong Delta region.

The Delta, which is the southeastern portion of the country, was within the military area labeled IV Corps by the Military Assistance Command, Vietnam. The region is formed by two of the world's great rivers: the Mekong and the Bassac, which run out of Cambodia parallel to each other. They cross the center of the Delta, splaying into numerous mouths as they near the sea. As one of the largest river delta systems in the world, the Mekong Delta, although predominantly flat, features wild regions of reed and grasslands, swamps, and forbidding dense mangrove swamps. At the heart of the Delta is a region that MACV identified as the Rung Sat Special Zone, aptly called by the Vietnamese "The Forest of Assassins."

All travel was done on a complex system of canals, rivers, creeks, and lesser tributaries. Few roads existed, even during the dry season. The Viet Cong found it the perfect place for sanctuaries and for exercising control of populated areas. Accordingly, MACV adopted a doctrine to protect the populace, restrict enemy movement, and deny him sanctuary. Unfortunately, control of the Delta fell outside of the Army's traditional methods and equipment. Land mobility did not exist and all movement was made by water or air. Control of the Delta was dependent upon control of the waterways. The Navy would exploit such unique conditions by forming its "Brown Water Navy" as part of Task Force 116 (TF 116), code named *Game Warden*.

Established in December 1965, this riverine force initially comprised fast river patrol boats, amphibious landing craft, and repair ships, along with a variety of interesting prototype craft. The patrol boat—called PBR for Patrol Boat, River, or "Pibber"—was a 31-foot fiberglass, shallow-draft boat built on a pleasure craft hull. Although fast and heavily armed with .50-cal. and M-60 machine guns, 81mm or 60mm mortars, a Honeywell Mk-18 grenade launcher, and a host of lighter weapons, the boats often

The twin .30-cal. gun installation mounted on a fire team's trail aircraft, although effective, would be replaced by crew-operated miniguns. The standard door gun mount was the adjustable and swivel-type Sagami mount, familiar to Army gunships. Heavy door gun weaponry usually precluded use of mounted quad machine guns, and later, miniguns. (Bruce Boissey Collection)

Vital to the Seawolves' armament package was the crew-operated M-60 machine gun. It is seen here in its typical mode as a Free 60 stripped down infantry version, which was fired sideways with the aid of a pistol grip. Seawolf door gunner/crew chief ADJ3 Bruce Boissey demonstrates how the gun was fired while ammunition fed upward from a large container secured to the cabin floor. (Bruce Boissey Collection)

were no match for well-planned, coordinated attacks from shore. When boat patrols began in April 1966, they met with intense firefights, proving the glaring need for close air support with heavy hitting firepower. Air assets, most notably North American OV-10A Broncos and helicopter gunships, would eventually join the Brown Water Navy.

Since the United States and its allies enjoyed air superiority over South Vietnam, the enemy used the cover of darkness to travel the Delta's waterways. Quick reaction night air support of the Brown Water Navy was not a strong point of Army aviation during that time; few Army helicopter pilots were instrument rated, and most units were centrally located and controlled. Although some Army helicopter detachments operated from remote strips to support Delta operations, they could not adequately cover aggressive and frequent patrolling, which often resulted in fierce firefights that required immediate air support. In addition, the Army was accustomed to a command and control presence, especially at night and in populated areas. Army Forward Air Controllers (FACs)

The time-honored Browning .50-cal. machine gun was used on nearly every HA(L)-3 Huey, normally on the lead aircraft of a fire team. This is the AN/MB style gun, which had a firing rate of 850 to 950 spm. The 7-tube XM-157 or XM-158 2.75-inch rocket launcher was a Seawolf standard. The 19-tube XM-200 launcher could not be used aboard ships due to radiation hazards. (Author's Collection)

The short-barrel AN/M2 HB Fifty normally had a higher rate of fire than long-barrel ground versions. This aviation version's Sagami mount incorporates a standard size ammunition can. (Henry E. Livingstone)

A Seawolf UH-1B of Det. 8, HA(L)-3 based at Vinh Long unleashes a 2.75-inch FFAR while supporting river patrol boats (PBRs, or "Pibbers") on the Co Chien River during May 1968. (U.S. Navy)

were spread thin and, therefore, hard pressed to provide continuous patrol.

The need existed for instrument-rated pilots who could launch from nearby locations to work closely with riverine forces, and who could exercise command at the lowest tactical level without FACs. The solution would have to come from the Navy itself.

During the early 1960s, Navy officers, in particular CAPT John T. Shepherd of the U.S. Naval Forces office in Saigon, had watched closely the Army's work with helicopter gunships. The Navy "brass" was receptive to Shepherd's nudging for Navy gunship helicopters. Since the concept went far beyond the realm of torpedo-armed helicopters, equipping and training a gunship squadron would have to start from scratch.

The obvious tutor was the Army, which assigned its gunship-pioneering 197th AHC not only in an advisement capacity, but to provide aircraft. Eight UH-1B Hueys were loaned to the Navy, and, once again, Helicopter Combat Support Squadron One (HC-1) at NAS Ream Field, Imperial Beach, California, would expand its mission by providing crews for the Hueys. Four detachments were formed, each with eight pilots and eight crewmen, all volunteers, whose training had included over-water operations and night and instrument flying. The Army's 10th

Aviation Group at Ft. Benning, Georgia, agreed to establish a special program to train Navy gunship pilots in tactics, and in the aircraft and weapons. Enlisted crew underwent aircraft maintenance and gunnery training alongside Army trainees at Fort Rucker, Alabama.

The first element, called Detachment 29 of HC-1, arrived at Vung Tau, South Vietnam, on 4 July 1966, and went aboard dock landing ship USS *Tortuga* (LSD-26) in mid August. Named "Rockwell's Rats" after detachment commander LCDR William A. Rockwell, the unit flew combat missions with, and then replaced, a contingent of Army Huey gunships of the 145th Aviation Battalion. In September, the unit, which the Army had named "Seawolves," was divided into four detachments of two Hueys each at Vung Tau, Nha Be, Vinh Long, and aboard USS *Comstock* (LSD-19). They began support of riverine forces, with the first major engagement occurring on 31 October when they joined PBRs to destroy 50 enemy sampans on the My Tho River.

Besides the *Tortuga* and *Comstock*, the USS *Belle Grove* (LSD-2) and USS *Floyd County* (LSD-762) had also been modified with helicopter pads pending the arrival of specially configured tank landing ships (LSTs). In November 1966, the USS *Jennings County* (LST-846) arrived off Vung Tau to serve as a base for Seawolf detachments and PBRs. The LSTs anchored in the lower Bassac, Co Chien (USS *Garrett County* LST-786), and Ham Luong (USS *Harnett County* LST-821) Rivers, moving periodically to thwart saboteurs and to be close to the action. The USS *Hunterdon County* (LST-838) would join

Not all weapons carried by Seawolves were of the lethal variety. Attached to the nose of this UH-1B is a siren and air horns, which proved as much a psychological effect on the enemy as firepower. (Henry E. Livingstone)

the trio and they would later be designated Patrol Craft Tenders (AGPs). On 1 April 1967 the four detachments became Helicopter Attack (Light) Squadron Three, or HA(L)-3. That summer, UH-1Bs from the Army's 1st Cavalry Division were added, and by the end of 1967, 22 Huey gunships were operational with seven detachments.

Since the UH-1Bs officially belonged to the Army, maintenance had to be done through Army channels, often making it difficult for HA(L)-3 personnel to keep them flying. Those that had come from Army units in country had seen hard use, while Hueys received later from the Army's overhaul depot at Corpus Christi, Texas, were in much better condition. Bringing the aircraft up to Navy standards involved mainly fitting them with specialized door gun mounts and radar altimeters. The altimeter provided exact altitude readouts, which were necessary for operations in bad weather, at night, and when landing aboard support ships. Since they were in short supply, the crucial instrument was priority-installed in aircraft operating from ships.

During their first months of combat operations, Seawolf personnel experimented with a variety of combinations of weapon systems. Heavy firepower was the name of the game, and crews favored door gun installations of .50-cal. and twin .30-cal. machine guns. Despite

Beginning in 1969, the XM-21 system replaced the XM-16 quad M-60C system on Seawolf gunships. The XM-21 incorporated an M134 minigun and 7-tube rocket launcher. The 2.75-inch rockets in this XM-158 launcher are not inserted fully so that their folding fins can be displayed. (Henry E. Livingstone)

the proliferation of Army Huey gunships, Army units generally avoided large crew-served weapons. Seawolf detachments had different preferences for armament, which often depended upon the main type of mission they flew. Weapon systems, however, mounted to the hard points of Seawolf UH-1Bs mimicked those used by Army Hueys, those being 7-tube 2.75-inch rocket launchers and quad 7.62mm machine guns. The quad XM-16 system would be replaced in 1969 by the XM-21 system, which used the M134 minigun—the first minigun was actually acquired by the Seawolves in 1968; however, it was quietly returned when the Army discovered it missing.

The firepower that made Seawolves fearsome centered around four weapons: the minigun, M-60 machine gun, 7-tube 2.75-inch rocket launcher, and .50-cal. machine gun. The time-honored Browning "Fifty," against which all other weapons have been measured, was a mainstay, thanks to its durability and reliability. It was used throughout HA(L)-3's tenure, and on nearly every aircraft. Used exclusively as a door gun, the .50-cal. often was favored over the minigun for its accuracy and hitting power, not to mention the minigun's tendency to jam. Both long-barrel and aviation short-barrel types were used. Ammunition was plentiful, often coming from stocks left over from World War II. Dated ammunition

frequently caused gun jams or were duds, but the order had been given to use it all up.

Miniguns were used both fix-mounted to the standard XM-156 universal mount and as pintle-mounted door guns. In the latter mode, the minigun was seen in a variety of configurations, most of which were fabricated according to a detachment's preference. In view of the frequency of night operations, all were tipped with muzzle flash suppressors. When a .50-cal. or minigun was used as a door gun, it replaced the fixed minigun on the side it was mounted. Typically, the lead aircraft mounted the .50, with about 1,000 rounds of ammunition, with the door minigun and about 1,500 rounds used on the trail aircraft.

Seawolf aircraft relied on the 7-tube version of rocket launchers since the Marines had discovered the hard way that the 19-tube version was sensitive to shipboard radiation hazards. Among the variety of warheads available, the HE fragmentation was most commonly used. Seawolf crews preferred the 10-pound warhead to the 17-pounder since the former's ballistics were more predictable than the latter's. Because of the different ballistics and the inherent difficulty in hitting targets with rockets, Seawolf crews found that mixing warheads was a bad idea. Another favorite was the flechette, or "nail," warhead if the pinpoint accuracy of close support was not

Miniguns used as door guns on Seawolf Hueys took many forms, depending on a detachment's preference. This version was used on a trail ship of Det. 3, whose emblem is painted on the dust cover of the universal mount.
(U.S. Army)

required. Crews also favored proximity fuses over point detonation types since the latter's effect was absorbed by the Delta's pervasive mud and water. Point fuses, on the other hand, were better for penetrating forested canopies.

Much like Army and Marine gunship crews in Vietnam, Seawolf crewmen used the M-60 machine gun, more often as a chopped down free weapon than pintle-mounted, giving the gunner more latitude and greater fields of fire. Normally, about 1,000 rounds of ammunition were carried as one continuous linked belt. When a crew-operated minigun or .50-cal. machine gun was used, a backup M-60 was nearby.

Personal weapons used by Seawolf crews ran the gamut from handguns to rifles, and everything in between. If the squadron armory didn't have whatever crewmen preferred, the black market offered an amazing selection and quantity of guns. As an Army Huey crew chief whose unit often worked missions with Seawolves, this writer found the widest variety of exotic weapons available at Special Forces and Seawolf bases. Standard on every Seawolf aircraft was the 40mm M-79 grenade launcher, which fired a variety of rounds, including anti-personnel and tear gas. Hand grenades and hand-fired flares were abundant on the aircraft. Not only were personal weapons fired from the air, they were insurance in the event the aircraft was downed.

In combat the basic Seawolf unit was the fire team, comprising two Hueys. A seasoned Fire Team Leader flew the lead ship, with an experienced copilot navigating and pinpointing targets. The trail aircraft, which was responsible for covering the pair, was flown by an Attack Helicopter Aircraft Commander, with his copilot in the learning seat. Like Army policy, a crew chief and gunner operated weapons and performed maintenance. The most experienced gunners flew aboard the trail Huey. Gun runs on targets generally began at about 1,200 feet with pullouts approaching 500 feet. Patrols were flown at 1,000 to 1,500 feet at 70 knots. Low-level reconnaissance was done at 100 feet or below.

Sometimes the aircraft were used as bait to draw fire. Flying at night with lights on, the lead ship flew at 500 feet, while the trail Huey flew behind and higher, blacked out. If the lead ship was fired upon, it broke into an orbit as the trail ship dropped down to engage. Meanwhile, the lead aircraft was completing its circle to attack. This racetrack pattern kept the enemy continuously under fire.

Since 14 of the 22 Hueys had to be operational at all times, two crews alternated 24-hour alerts and patrols,

This UH-1B of HA(L)-3 is armed with the XM-16 quad guns and XM-158 rocket systems. Most aircraft wore the Seawolf emblem on the nose and carried armor panels in the chin bubbles. On this Huey, which had a Greenhouse window replaced, pilot doors were removed for air movement, increased visibility, and for quick egress in case the helicopter was downed. Like Army gunships, this aircraft had a wind baffle installed on the forward edge of the cabin doorway. (Author's Collection)

Seawolf Mike Worthington shows the amount of ammunition links and cartridges produced by his minigun during a night mission. (Seawolf Mike Worthington Collection)

Modifications of weapon systems were limited only by Seawolves' imaginations. This Det. 2 Huey at Nha Be in 1969 had a large screen installed to prevent ejected shell casings and links from damaging the tail rotor. Written atop the minigun's frame is "The Judge." (Henry E. Livingstone)

while maintenance personnel toiled to keep the aircraft flying. The night flying skills of pilots paid dividends since night patrols accounted for between one-third and one-half the total flown. Besides supporting PBRs and the Vietnamese Navy's River Assault Group, Seawolves supported SEAL commandos, performed medevac, and provided cover for downed aircraft and crew recovery. They earned the respect of American and Vietnamese troops at outposts they often supported. By the end of 1967, Seawolves had flown more than 9,700 hours during more than 7,300 missions; seven crewmen had been killed and 50 wounded.

When the enemy's 1968 Tet Offensive swept through South Vietnam, fire support from Seawolves was credited with saving outposts that otherwise would have been overrun. At Ben Tre, PBRs and HA(L)-3's Hueys waged a 36-hour battle, preventing the city from being taken by enemy forces. Later that year river patrol forces ratcheted up the campaign to interdict enemy troop and supply movement into the Delta. The squadron's effectiveness was limited only by its small number of helicopters, prompting the Navy to seek more gunships for HA(L)-3.

Changes for the Seawolves during early 1969 included the move to a new headquarters and maintenance facility at Binh Thuy, and increasing to 33 the number of UH-1Bs authorized. The additional aircraft became available when

Army gunship units began exchanging their B Model Hueys for UH-1Cs. In November, the Seawolves would receive their first two Charlie models, whose performance was far superior to that of the UH-1B. The year 1969 also marked a new mission for HA(L)-3 when the transport duties of White Hat Airlines, Vietnam's Naval Air Facility detachment flying UH-34Ds and C-117Ds, were turned over to the squadron. To carry out the mission, the squadron was assigned its third and newest model Huey, the UH-1L.

As the first Navy-owned Huey, the UH-1L combined features of the UH-1C and Marine UH-1E, being powered by the L-13 engine. Immediately upon delivery in November 1969, the first four UH-1Ls were sent to Vietnam, where they formed the "Sealords" section of HA(L)-3. Another four arrived in January 1970. Although intended as a utility aircraft, the UH-1L's mission was quickly expanded to include combat support and they were adapted to mount weapon systems. Only eight UH-1Ls were built, all of which served in Vietnam, where six were destroyed or damaged.

By the end of 1969, *Operation Game Warden* strength had peaked with more than 20 squadrons of PBRs and a variety of floating support bases to ensure coverage of the Delta. The Seawolves grew to nine detachments that moved with the changing tactical environment, including

A black-painted UH-1B departs a patrol craft tender. Mounted above its rocket launcher is a quad M-60 XM-16 gun system. Seawolf Hueys spent equal amounts of time aboard ships and on land bases. (Gerald O. Busic)

the 1970 invasion of Cambodia. Seawolf Hueys would be the first American helicopters to reach the nation's capitol, Phnom Penh, and before the operation ended, three Seawolf detachments would log more than 700 hours flying strike missions in Cambodia. Squadron growth was also marked by new Huey helicopter models joining the fleet of more than 30 Hueys.

During late 1970, the Sealords received a pair of HH-1Ks. Based on the UH-1E and powered by the L-13 engine, the HH-1K had improved avionics and was intended as a search and rescue platform. Both were lost in crashes and another pair was sent to Vietnam in November 1971. In June of that year, the squadron had received its fifth and final Huey model, the UH-1M. Basically a UH-1C with the more powerful 1,400-shp L-13 engine and increased fuel capacity, the Mike model boosted the squadron's overall performance since aircraft commonly were flown at redline gross weights. The plan to equip the entire squadron with UH-1Ms fell short due to the heavy demand for the L-13 engine, which powered hundreds of Army helicopters. The Navy was low on the priority list and the Seawolves would receive a total of only 11 UH-1M gunships by the end of 1971.

As with earlier model Hueys flown by the Seawolves, later models were fitted with both fix-mounted and crew-operated miniguns, rocket launchers, and .50-cal. door guns. The most unusual fits were made to the Sealords' UH-1Ls and HH-1Ks. Enthusiastic about the track record of their Huey gunships in Vietnam, and given the power range of the HH-1K, the Navy and Marines decided to evaluate its potential as a heavy weapons platform. During 1970 and 1971, experiments were conducted at China Lake, California, mounting FAEs and AIM-9

Installation of the more powerful L-13 engine in the HH-1K enabled it to test the Mass Air Delivered Fuel-Air Explosive Unit. Here, HH-1K BuNo. 157193 prepares to lift the large ordnance at NOTS China Lake, California. (U.S. Navy)

Developed by the Navy, this ordnance rack of the HH-1K was used to mount non-standard weapons such as iron bombs and fuel-air explosives. Much of the special testing was done at NOTS China Lake, California. (U.S. Navy)

Long before HA(L)-3 was established, the Navy tested the Mk 115 Helicopter Trap Weapon at China Lake in 1963. The weapon, which was parachute-retarded, was to be dropped in clusters from fixed-wing or rotary-wing aircraft. Immediately upon impact in a forested region, the weapon's HE detonation cleared helicopter landing areas. During Navy tests, four Mk 115s were carried on a single rack mounted to a UH-1B, which made the first drop in 1965. (U.S. Navy)

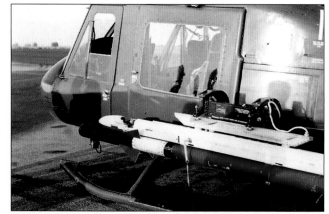

While HH-1K Hueys went to war with HA(L)-3 Sealords in Vietnam, some stayed in the States for ordnance testing. BuNo 157194 seen here tested an AIM-9B Sidewinder missile at China Lake in September 1971. (U.S. Navy)

Sidewinder missiles to the K model Huey. While tests were somewhat successful, opposition from the Air Force, which had gone numerous rounds with the Army over the issue of heavily armed aircraft, brought further testing to a halt. Evaluations did, however, reach the point where Sealord UH-1Ls and HH-1Ks were modified to carry FAEs and 500-pound general-purpose bombs. No records have surfaced indicating that they were used operationally.

To enable the South Vietnamese to continue the Seawolf mission, HA(L)-3 personnel began training members of the Vietnamese Air Force in mid 1971. The Seawolves were disestablished on 26 January 1972 after six years of continually demonstrating its mobility, versatility, and firepower with Huey gunships. During that time, the exclusively Huey Seawolves would operate nearly 80 aircraft of five models, the bulk of which were UH-1Bs; a total of 49 B models are recorded, along with six C models, 11 M models, eight UH-1Ls, and four HH-1Ks. The squadron's impressive accomplishments include more than 112,000 flight hours during which more than 4,000 enemy were confirmed killed, nearly 7,000 sampans destroyed, and over 4,000 enemy structures destroyed. A total of 1,530 medical evacuations had been flown. A total of 44 members of HA(L)-3 were killed.

The Seawolves knew that the attack helicopter was not a replacement for fixed-wing aircraft, and that neither was a replacement for artillery or ship's guns. Yet, as a quick-reaction weapon, the attack helicopter had no equal. Despite this, in the overall scheme of things, it appeared that the Navy did not fully embrace attack helicopter doctrine, having made no future plans for helicopter gunships when HA(L)-3 closed its doors. The Army's commitment to attack helicopters had taken a quantum leap, since they offered more promise to the Army, which did not have the organic fixed-wing attack airpower the Navy enjoyed. Nevertheless, two Naval Reserve light attack helicopter squadrons were formed to support naval special warfare forces; HA(L)-4 was established at NAS Norfolk, Virginia, on 1 July 1976, and HA(L)-5 one year later at NAS Point Mugu, California. Both operated eight HH-1Ks whose gunship configuration paralleled that of the Seawolves. Both would evolve into combat support squadrons flying twin-engine Hueys and Seahawk helicopters in support of naval special operations.

In the span of two decades, the Navy had come a long way in the marriage of non-aviation ships and helicopters. The DASH met with an infamous end, and the LAMPS program with manned helicopters solved the unreliability problem of the DASH drones, while extending the eyes and ears of ships. Helicopters became regular occupants of ships, not only protecting them from submarines, missile, and mines, but also providing a regular means of transport. Navy helicopters evolved into responsive and aggressive gunships, and all remained capable of search and rescue. Navy helicopters not only have endured but have grown, thanks to technology and the imagination to use it effectively.

Seawolves Aircraft

Listed below are the various Huey models used by HA(L)-3. Following the Army serial numbers are known squadron aircraft numbers, which, normally, were worn in white on the tail fin.

UH-1B

62-1936	63-8547/312	64-13974
62-1970/327	63-8589/326	64-13975
62-1985	63-8666	64-13980
62-2025/309	63-8679	64-13990
62-2031	63-8715	64-14007
62-2034/321	63-8738	64-14020
62-2038/316	63-12923/324	64-14022
62-4567	63-12929/312	64-14031/315
62-4579/306	63-12930	64-14033
62-4597	63-12943	64-14070
62-4602/322	63-12946	64-14076
62-4604	64-12934	64-14081
62-12515/321	64-13911	64-14083/330
62-12542	64-13919	64-14087
62-12543	64-13939	64-14090
63-8540/312	64-13943/328	64-14091
63-8545/305	64-13948/322	

UH-1C

64-14145	66-546	66-15200/312
66-540	66-610	66-15977

UH-1M

64-14117	66-599	66-15111/302
65-9423	66-616/316	66-15236/312
65-9476/314	66-655	
65-9548	66-15017	

Sealords Aircraft

Sealords Hueys were assigned Navy BuNos and were differentiated from HA(L)-3 aircraft by tail code SL.

UH-1L

157851	157854	157857/SL7
157852	157855	157858/SL10
157853/SL3	157856/SL6	

HH-1K

157187/SL11	157202
157200/SL1	157203

CHAPTER SIX

GUNSHIP FEVER

Wearing camouflage and civil registration N6715A, the S-67 carries 16 dummy TOW missiles and AIM-9 Sidewinder missiles on its wingtips. Sikorsky began the single-built aircraft as a private venture in 1969 and first flew the aircraft in August 1970. Modified with a ducted tail rotor, the S-67 set a world speed record of 216 mph in 1974. (Igor I. Sikorsky Historical Archives, Inc.)

In the early stages of the Vietnam War, the Army was fast becoming sold on the helicopter gunship concept, which it embraced to identify its quest for becoming a leading, autonomous air arm. When Secretary of the Army Cyrus R. Vance expressed disapproval of procuring an interim off-the-shelf gunship, he challenged planners to come up with a more advanced system. That set the Combat Developments Command off on a search in 1963 for a new armed helicopter. The momentum continued with the new AAFSS project manager directed to study the best technology available for arming helicopters. Faced with the choice of choosing Bell's proposed Cobra or developing a new advanced system, Army planners chose both.

The specifications outlined by the Army were indeed challenging. They called for phenomenal capabilities such as a top speed of 252 mph, a night targeting system, the latest in avionics, and an armament package comprising a grenade launcher, 30mm cannon, and six anti-tank missiles.

While Bell went to work on the Cobra, the Army sent to industry a Request for Proposals in August 1964. Proposals from 12 companies were submitted by the 23 November deadline. Similar compound rotor, tandem-seat designs by Lockheed and Sikorsky edged out the others, leading to contracts for both in February 1965.

This would be Lockheed's first major helicopter project, having conducted only limited research in the rotary-wing field. The firm's Model CL-840 featured wings that unloaded the main rotor at high speeds. Its glowing feature was a rigid rotor, which coupled speed and stability with maneuverability. Although having earned a reputation for being prone to failure, the rigid rotor was simple and lightweight. Besides a conventional tail rotor, a thrust propeller was attached to the rear of the fuselage. The CL-840 delivered the Army's required speed of 252 mph, along with a 3,420-fpm climb rate.

Sikorsky's competing design, the S-66, was a combination of its S-61F high-speed research helicopter and numerous experiments conducted since 1961. These included high-speed rotor systems, a rigid rotor flight simulator, weapon systems, and tilt-propeller model tests. Winged helicopter experiments began with the S-55 in 1959, and its swiveling tail rotor Rotoprop was tried on the S-61A during interim gunship competition. Sikorsky's first experiments with a swivel tail date as far back as 1945 when the concept was tried on an R-4.

After a development study of both entries was completed, on 3 November 1965 the Army announced Lockheed as the winner. The rigid rotor of Lockheed's design was cited as the determining factor in its selection over Sikorsky's S-66. Power was derived from a GE T64-GE-716 (ST) engine rated at 4,275 shp. Internal armament consisted of belly and nose turrets, while four wing pylons carried a variety of stores combinations. When the engineering contract for 10 prototypes was signed in March 1966, the gunship was designated AH-56A, with the 10 machines given serial numbers 66-8826 through -8835. One would be a ground test vehicle,

Undoubtedly the most unusual entry in the Army's Advanced Aerial Fire Support System (AAFSS) competition was Convair's Model 49. Drawing from its experience with the XFY-1 Pogo, Convair's oddity had three turbine engines driving counter-rotating propellers within a huge shroud. A crew of two occupied the capsule that articulated for flight and the upright firing mode seen here. The heavily armed craft featured outboard turrets for miniguns or grenade launchers, while the center turret housed two XM-140 30mm cannon, or 500 WASP rockets. Hard points on two engine nacelles accommodated three TOW or Shillelagh missiles, or a single 106mm cannon with an effective range of 10,000 yards. Hard points rotated to adjust to wind or flight modes. Although Convair felt the project was low risk, it was deemed too radical a concept to pursue. (U.S. Army)

one a flying model with no weapons or fire control system, and the remaining eight built to near operational standards.

When the ground test vehicle was rolled out in April 1967, it was named Cheyenne, a noteworthy deviation from Lockheed's practice of naming its aircraft with a celestial theme. The second prototype flew on 21 September. A full-scale mockup arrived for tests at Eglin AFB, Florida, on 5 December. The following month, the Army exercised an option to procure the first batch of a total of 375 Cheyennes, with production totals expected to exceed 1,000 aircraft.

The conflict in Vietnam drove the need for the Cheyenne; however, the cost of the war made it difficult to justify the Cheyenne's steadily increasing cost. Funds became available to support the program, but not without rumblings by Air Force representatives in Washington;

Retractable main landing gear helped the S-67 achieve airplane-like high speeds and performance. The Blackhawk tested a wide range of weapons including the 20mm cannon turret seen here. The S-67's size provided ample room for a center-fuselage bay with room for six passengers. (Igor I. Sikorsky Historical Archives, Inc.)

Sikorsky's S-67 Blackhawk, not to be confused with the firm's later H-60 Blackhawk, was a large tandem-seat gunship, which had the ability to perform aerobatic maneuvers. Large wings allowed this load of 152 2.75-inch rockets, in addition to the nose turret. (United Technologies Corporation/Don Brabec Collection)

For the AAFSS competition, Sikorsky proposed its S-61 with tail boom extensively modified for a unique Rotoprop swing-tail. The prop rotated 90 degrees to convert from conventional tail rotor to thrust propeller. Here, the S-61 is secured to test the Rotoprop in propeller mode in June 1965. Although eliminated from the AAFSS competition, Sikorsky used the demonstrator as a test bed for its S-66, which competed against Lockheed's Cheyenne. The aircraft was painted gloss **Olive Drab.** (Igor I. Sikorsky Historical Archives, Inc.)

Bell Helicopter's one-of-a-kind twin-engine Model 309 KingCobra led to development of the Marine Corps AH-1T, which was TOW-equipped. Much larger than the popular AH-1G, the KingCobra never made it to production. As a company project, the aircraft wore barely visible civil registration N309J on its tail fin. (Bell Helicopter)

such opposition elicited little response at first, but it was enough to raise questions. Flight testing continued as the Army enthusiastically went about the business of preparing to establish its AH-56A training program. At 450 test hours into the program, on 12 March 1969, the number three prototype crashed on a test flight. The disaster was costly not only in terms of the loss of the test pilot, but in spurring design changes.

The Cheyenne's rising cost and schedule slippage was compounded by President Nixon's desire to undo outgoing President Johnson's procurement policies. And it was no secret that the Army found the Cheyenne too sophisticated, or that the Air Force, having seen the Cheyenne's airplane-like air support capabilities, lobbied even harder for its A-10 program to shut out the Cheyenne.

On 19 May 1969, Army Secretary Stanley R. Resor announced the cancellation of the AH-56A program, claiming that Lockheed failed to meet original

The Model 309 KingCobras, called by Bell employees Ships 1 and 2, are made ready for rollout in September 1971. The AH-1G lineage is obvious in both. (Bell Helicopter)

Armed with three-barrel 20mm cannons in nose turrets, the single- and twin-engine KingCobras are test flown shortly after their debut. The single-engine Model 309 crashed during April 1972. It was not rebuilt; however, the twin-engine ship led to development of the Marine AH-1T. (Bell Helicopter)

specifications. The aircraft itself remained active, in fact, becoming the first helicopter, other than the Huey, to fire TOW missiles. The successful firing in July 1970, which scored a direct hit on a Sherman tank, spurred the Army to arm its Cobras with TOW missiles.

While the Army and Lockheed began months of deliberation over the issue, Sikorsky saw this as an opportunity to present the follow-on design to its original S-66 proposal. Begun in August 1969, the design combined the dynamics of the S-61, features of the S-66, and the compound aspects of its S-61F. Construction began in November and the first flight was made on 20 August 1970. Called the S-67 Blackhawk, the aircraft used the S-61R's T58-GE-5 turboshafts driving a five-blade main and tail rotor.

The Blackhawk was a large aircraft, measuring more than 64 feet in length and having a wingspan of 27 feet, 4 inches. A personnel bay in its center fuselage could accommodate six passengers. Especially impressive was the Blackhawk's armament, which included one or two 20mm

or 30mm turrets, a variety of missiles, as well as a wide variety of wing stores. A door gunner could be positioned in a rear compartment, facing rearward or out a side doorway.

Only one Blackhawk was built, which reached speeds exceeding 200 mph, and performed rolls and split-S turns without difficulty.

Bell officials had also watched closely the slow death of the Cheyenne, having undertaken low-profile development of its Model 309 KingCobra. The design expanded the AH-1G and AH-1J concept with emphasis on night capability, while taking advantage of production hardware and proven systems. Bell hoped that the Marines would show interest in the KingCobra, while edging out the Cheyenne and Blackhawk.

Two KingCobras were built: one powered by Pratt & Whitney's Twin-Pac, which was standard in the AH-1J, and the other a single-engine version powered by a 2,850-shp Lycoming T55-L-7C. To handle a gross weight of 14,000 pounds and higher speeds, the Model 309 was

The Cheyenne featured both internal and external armament, having two fuselage pylons and four wing pylons. This AH-56A is firing 2.75-inch rockets, while TOW launchers with breakaway covers are mounted on inboard stations. (U.S. Army)

Similar in appearance to Sikorsky's S-66, the Cheyenne presented as a large-winged aircraft. Lift from its wings increased as speed increased. Sponsons alongside the fuselage held retracted main landing gear, and housed fuel tanks, an APU, and an environmental control unit. The tail wheel retracted into the vertical stabilizer. (U.S. Army)

In the Cheyenne's front cockpit was a General Electric swiveling gunner's station, which allowed a stabilized line of sight for 360-degree coverage in azimuth to engage targets. A large cockpit provided ample room and visibility. (Author)

larger and stronger than the AH-1G. Wider chord rotor blades with swept tips reduced noise and improved performance. And it was more sophisticated than the HueyCobra with systems that included Low Light Level Television (LLTV), Forward Looking Infrared Radar (FLIR), helmet sights, and a multi-sensor fire control system. A GE turret with a 20mm cannon and 1,345 rounds of ammunition, or a 30mm cannon and 3,000 rounds could be mounted. Stout wings that spanned 13 feet could carry 16 TOW missiles or the usual array of weapon stores.

The Twin-Pac KingCobra was rolled out on 1 September 1971, with the first flight made just days later. The machine dove at 230 mph and it performed 3g maneuvers with ease. The single-engine Model 309 was rolled out on 1 November but crashed on 11 April 1972. Navy evaluation of the remaining aircraft in 1974 led to development of the Marine AH-1T.

The year 1971 ended without a production contract for an attack helicopter, prompting the Army to take a new direction. In January 1972, the Advanced Attack Helicopter Task Force (AAHTF) was established. Not only was

The beginning of the end of the Cheyenne may have occurred on 12 March 1969 when the Number Three prototype (S/N 66-8828) went out of control and crashed into the Pacific. Test pilot David Beil was lost and the aircraft destroyed. (U.S. Army)

the Cheyenne still in the running, it was one of three designs examined by the Task Force Risk Assessment Team. In a detailed report submitted in July 1972 by the AAHTF, the Cheyenne was weighed against Bell's King-Cobra and Sikorsky's Blackhawk in the areas of performance, survivability, maintainability, and armament. But the curtain would be drawn on all three types when, the following month, in conjunction with the Secretary of the Army's termination of the Cheyenne program, the task force identified the capabilities desired in an advanced attack helicopter that could be available in the late 1970s.

The program was aptly labeled *New Start* and called for a gunship that would be more agile, smaller, slower, and have less sophisticated fire control and navigation gear than the requirements the Cheyenne was expected to meet. Within that time frame, the Army initiated other New Start programs, the requirements of which intertwined with gunship improvements. It was thought that broadening research and development would benefit all programs. Priority programs were the Utility Tactical Transport Aircraft System (UTTAS), begun in 1972 and intended to replace the Huey, and the ASH program to upgrade OH-6A and OH-58A scout helicopters. The latter was short-lived due to funding denials. Gunship

Requests for Proposals went out in November, and in December, the Helicopter-Launched Fire and Forget (Hellfire) advanced anti-tank air-to-ground missile was approved.

Development of the Hellfire, which far out-ranges wire-guided missiles, began during the early 1960s when North American Rockwell ambitiously pursued a helicopter-launched anti-tank missile, then called the Hornet. The notice to manufacturers allowed them to select any twin-engine arrangement that would enable their design to cruise at 145 knots, climb 450 fpm, hover out of ground effect at 4,000 feet at 95 degrees F, and carry a 1,300-pound weapon load. In addition, the AAH was required to have IR protection, IR night vision, 30mm cannon, TOW missiles then qualified for the AH-1Q, 2.75-inch rocket launchers, a laser rangefinder, LORAN navigation, and a fire control computer. By 15 February 1973, the Army had received six proposals from five firms.

Bell's design was called the Model 409, Hughes the Model 77, Boeing Vertol's the Model 235, and Sikorsky's the S-71. Lockheed submitted two designs similar to the Cheyenne and labeled CL-1700.

In Bell's design, the only two-blade entry, the company's prior gunship experience was obvious; its Model 409

Lockheed built its Model 186 to satisfy a 1960 Army-Navy search for a high-speed, highly maneuverable research helicopter. Two machines, designated XH-51A, were built, with the first flight made in November 1962. The second-built of the rigid rotor machines was converted to a compound craft with wings and a turbojet on the left side of its fuselage. The compound XH-51A pioneered many of the features carried over into the Cheyenne. Some of its demonstrations included firing of a side-mounted .30-cal. machine gun. (Stephen Miller Collection)

Boeing's design entry in the Advanced Attack Helicopter (AAH) competition was its Model 235, a most unusual configuration featuring a non-symmetrical fuselage, which positioned the gunner forward and offset from the pilot. This design bore similarities to the UTTAS design. (U.S. Army)

Sikorsky's entry in the AAH competition was its S-71 seen here in mockup stage. The design, which was patterned after the UTTAS airframe, is armed with a TAT-300 turret with XM-188 30mm gun. The smaller unit forward of the TOW stabilized sight under the nose is a pilot's night vision system sensor. Armament includes a 30mm chin turret, and under-wing TOW missile and rocket launchers. (Don Brabec Collection)

High-quality concept art was commonly used by companies to project operational use of their aircraft. Much of the art showed gunships in a tank-killing role over terrain that could be construed as European. A Sikorsky artist painted this impressive rendition of the firm's design submitted for the AAH competition. (Don Brabec Collection)

This was the final version of Sikorsky's S-71 featuring airplane-like landing gear and a ventral enclosure for turret ammunition. Under-wing is a TOW unit and 19-tube 2.75-inch rocket launcher. Dazzling camouflage schemes often were applied to competition designs to enhance their appeal and suggest readiness for combat. (U.S. Army)

Bell's AAH entry was its Model 409, which was given serial number 73-22246. Since combat experience with the Cobra had proven the value of a turret weapon, the AAH team made it a requirement, although of 30mm strength. A major change from the Cobra, however, was Bell's placement of the pilot in the front cockpit, with the gunner/copilot behind. It was felt that the reversal was a detriment to Bell's competitive design. (Bell Helicopter)

Two Model 409 prototypes were built and powered by General Electric T700-GE-700 engines rated at 1,536 shp. The first flight was made on 1 October 1975 and the second prototype flew on 21 December. Of interest is the tail rotor guard and the fact that all aircraft components were included in the camouflage scheme. The spurious tail number, 74409, likely was derived from the year of construction and model number. (Bell Helicopter)

came out on top, having met or exceeded all the Army requirements. The design, which featured blade fold and retractable rotor mast, was found rugged and simple. Hughes' design also met the requirements, but was found lacking in ballistics tolerance and crew protection. Boeing's Model 235 came in third since its engine ran hot and would lag in production. Sikorsky was fourth due to minimum engine power, and Lockheed's design was found unsuitable in view of its heavy armor, which affected performance.

All of these manufacturers selected either the TAT-140 or XM-188 30mm cannon, with the exception of Hughes, which relied upon its own chain gun. The gun was the most reliable as it used fewer parts and had no critical timing requirements. All chose the TOW as a point weapon; however, Hughes added an improved TOW launcher. Hughes' Model 77 also gained points by having a low-noise tail rotor.

Events moved slowly and it wasn't until 22 June 1974 that contracts were awarded Bell Helicopter Textron and

The engineering model of Hughes' Model 77 design for the AAH competition gave an early indication of its basic shape and component layout. An aerodynamic TOW missile pod was an early consideration. The T-tail would prove problematic. The empennage guard is assumed to have been a protective device for the low-position tail rotor. (Hughes Helicopters/Don Brabec Collection)

From the start, Hughes designed its gunship with the electronics positioned high in the nose, reasoning that it was better to lose a $20,000 gun in a crash than an electronic suite that cost hundreds of thousands of dollars. The curved canopy seen here was changed to a flat-plate design. Moving the horizontal tail surface from its original site atop the fin to a low position minimized disturbance between main rotor downwash and the tail surface. (Hughes Helicopters/ Don Brabec Collection)

These mockups show the size comparison of the Hughes 30mm chain gun (left) and General Electric's XM-188 30mm gun, which fired 600 spm from a 1,200-round magazine. The Hughes gun was externally powered and electrically chain-driven, with a sprocket rotating bolt. It fires High Explosive (HE), High Explosive Dual Purpose (HEDP), and NATO standard ADEN/DEFA rounds. (Hughes Helicopters/Don Brabec Collection)

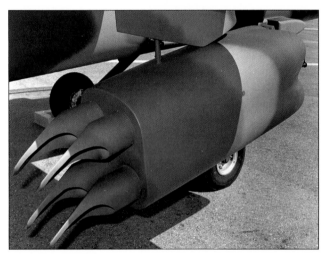

All of the TOW missile launchers considered for the Hughes Model 77 were of low-drag design. This mockup of a streamlined launcher featured debris deflectors. (Hughes Helicopters/Don Brabec Collection)

Hughes Helicopters for a ground test vehicle and two flying prototypes. Bell designed and built its Model 409 entry, designated the YAH-63, in-house using the firm's plant facilities and years of experience, whereas Hughes, which lacked this capacity, used a team approach, enlisting 12 contractors for its Model 77 design, assigned the designation YAH-64. Although more costly, this method pooled the expertise and experience of established firms.

Also in June, the stage was set for replacement of the TOW missile when Rockwell International received the development contract for the Hellfire. Hughes' prototype made its first flight on 30 September 1975, followed by Bell's on 1 October. Following extensive contractor tests, Bell and Hughes prototypes delivered their aircraft to the Army at Edwards AFB. The YAH-64 received higher

marks in the technical and operational suitability areas and it went on to the next phase of the AAH program.

Apache

The name Apache evokes images of a proud Native American tribe of the Southwest, whose warriors proved themselves fierce and skillful fighters during the Apache Wars of the late nineteenth century. The title also carried on the tradition of 1st Cavalry Apache scout and gunship helicopter crews who fought in Vietnam. The Apache helicopter identified with another link to that war; the slogan adopted by its fixed-wing gunship cousins: "Deny him the dark." The Apache would prove that an understatement after Iraq invaded Kuwait in 1990.

In the early morning hours of 17 January 1991, just hours after President Bush ordered *Operation Desert Storm*, the U.S. Air Force 20th Special Operations Squadron Green Hornets launched four MH-53J Pave Lows from Saudi Arabia. Following were two teams of four U.S. Army Apaches. Flying 50 feet above the desert, in total darkness, the armada headed toward western Iraq where they would punch a hole in the early warning screen of Saddam Hussein's air defenses. At the border, Pave Low crews used sophisticated systems to blind enemy radar and surface-to-air missile sites, allowing the Apaches to slip in and strike the first blow in the air campaign of the Persian Gulf War. Firing 27 Hellfire missiles, the Apaches destroyed the sites, clearing a path for more than 100 fighter-bombers to reach their targets. But their work wasn't over; they fired 100 rockets and 4,000 rounds of 30mm ammunition at targets during the 15-hour mission that covered nearly 1,000 nautical miles round-trip.

The Apache had to be, and was, a lot of things. The requirements for what would be billed as the world's deadliest helicopter were stringent, presenting a challenge for even the most experienced aircraft manufacturer. Its climb to status as the most advanced combat helicopter in the world was arduous, involving a long development process and political obstacles before the Army took delivery of the first production AH-64A on 26 January 1984.

Powered by a pair of 1,536-shp General Electric T700-GE-700 engines, also used to power UTTAS designs, the first Apache prototypes during demonstrations far exceeded the Army's climb rate. The engines gave the Apache a top speed of 180 mph at its maximum weight of 21,000 pounds. Production Apaches would receive 1,698-shp T700-GE-701 engines, which allowed a maximum dive speed of 197 knots with a full combat load. Thanks to an ingenious cooling system, the engine heat signature was so low that one could touch its exhaust barehanded. Designed with the knowledge that the Apache would fly in harm's way, the engines are widely separated to prevent even a 12.7mm shell hit from damaging both powerplants. A transparent acrylic blast panel separates the front and rear cockpits, ensuring that both crew members are not put out of commission.

Apache would not win any beauty contests, being void of the smooth aerodynamic contours desired in aircraft design, giving way instead to hard angles of stealth technology—the Apache is as mean as it looks. Other stealth qualities are built in; its four main rotor blades with swept tips, along with scissors-arranged tail rotor blades, generate half the noise made by two-bladed helicopters. Rather than creating the familiar thump of the Huey's rotors, the Apache's slice, rather than slap, the air, giving it a trademark low-pitch growl. Myriad defensive measures include flat canopy glass panels that reduce glint that can betray the aircraft's position. Even Apache's skin is painted with special paint that absorbs radar and reflects little light. An Aircraft Survivability Equipment System includes a passive radar warning receiver, IR jammer, radar jammer, and an M130 chaff/flare dispenser.

Its surveillance capabilities prove far beyond those of its predecessors. Inside its protective shell, miles of wiring link engines, avionics, system displays, and weapon systems to onboard computers. Apache crews find their prey using a Martin Marietta nose-mounted Target and Designation Sight/Pilot Night Vision Sensor (TADS/PNVS) system, which comprises an array of cameras. Its day TV camera magnifies subjects 127 times and its thermal camera can identify a human form at a distance of 6 miles, and spots of blood more than 1 mile away. As the most technologically advanced helicopter in the world, the Apache is the most difficult aircraft to fly, and only a small percentage of people can perform the simultaneous activities necessary to fly the machine. Most difficult to master is the demand for multi-tasking. The major challenge for pilots is being bombarded with information from flight instruments, radios, intercom, weapon systems, defensive systems, and radar. All need to be acted upon every few seconds.

The second most challenging aspect of flying the Apache is physical coordination. Hands, feet, and eyes are constantly busy. Seeing in the Apache world means training one's eyes to work independently of one another, with the left eye seeing outside the cockpit, while the right eye is slaved to a monocle that projects myriad images ranging from instrument readings to target information. The 1-square-inch lens is part of the Integrated Helmet and Display Sighting System (IHADSS), which slaves the Pilot's Night Vision Sensor (PNVS) turret to his line-of-sight. When the turret turns with the pilot's head, it becomes second nature to see in the dark.

Apache's destructive capabilities are unmatched. The machine's muscle takes the form of three weapon systems that strike with varying degrees of power, speed, and precision. First, its M230 30mm cannon is best for individual targets, firing 10 High-Explosive, Dual-Purpose (HEDP) rounds per second, accurate to within 3 meters. After their armor-piercing tips penetrate vehicles or buildings, their bodies fragment into shards, and then their incendiary charge sets the target afire. A total of 1,160 rounds can be fired in bursts of 10, 20, 50, 100, or more, or all at once.

Second, the time-honored area weapon, the 2.75-inch rocket (now termed the Hydra 70), is carried in 19-tube M261 launchers, which are pressed aluminum and made by Hughes. Mainly two types of rockets are used: the Flechette, containing 80 5-inch-long tungsten darts, and the HEISAP (High Explosive Incendiary Semi-Armor Piercing) for buildings, vehicles, or ships. The HEISAP has kinetic energy to penetrate 1/2 inch of steel, while its body contains explosive zirconium incendiary that adheres to light alloys and combustibles, furiously igniting them. Other warheads are available, including red phosphorous (which replaced white phosphorous), smoke, illumination, and chaff. Thanks to recommendations made years earlier by an AH-1 Cobra study group, rockets can be remotely fused from the cockpit.

Finally, the Semi-Active Laser Hellfire II air-to-ground missile carried on four-rail launchers. Laser-guided from the cockpit for pinpoint accuracy, the Hellfire's 20-pound HE, shaped charge warhead packs a five-million pound-per-square-inch punch on impact, destroying all known armor.

When the AH-64A became operational, the Army planned to form all of its Apache battalions at Fort Hood, Texas. Ten were to be newly activated, while existing units would begin trading in their Cobras. The first Apaches arrived on 25 March 1986 and the first unit to convert was 7th Battalion, 17th Cavalry Brigade. Next came the 1st and 2nd Battalions of the 6th Cavalry regiment, 6th Cavalry Brigade. In summer 1987, 38 Apaches from these units were shipped to West Germany to wage mock combat in Northern Europe as part of *Reforger 87*. As the pace of Apache production quickened, more were seen on the flight lines of Europe. A typical battalion consisted of 15 to 18 AH-64As, 13 OH-58Cs, and three UH-60A Black Hawks.

In a scenario reminiscent of the Cobra/Loach Pink Teams of the Vietnam War, Apache gunships teamed with OH-58D Scout helicopters for closely coordinated missions, which meant destroyed targets. By July 1988, seven Apache battalions had been fielded. The Army's modernization of its attack helicopter forces was not limited to front-line units in the United States and Europe; the North Carolina Army National Guard took delivery of new production AH-64As in November 1987, with South Carolina, Florida, Texas, Arizona, Utah, and Idaho National Guard units eventually flying Apaches.

As the threat of Warsaw Pact armor dwindled, the Apache was sent to other world trouble spots. Eleven AH-64As of the 1st Battalion, 82nd Aviation Regiment recorded 247 combat hours in Panama during *Operation Just Cause* in December 1989. Firing Hellfire missiles against Noriega's headquarters, the Apaches made a stellar combat debut, while learning lessons that would pay dividends one year later when Iraq invaded Kuwait.

When the AH-64D came on line in 1998, it was considered hundreds of times more deadly and more survivable than its predecessor. Its most significant improvement was the Longbow Radar, which can operate in all weather, day or night. It possesses the amazing ability

The Apache is as mean as it looks. The ferocious jaws of this AH-64A only add to its character. Carrying half loaded Hellfire missile launchers and empty Hydra rocket launchers suggest that this Apache may be returning from a strike mission. (Steve Van Allen)

to simultaneously detect over 1,000 potential targets, moving or stationary, up to more than 12 miles distant, classify the top 250, and display the 16 most threatening for destruction—all in three seconds. Twenty-five seconds later, all could be destroyed by an Apache's Hellfires. Eight Longbow Apaches working in unison can obliterate 128 tanks in 28 seconds simply by one Apache raising its radar from hiding for a few seconds.

Other improvements include upgraded T700-GE-701C engines, an updated glass cockpit, and new avionics. Following its first flight on 17 March 1997, the first production AH-64D, S/N 96-5001, was rolled out on the 21st. The Apache was remanufactured from 10-year-old AH-64A S/N 85-25387, and was among six Longbow prototypes flown as part of the development program.

Despite its positive features, the Longbow Apache had shortcomings; it couldn't operate from ships and it didn't have the power to carry large ordnance and fuel

loads. British Army officials and Westland went to work to address these, and came up with significant changes to the American Apache. They switched to Rolls-Royce RTM 322 engines, which increased power by 30 percent, thereby allowing them to fly farther, higher, and carry larger loads. Even more sophisticated countermeasure suites were added, permitting flight into lethal SAM zones. Blade-folding devices were added for shipboard operation, along with Saturn radios that defy intercept, and a unique health monitoring system.

Gradually, the U.S. government allowed close allies to acquire Apaches. Israel was first, followed by the Netherlands, Saudi Arabia, Singapore, Egypt, Japan, Kuwait, South Korea, and the United Arab Emirates (UAE). The British didn't join the group until the late 1990s, with the United Kingdom's purchase of 67 Westland AH Mk1 Apaches. Eventually, more than 1,000 Apaches were exported.

One of four prototype Longbow Apaches with Hellfire missiles and Hydra 70 rocket launchers. Longbow radar is housed in the dome above the main rotor mast. The first AH-64D was unveiled to the public by McDonnell Douglas at Mesa, Arizona, on 21 March 1997. (Westland Helicopters Ltd.)

CHAPTER SEVEN

GUNSHIP GROWTH AND NEW MISSIONS

A SuperCobra displays its arsenal. Centered behind more than 500 rounds of 20mm ammunition is a pair of Sidearm missiles, flanked by Sidewinders and TOW missiles. Behind them is a row of 2.75-inch rocket launchers, and 100-gallon fuel tanks. One live and three dummy Hellfire missiles occupy the right outboard station, with four TOW missiles opposite. (Bell Helicopter)

Although the U.S. military used the period immediately following the Vietnam War to reassess its performance, it had begun studies and had implemented changes while helicopters were still flying combat missions from bases throughout Southeast Asia. The lessons most ingrained in the minds of military leaders were those written in blood; but there were others that opened the door to new technology, and a fresh approach to the process of designing, acquiring, and fielding armed helicopters. Having the most at stake with the largest number of gunships, the Army wasted little time in establishing a review process of the AH-1G Cobra's performance and subsequent need for improvements.

When the Army first acquired the AH-1G in 1966, its mission weight was 8,180 pounds, which left 1,320 pounds for ammunition to bring the aircraft up to its maximum gross weight of 9,500 pounds. Not only was the 9,500-pound load common, it was often exceeded. At such weights, hovering, whether in or out of ground effect, in Vietnam's heat, was impossible. Since the main threat

during the early part of the war was small arms fire, Cobras generally dove on their targets from 1,200 to 1,500 feet, or higher, so there was no need to hover. The most troublesome portion of the mission for heavily loaded Cobras, in terms of flight performance, often was doing the "hover dance" out of revetments and to the takeoff point.

Improvements were made in Cobras acquired until 1972; these were changes made in the structure, propulsion, armament, flight control, and cockpit air conditioner. All came with a weight penalty, which reduced the amount of ammunition that could be carried. After the six years of growth, the ammunition capacity had shrunk by 30 percent; even when dive tactics were used, the minimum ammunition load was insufficient. In 1972, when enemy air defenses became more sophisticated and pervasive, it became obvious that flight above 100 feet was disastrous, and the answer to survival lay in firing while hugging terrain, and in a hover. Much more power is needed to hover out of ground effect than is needed for forward flight. The Cobra could only hover out of ground effect at

The first YAH-1Q (S/N 70-16055) was basically an AH-1G with TOW system and associated structural strengthening. The TOW's M56 Telescopic Sight Unit in the nose necessitated relocating the pitot tube to the rotor pylon. Although the TOW system gave the Cobra anti-armor capability, the aircraft remained underpowered. By the end of 1977, approximately 230 Qs were in Europe, with the first examples having been assigned to the Germany-based 11th and 2nd Armored Cavalry Regiments. (Bell Helicopter)

4,000 feet, at 95 degrees F, with a gross weight of 7,500 pounds. That meant that no ammunition could be carried, plus more than 1,000 pounds of other weight had to be left off of the aircraft. This was totally unacceptable.

Since the Cobra was expected to be in for the long haul, pending the arrival of the AAH, changes had to be made. Not only did the Army plan to keep the Cobra into the 1980s to supplement the AAH force in the anti-armor, suppression, and armed escort mission, it planned to acquire 305 new Cobras between 1977 and 1981. Given that improvements add weight, all aspects of the AH-1G would have to be thoroughly examined.

With the AH-56A program canceled, the Army was short the number of helicopter gunships it needed to counter the threat posed by the Warsaw Pact's growing armor inventory. The solution, Army officials felt, was converting half of the Cobra fleet to tank killers. Under the Improved Cobra Armament Program (ICAP), the TOW missile system would be integrated into the AH-1G. The Army's Missile Command had first shown interest in the TOW missile concept in 1962.

The following year, tests were conducted with a UH-1B, and in 1966, Hughes was awarded the research and development contract for the system, which was designated XM-26. Sighting the missiles would be accomplished with a Sperry Rand XM-128 Helmet-Directed Fire Control Subsystem. The TOW Cobra's weapon load would consist of eight missiles and two inboard rocket launchers, while retaining the G model's nose turret.

Two years later, work on the TOW system became part of the AH-56A Cheyenne program. Finally, in 1970, the system was considered for the Cobra. Mindful of Bell's success in mating the TOW system with its KingCobra in 1971, Army leaders felt confident awarding the company a contract in 1972.

Eight AH-1Gs would be modified with the missile and sighting systems, as well as a nose-mounted telescoping sight unit. Since the first ground firing caused structural damage, the airframe was beefed up and the first YAH-1Q was delivered to the Army in February 1973. Helicopter combat operations had ceased in Vietnam the month before, so it is unlikely that the new system was shipped there for evaluation. The first machine went to Fort Hood, Texas, for assignment to the 6th Air Cavalry Combat Brigade. Others followed and in August the TOW aircraft participated in war-games that highlighted shortcomings in the high-threat environment. Of special concern was the inability of the AH-1G and AH-1Q to hover fully loaded out of ground effect in hot and high conditions. The range and armor penetrating ability of the M28A1 turret weapons were not considered adequate, as demonstrated during the 1973 Mideast War.

For the solution, the Army reverted to a 1970 study that found a lighter-weight 30mm turret weapon ideal. Since the TOW Cobra was deemed an urgent requirement, and follow-on contracts for nearly 300 AH-1Qs were in the works, a study group identified a number of changes needed to maximize the gunship's firepower, endurance, and survivability in high threat environments.

Under the Improved Cobra Agility and Maneuverability (ICAM) program, two aircraft would be modified: one AH-1G upgraded to ICAM standards without the TOW and labeled YAH-1R, and the other a YAH-1Q with TOW upgraded to ICAM standards and designated YAH-1S. Foremost among the changes necessary to handle the 500-pound TOW system was the switch to a more powerful engine. Lycoming went to work adding 400 hp to its stalwart L-13B engine, which resulted in the 1,800-shp T53-L-703. For good measure, Bell added the stronger transmission of the AH-1J, along with its tail rotor group, bringing the maximum gross weight of both test aircraft up to 10,000 pounds.

Concurrent with Cobra updates, a search was begun for new rotor blades that not only would provide more lift, but also last longer and be more resistant to gunfire. The Kaman Aircraft Corporation, which also had proven itself to be a leader in the helicopter industry, was selected in 1975 to produce the new blades, which were of composite fiberglass construction.

Another major shortcoming addressed in transforming the Cobra was armament. The M28A1 was the only turret subsystem qualified for the AH-1G, Q, R, and S versions. Not only did the turret weapons lack standoff range, only 100 turrets were available for arming new AH-1S models slated for delivery beginning in April 1977; it was recommended that all TOW Cobras, which would account for 60 percent of the AH-1 fleet, be up to ICAM standard by 1981.

The study group considered four turret systems, two of which were 20mm and the other two 30mm. Those in the 30mm category, the XM-188 and XM230, were tied to the AAH program, and would not be decided upon until late 1976. The study group felt that the gun system chosen for the AAH might be a candidate for the Cobra as well. Most appealing to the group was the XM-97 turret with XM-197 three-barrel, 20mm cannon then in use with the Marine AH-1J, the Iranian International AH-1J, and the Marine OV-10A Bronco. Although it was heavy at 1,000 pounds, and suffered feed and cartridge ejection problems, the gun system's developmental lead-time was shorter and it cost less than other systems under review. The other 20mm weapon was a modification of the AH-1G's turret and designated M28MOD/XM197. The lightweight among the four was Hughes' XM230 chain gun, which also was compatible with the turret. Regardless the system used, all created risk areas of torque, blast, vibration, and debris.

The study group also examined the 2.75-inch rocket, which saw extensive use in Southeast Asia on a wide variety of aircraft. Although reliable and simple to use, the rocket was generally inaccurate and was used only against targets at relative short ranges. It had become obvious that if the rocket system was to be of value on the high threat battlefield, it required improvements in warheads, fusing, ranging, aiming, and motor function.

After SA-7 shoulder-launched missiles shot down two Cobra gunships during the North Vietnamese Army's 1972 Spring Offensive, some Cobras were fitted with toilet bowl exhaust and Disco Light IR jammers atop the engine cowl. Other countermeasures apparent on this AH-1R are a low-glint canopy and radar-reflective paint. Post-Vietnam development of the AH-1G resulted in the Q and S Cobra TOW versions, while the G and R versions were rocket-armed. (Bell Helicopter)

The standard Mk 40 rocket motor gave way to the Navy Mk 66 motor, which was longer, had more thrust, and powered rockets fired from LAU-61, -68, and -69 launchers. Replacing the Mk 1 rocket for use in Southeast Asia was the Army-developed M151 10-pound warhead. The M229 HE 17-pound warhead, which was actually 16.1 pounds, was more destructive. Flechette warheads used during the war were Air Force-developed and came in two types: the WDU4A/A containing 2,200 20-grain steel darts, and the WDU13/A containing 700 60-grain darts for use against vehicles. Other common rocket warheads then in use were the M156 smoke for marking targets, and the XM245 CS (tear gas). Smoke screening, chaff, illumination, and sub-munitions warheads were also available.

Since the AH-1G's external stores management system was deemed inflexible, it too was marked for revamping. With this system, the pilot was limited to selecting only inboard or outboard stores. It was preferred that the pilot be able to select and fire various rocket types,

and know how many of each type remained and their location on the pylons. Also important was in-flight remote fusing, which enabled the pilot to select point or delay detonation of the rocket. Ordinarily, rocket fuses were set for point detonation or airburst when the rockets were loaded for an expected type of target. Remote fusing would reduce the different types of warheads carried.

A particularly interesting aspect of this study was an in-flight escape system designed by an Army-Navy project team. The system was designed to explosively sever the main rotor blades, shut off the engine, retract the cockpit pantograph sight, and jettison the canopy—all within seconds. The project was discontinued when the system's weight of 130 pounds was deemed too heavy for the AH-1. Although 78 systems reportedly were built, none are known to have been used operationally.

Until 1979, the Army's Cobra program was in a constant state of flux, challenging even the keen observer to keep track of modifications and designations. All

This Cobra (S/N 68-15086) started life as an AH-1G, and was later converted to AH-1S, seen here in 1991 while assigned to the 40th Assault Helicopter Battalion of the California National Guard. Later, the Cobra would undergo conversion to AH-1F. (Author's Collection)

AH-1Qs brought up to ICAM standards, along with AH-1Gs slated for conversion, were designated AH-1S Modified (MOD). Many of the converted Cobras were sent to Europe to bolster the attack helicopter force. To facilitate the conversion of 62 AH-1Qs based in Germany, the in-country firm Dornier Reparaturwerft GmbH was contracted to convert them to AH-1S (MOD)s. Additional modifications led to a contract for 100 new production Cobras designated AH-1S Production (PROD). This variant introduced a revised nap-of-the-earth (NOE) cockpit with flat-plate canopy, new navigation and avionics suites, and an infrared signature exhaust suppressor. Deliveries of the AH-1S (PROD) were completed by August 1978, and in March 1987, the type was re-designated the AH-1P.

Of the original order for 297 anti-armor Cobras, the 101st machine (S/N 77-22763) became the first of 98 AH-1S Enhanced Cobra Armament System (ECAS) aircraft, also termed the "Up-Gun" Cobra. Re-designated AH-1E during March 1978, this version was basically an AH-1P with the M197 20mm cannon, a new rocket management system, and composite main rotor blades. Deliveries of the AH-1E were completed by October 1979.

The last of the Army's Cobra line was the AH-1S Modernized Cobra (MC), which became the AH-1F in March 1987. Serving as prototypes for the F Model were two AH-1Ps (S/Ns 76-22567 and -22600), which began trials in July 1979. Major improvements in the F Model included a Kaiser Head-Up Display (HUD), ballistics computer, low airspeed data probe, a more efficient IR suppressor, secure voice communication, and Doppler navigation. An AN/ALQ-144 IR jammer was mounted atop the engine cowling, and a fire control system incorporated a laser rangefinder and tracker, which was evident as a radome on the front of the rotor pylon. The tracker not only searches for, locks onto, and tracks targets, it displays the data on the HUD and cues the Telescopic Sight Unit (TSU) to the target.

By March 1981, Bell had delivered 99 AH-1Fs. A follow-on contract brought an additional 50 for the National Guard. After 378 AH-1Gs were brought up to F standards, the Army possessed 529. When the last Cobra was delivered in 1986, nearly 1,100 Cobras were on the Army inventory. A later improvement had AH-1Fs equipped with Hughes Cobra-Nite (C-Nite) targeting systems. This allowed Cobra crews to fire and track TOW missiles in day or night, through smoke, dust, and foul weather. By 1990, the AH-1F force based in South Korea had been equipped with C-Nite.

As more AH-64A Apaches came on line, they would replace the Cobras; it wasn't lost on the old hands in Army aviation, who transitioned from Cobras to Apaches, that the Cobra's extensive combat experience in Vietnam made the Apache possible.

New Start and the Kiowa

Since Army aviation was developing on different fronts during the early 1970s, test programs for hardware that was closely related often were combined for cost effectiveness and to gain maximum benefit from all studies. Such was the case when the Army formed a special task force to combine testing of the Hellfire missile and an Advanced Scout Helicopter (ASH) with the AAH Apache. It was estimated that combining the three would reduce the number of ASH test hours flown, and reduce the original number of missile firings required from 317 to 227. Hellfires were expensive and eliminating 90 firings, alone, would save more than $3 million.

The Advanced Scout Helicopter was to be a multi-mission aircraft in the 6,000- to 7,000-pound weight class. It would rely upon the same Target Acquisition Designation System used in the Apache, and some, therefore,

could be armed with Hellfire missiles. Since the Hellfire's target was "painted" by a laser, this could be done by the gunship, the scout helicopter, or a ground-directed laser. The program would have the added benefit of improving scout helicopters with stabilized optics, night vision, computerized navigation, and greater survivability.

The ASH contract was scheduled for mid 1978, with fielding to take place in the 1980 to 1990 time frame; it was then, strategists predicted, that hordes of Soviet armor would be encountered on a mid-intensity battlefield in Central Europe. The strongest argument for the ASH/HELLFIRE/AAH program was the Army's identification of Soviet weapons that most threatened Army aviation. The list included T-62 and T-72 medium tanks, the BMD and BMP series of combat vehicles, towed and self-propelled 122mm and 153mm artillery, the BRDM family of reconnaissance/anti-tank missile carriers, the ZSU-23-4 and S-60 AAA systems, and the SA-6, -8, and -9 SAM systems. The list included HIND and follow-on attack helicopters and high-performance aircraft such as Fishbed, Fitter, and Flogger, all equipped for anti-helicopter operations.

As part of the 1981 Army Helicopter Improvement Program (AHIP), Hughes came up with this enhanced version of its OH-6A, called the OH-6D. Incorporating components of its Model 500D, Hughes added a mast-mounted sight, wire strike protection kit, Black Hole exhaust, four-blade rotor, and a modernized cockpit. It is armed with Stinger missiles. (U.S. Army)

This Bell artist's rendering of the company's AHIP entry shows obvious features, such as mast-mounted sight, four-blade main rotor, and IR exhaust suppressors. Armament is General Dynamics' AIM-92 Stinger, or Air-to-Air Stinger (ATAS) in a twin-box launcher. A derivative of this design, the OH-58C, won the eight-month AHIP competition. (Bell Helicopter)

The ASH program faltered throughout the 1970s, finally leading to the AHIP program. The ASH design was to be heavily armed and use the Apache's TADS to designate targets. Bell proposed this sleek design, which featured dual tail rotors and a retractable cannon in the belly. (Ned Gilliand Collection)

Shortly after taking over Hughes in 1984, the McDonnell Douglas Helicopter Company began aggressively marketing its new Defender series, which included this Model 500MD/TOW. The company offered the Defender line with a wide variety of mission configurations. This prototype features T-tail, mast-mounted sight, Black Hole exhaust, and streamlined TOW launchers. (McDonnell Douglas Helicopter Company)

In 1979, Bell used this OH-58C to test a variety of weapons. Named Killer Rabbit by the aircraft's project pilot and flight test engineer, the helicopter is seen here test firing the FFV Uni-Pod 0127, which housed a 12.7mm M3M machine gun. FN Herstal built the gun, which has seen global use. This upgraded military version of Bell's versatile JetRanger series nicely proved that a well-designed aircraft can be adapted for a wide variety of different uses. (Bell Helicopter)

The prototype for Bell's Model 206L was a stretched JetRanger, which first flew in September 1974. It became the prototype Model 206L-1 LongRanger II, and in 1980 Bell converted it into the TexasRanger gunship. Powered by a 650-shp Allison turboshaft, the aircraft had provisions for four TOW missiles or 2.75-inch rockets. Despite a world tour, the gunship drew little interest. (Bell Helicopter)

The ASH program was denied funding in 1972, the same year it was begun, however, Congress in 1976 allowed the Army to redefine the requirements, although with a list of constraints drawn up by the Secretary of Defense.

The ASH program again was terminated within months of gaining a foothold. In May 1978, both the House and the Senate Armed Services Committee directed the Army to study the feasibility of adapting an existing aircraft as a "Near Term Scout Helicopter" for the Army Helicopter Improvement Program (AHIP), the development of which would coincide with fielding of the AAH. Requests for Proposals went out in January 1981, and in July, the decision was made to develop and field an improved scout helicopter by pitting the OH-6A and OH-58 against each other. During the previous two years, both types had been modified in-house and demonstrated with updated weapons, avionics, and flight performance to broaden their market appeal.

During the post-Vietnam period, Hughes not only made vast improvements to its OH-6A for widespread use by the Army National Guard, it focused on commercial and global military sales. Flexibility became a byword at Hughes as the company overlapped development of various models and systems. Its AHIP entry would incorporate components of the OH-6A and Model 500D; from the Apache came the Mast-Mounted Sight, FLIR, and laser designator/range finder. The only new component that Hughes planned for its ASH contender, called the OH-6D, was a five-blade composite rotor system. Hughes' work on an OH-6C, which it offered to the Army not only as the ASH prototype, but in Quiet and Armed scout versions, led to development of the military Model 500D. From this model evolved a line of "Defender" aircraft, which could be armed with a variety of weapon packages. These included a side-mounted 30mm chain gun developed for the Apache, and smaller Hughes-developed chain guns mounted as extendable turrets on the aircraft's belly. The Defender was mated with the TOW missile system in 1977, and in 1981 a Mast-Mounted Sight (MMS) was added, resulting in the designation 500MD/MMS-TOW.

Likewise, Bell had invested a great deal of time and effort experimentally modifying its Models 206B JetRanger series and 206L LongRanger and TexasRanger with various combinations of sensors and weapon systems. After replacing most of the Army's OH-6As, the OH-58A, which was based on the 206A, was modified into OH-58C. Its improvements included an uprated engine, IR suppression exhaust section, and flat-plate canopy. Later models reverted to the full span windscreen, since the advantage of supreme visibility far outweighed the low-glint qualities of the flat glass panels. The OH-58C also featured a night vision-compatible enlarged instrument panel. Bell's AHIP contender was an outgrowth of the OH-58C, which was named the winner of the competition, ultimately becoming the OH-58D Kiowa Warrior, which Bell labeled its Model 406. The AHIP

OH-58D, which was not armed, first flew on 6 October 1983, and entered service in 1985.

Powering the OH-58D was a 650-shp Allison 250-C30R (T703-AD-700) turboshaft driving a 35-foot-diameter, four-blade main rotor. At its gross weight of 5,500 pounds, the OH-58D cruised at 130 mph. With its dominant feature being the MMS to serve as the eyes and ears of commanders, the type was slated for operations with attack helicopters in air cavalry and field artillery units. Armament, which was not initially a consideration, included four Stinger or Hellfire missiles, rocket launchers, or two M296 .50-cal. machine gun systems. A total of 578 OH-58Ds were slated for delivery to the Army by 1991. Trouble in the Middle East, however, not only would alter that schedule, it gave the Army an early opportunity to prove the type's reputation as a formidable gunship.

As part of *Operation Earnest Will*, in August 1987 AH-6 gunships of the Army Task Force 160 were sent to protect reflagged Kuwaiti oil tankers in the Persian Gulf. Since shipboard weapons were of little use against fast gunboats, and Navy and Marine helicopters did not have night attack capability, the AH-6s flew armed surveillance missions from Navy ships. Although highly successful, the specialized attack helicopters were few in number and could not be committed to indefinite Gulf duty.

In seeking an alternative, the Joint Chiefs of Staff leaned on the Army to quickly prepare 15 OH-58Ds and crews to replace the AH-6s. While being rushed through a weapons program, the aircraft were given radar warning

This OH-58A (S/N 70-15215) was temporarily converted to a JOH-58C to evaluate its use against Iranian gunboats. An M197 20mm cannon occupied the copilot's station, with its barrels protruding through the nose. Its ammunition belt went over the seat to a large container in the rear cabin. The aircraft's Light Combat Helicopter kit included folding skids, elevators, and vertical fin for transport in cargo aircraft. A gun sight/video camera was mounted on top of the cockpit. An SCAS was to compensate for gun recoil; however, it pitched the nose sharply downward. Another major drawback was excess gun gasses in the cockpit. Early conversions from A to C models featured flat plate canopy glass. (Ned Gilliand Collection)

Armed with a rocket launcher, the OH-58X demonstrator (S/N 69-16322) was converted from an OH-58D with a night flying system and FLIR. Avionics were located in the nose to enlarge the cabin area. Wearing a striking Kiowa Warrior motif, this one-of-a-kind demonstrator is seen in 1992. (Bell Helicopter)

The OH-58D Kiowa Warrior differed dramatically from the first OH-58 Kiowas. The clean surfaces of the A and B models gave way, of necessity, to myriad offensive and defensive systems. Apparent on this OH-58D (S/N 91-0564) of the Arkansas National Guard is an M296 .50-cal. gun system, mast-mounted sight, beefier engine area, kneeling skid gear, wire strike protection kit, IR jammer, and various antennae. (Matt Ellis)

A pair of 160th SOAR AH-6Js practice firing Hydra 70 rockets in the low-level environment at Yuma Proving Ground. The lead Little Bird has the Black Hole IR resistive exhaust, while the trail aircraft has the standard exhaust. (U.S. Army)

Previously a Hughes OH-6C, serial number 65-12951 served as the test bed for the secret NOH-6P. Two OH-6As underwent a number of changes to produce these quiet aircraft for use by the CIA. This aircraft is armed with the Hughes-developed HGS-22 gun system, which extended from the belly to provide 360-degree coverage. The gun elevated 5 degrees and depressed 60 degrees. (Hughes)

The attack series of Little Birds of the 160th SOAR rely upon miniguns and 7-tube Hydra rocket launchers. In keeping with their classified nature, Night Stalker helicopters are painted black and bristle with antennae that correspond to their special electronics equipment. (Author's Collection)

receivers and additional avionics. Every chance of survival for the two pilots was built into the Kiowa Warrior, including ALQ-144 jammers, and a 15-foot caving ladder that could be released by a pull-cable in the cockpit. Within two months of beginning modifications, Bell delivered the first OH-58D (Armed) in November 1987, and all were completed by April 1988. The program was named *Operation Prime Chance* and the previously unarmed OH-58D was now named Kiowa Warrior.

The aircraft and specially trained pilots formed Task Force 118, which shared cramped space with LAMPS III SH-60 elements aboard FFG-class frigates and DDG-class destroyers. From blacked-out decks, the pilots relied upon

Although a far cry from the heavily armed Chinook gunships of the Vietnam War, special operations CH-47s are well protected with crew-operated improved miniguns. The miniguns of this 160th SOAR MH-47E requires a lengthy chute to ensure that ammunition casings fall well clear of the aircraft. (Author)

Thanks to its punch, accuracy, and reliability, the time-honored .50-cal. made a comeback on special operations AH-6s of the Army's 160th SOAR Night Stalkers. This is General Dynamics' GAU-19/A, which fires at a rate of 1,000 or 2,000 spm. Although the details remain classified, a 160th Little Bird is credited with an air-to-air kill of a helicopter using the .50-cal. gun. (U.S. Army)

night vision goggles to fly less than 50 feet off the water, using their MMSs to find, identify, and destroy targets at long range. Although they operated in secrecy, their hard evidence of gunboats operating in the Gulf was shown to a watching world. Their mission ceased in early 1990; however, they were kept at the ready aboard ships to investigate occasional contacts. Keeping the Kiowa Warriors in the Gulf proved a wise decision; months later Iraq invaded Kuwait and Task Force 118 would become participants in *Operation Desert Storm*.

Night Stalkers

The versatile OH-6A Cayuse and its derivatives easily fit into the shadowy world of special operations. The Cayuse was no stranger to Black operations, having been successfully modified for low noise levels, and having undergone extensive alterations to carry out CIA-sponsored missions during the latter part of the war in Southeast Asia. Despite such successes, it wasn't until the failed attempt to rescue American hostages in Iran in 1980 that special operations aviation came into its own. A special Army helicopter unit was formed for a second rescue attempt, but the hostages were released.

Since the United States did not have an air unit with nighttime deep penetration capability, the unit did not disband, but went on to become a most capable, all-volunteer task force within the emerging Special Operations Force. Designated Task Force 160 and named "Night Stalkers," the highly trained unit and their modified "Little Birds" became known as a unit that could get the job done. TF 160's range of missions, nearly all of which are clandestine, are unlimited. Besides specially modified Blackhawk and Chinook helicopters, the unit was equipped with vastly altered OH-6As for light assault transport or light attack roles.

Re-designated as the 160th Special Operations Aviation Regiment (SOAR) in 1990, the unit participated in every major conflict, and as many that escaped the attention of the media. The unit's Little Bird element remained the basic OH-6A airframe, which was continually upgraded to best accomplish the mission. Hughes' work with its Model 500D Defender led to a tough, maneuverable MH-6 assault transport helicopters, while those armed with miniguns and rocket launchers were termed AH-6s. After numerous enhancements, the two Little Bird types were MH-6H and -6Js for combat assault, and AH-6G and -6J for attack. All became J models in 1995

Some 20th SOS UH-1Ns were armed with TAT-102 type turrets that used a single minigun. The turret was stowed upward for ground clearance, and in use, extended 12 inches below the skids for 360-degree coverage. During J-CATCH exercises, the gun was replaced by a video camera that scored hits against opposing Army helicopters. (U.S. Air Force)

Both UH-1Ns and CH-3Es of the 20th SOS wore this leopard camouflage for their role as aggressors during J-CATCH. The scheme was so popular that it was retained into the 1980s. Like the Green Hornet UH-1Ns of a decade earlier in Vietnam, this UH-1N (S/N 69-6654) was armed with rocket launchers and crew-operated XM-93 miniguns. (U.S. Air Force)

to standardize cockpits and revert to the Model 530FF airframe, which used the 650-shp 250-C30 engine and distinctive T-tail. The AH-6J's basic weapons package consisted of 70mm rocket launchers, miniguns, and GAU-19/A .50-cal. machine gun. After being fielded in 1994, the gun fast became a favorite, often being used in place of the minigun. Other weapons available were the Mk 19 40mm grenade launcher, and Stinger and Hellfire missiles.

Beginning in 1983, the Night Stalkers began racking up major engagements, with combat hours flown in Grenada, the Persian Gulf, Panama, Somalia, Haiti, and finally Iraq and Afghanistan. While many locations remain elusive, world trouble spots have been the flames to which the Little Birds seem naturally attracted.

Air Commando Updates

Air Force involvement in special operations aviation also regained high priority levels following a lull after the Vietnam War. Helicopter gunships once again became part of the Air Force inventory with reactivation of the 20th Special Operations Squadron Green Hornets in January 1976. Using a small force of UH-1Ns and CH-3Es, the squadron was first assigned the task of supporting ground elements of the 1st Special Operations Wing (SOW). After becoming the first Air Force unit to become qualified to fly with night vision goggles, the 20th became involved with tests aimed at improving the helicopter's air-to-air capability. Since unconventional warfare and low-level navigation was their stock in trade, the 20th SOS assumed the role of aggressors in secret exercises that pitted Army helicopters and high-performance fixed-wing aircraft against threat helicopters. Called J-CATCH, for Joint Countering Attack Helicopters, the study was conducted during the late 1970s.

After the failed Iran hostage mission, the Vice Chief of Staff of the Air Force in May 1980 ordered the immediate reassignment of nine Sikorsky HH-53 helicopters from

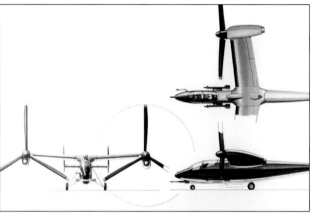

Throughout most of its years in the field of rotary-wing aircraft, Bell Helicopter studied tilt-rotor technology. The company applied many of its designs to the myriad gunship programs, such as AAH, ASH, and LHX. These concept renderings show versions of tilt-rotor gunships based on Bell's XV-15 research vehicle. (Bell Helicopter)

In its quest to add realism to training exercises that would prepare forces for the Soviet threat, the Army modified six UH-1H Hueys to resemble Soviet HIND helicopters. The not-too-convincing JUH-1H look-alikes were used in the 1980s at the National Training Center at Fort Irwin in California as the opposing forces (OPFOR). (Bob Niedermeier)

Air Rescue to the 1st SOW. The large aircraft would provide special operations with long-range, heavy lift capabilities. As part of a major modification program called *Pave Low*, the aircraft received a sophisticated electronics suite and crew-operated miniguns. The 20th's CH-3Es were transferred to other units and Pave Lows joined the mix of aircraft gathered to train for a second hostage attempt named *Honey Badger*.

During the early 1980s, the Huey element of the Green Hornets joined the task force on drugs, flying in *Operation BAT*, which stood for Bahamas, Antilles, and Turks and Caicos Islands. While armed Green Hornet Huey crews chased drug smugglers, the Pave Low section stayed busy training on worldwide deployment exercises. The HH-53s were continually updated, becoming MH-53Hs in 1987, with the fleet of 22 eventually upgraded to MH-53Js. Fit with armor and armed with crew-operated miniguns and .50-cal. machine guns, Pave Lows flew low-level, long-range undetected penetration into denied areas, day or night, in any weather, usually for infiltration, extraction, and re-supply of special operations forces. The MH-53Js logged combat hours in Panama, which would prove to be a primer for forthcoming missions in the Middle East.

Red Star Gunships

Although the Army diligently maintained a secret list of opposition hardware it considered threatening to its forces, it went the distance to simulate Soviet military equipment. The Army's ultimate quest, however, was getting its hands on the real thing.

In the post-Vietnam period, Army planners recognized the growing threat of attack helicopters that equipped air arms of Eastern Bloc and Third World countries. After analyzing successes and failures, the U.S. Air Force, Navy, and Marines had established combat training programs, complete with "aggressor" equipment, to realistically simulate opposition forces. The Army's first major involvement with realistic training was establishment of the National Training Center (NTC) at Fort Irwin, California. In the desert of Fort Irwin, armor and infantry units waged mock war against OPFOR that represented Soviet and Warsaw Pact armies.

Since only helicopter gunships were missing from the simulated battlefields, six UH-1H Hueys were modified to simulate Soviet-built Mi-24 HIND gunships. The NTC eventually passed operation of the JUH-1H HINDs to the Army Reserve's 159th Aviation Regiment. While not

Much to the Army's satisfaction, Russian-built HINDs became available for realistic training during the early 1990s. This HIND Mi-24 was operated by the Army Test and Evaluation Center, Threat Support Activity at NAS Fallon, Nevada. The aircraft simulated hostile threats to search and rescue training operations during Desert Rescue, a joint SAR exercise. (Author's Collection)

HELICOPTER GUNSHIPS: DEADLY COMBAT WEAPON SYSTEMS

Although tests with the AIM-9L Sidewinder were successful, and the Marines insisted that their AH-1Ts be so equipped, budget constraints allowed only limited use of the missile. This is the Sidewinder installation of AH-1J BuNo 159228 of VX-5 at China Lake, where most of the tests took place. (Robert Ziesler/Gary Verver Collection)

look-alikes, the Huey HINDs maintained an ad hoc Soviet presence on the battlefield, using onboard tracking gear to record armor engagements. They were deemed a poor substitute for Mi-24s, prompting a search for a machine that more closely resembled the HIND.

In 1987, the Army's Missile Command contracted with Orlando Helicopter Airways (OHA) to transform 15 Sikorsky S-55s into HIND-E look-alikes. The result would require a double take from even a keen observer to realize that the aircraft was a fake. The HINDs, which were designated QS-55s, were delivered to the Army in 1990. Concurrent with the OHA contract, Honeywell was contracted to install the same drone system of the QF-106A. While that ensured their usefulness as realistic HIND targets for ground-to-air systems being tested at White Sands Missile Range, it detracted from their use as battlefield simulators.

The QS-55s served the air defense community well, but it only meant that the Army had to resume the hunt for more HIND look-alikes. Since OHA had run into legal difficulties, the search for an alternative source led Army officials to the Air Force, which had surplus Sikorsky CH/HH-3Es it was willing to part with. By

1992, the Army had accepted nine CH-3Es and 12 HH-3Es, which were earmarked for conversion to facsimiles called HIND-Xs. Only three of the aircraft were kept flyable at Fort Rucker until 1993, when the project was shelved and the airframes placed in storage.

Still in need of Soviet helicopter look-alikes, personnel at the NTC had their hopes raised as the prospect of obtaining the real thing loomed. Two Afghan pilots had defected with their Mi-24s to Pakistan, a Libyan Mi-24 had been captured by Chadian forces, the reunification of Germany made available a variety of Soviet-built helicopters, and Iraqi Air Force HINDs were captured during *Operation Desert Storm*. Within a short period of time, the Army would have its real HINDs.

The objectives of different commands that sought specific equipment of potential adversaries were coordinated by the Operational Test and Evaluation Command (OPTEC) established in November 1990. Soviet aircraft and air defense systems would be governed by OPTEC's Threat Support Activity at Fort Bliss, Texas, which bordered the vast White Sands Missile Range. By 1995, OPTEC boasted nine Soviet-built helicopters, the most intimidating of the group being the prized Mi-24F HIND

Painted Dark Desert Tan and equipped with 20mm cannon and TOW missile launchers, this pair of AH-1Ts (BuNos 161015 and 160826) are test flown by Bell production test pilots Gilliand and Bailey in 1979. The Tango was a larger, more powerful aircraft; a development of the AH-1J intended to handle emerging anti-armor missile systems. (Bell Helicopter)

To give the AH-1W night targeting capability, Bell installed a Texas Instruments FLIR into the nose of AH-1T BuNo 159228. Called the Viper, the system did not go beyond the research stage. With the cover off of the M197 turret, the motor and drive system is visible. The side bulge is an AN/APR-39 radar warning receiver. (Bell Helicopter)

named *Patience*, and an Mi-25 in Iraqi war paint named *Warlord*. The pair is considered an extremely valuable training tool since, at the beginning of the twenty-first century, more than 2,000 HINDs are known to be in use worldwide.

The Army was not alone in its quest for Soviet-built helicopters. To best perform its mission of assisting and training allied air arms, the Air Force 6th Special Operations Squadron at Hurlburt Field, Florida, acquired Soviet-built helicopter gunships to add to its unusual stable of aircraft, which included a pair of Bell UH-1N gunships.

More Marine Cobras

The rotary-wing branches of the U.S. Army and Marines shared common aircraft types until the end of the Vietnam War, when their direction down different paths became obvious. Notably dissimilar was their choice of gunship and how they planned to adapt it to their tactical doctrine. Although the Marines were quite satisfied with the AH-1J, the type required major improvements with the advent of anti-armor missile systems. The conversion centered on the TOW system, with Bell engineers drawing from their experience with the Model 309 KingCobra and Model 214 HueyPlus. Improvements were sufficient to warrant the new designation, AH-1T. To arrive at the Tango model, the basic AH-1J fuselage was lengthened 12 inches behind the cockpit to counterbalance the additional weight of electronic equipment necessary for the anti-armor mission. The aft ventral portion of the tail boom was swept upward and a ventral fin added to improve stability.

KingCobra technology was used throughout, with a larger tail rotor and 33-inch wide chord main rotor blades borrowed from the Model 214. Given the weight of the aircraft and the TOW system, the switch was made to a Pratt & Whitney T400-WV-402 Twin-Pac rated at 1,970 shp. Bell introduced the powerful engine in its TOW-armed AH-1J International specially built for Iran. In preparation for the AH-1T, AH-1Js at China Lake underwent extensive trials with various systems, especially Sidewinder and Sidearm missiles.

The last two production AH-1Js underwent conversion to Tangos, with the first flight made on 20 May 1976. The Marine Corps ordered 55 AH-1Ts and accepted the first example (BuNo 159228) in October 1977. Deliveries to HMA-269 began during December 1978. The first 33 Tangos were delivered without TOW systems, and as they were being retrofit, Bell completed work on an advanced version of the AH-1T. Engineers had experimentally mated a 3,250-shp GE T700-401 Twin-Pac with an AH-1T. The test Cobra weighed in at 15,000 pounds but when first flown in April 1980, reached a speed of 193 mph.

That stirred enough interest for two months of evaluation by Marine and Navy test pilots. Encouraged by the results, proposals were discussed, but the SuperCobra was converted back to its original configuration when funds to proceed with the project were denied. Marine leadership persisted and in 1983, 44 SuperCobras were approved, with the second half of the order contingent on field evaluation. Later that year, on 16 November, the AH-1T BuNo 161022, which had been converted to a Plus SuperCobra and painted in a striking black and gold scheme, made its first flight. Approval for the new Cobra would come in May 1984, a clear indication that the Cobra was in the Marines to stay.

Whiskey Cobra

Marine aviators welcomed the new Cobra since, from the start, the 530-pound TOW system taxed the AH-1T, especially in hot and high conditions. This marginal performance placed strain on the mission of the Marine Rapid Deployment Force and became the driving force that finally opened funding for the new Cobra. The AH-1T was so extensively reworked to create the SuperCobra that it was given the new designation AH-1W, called simply the Whiskey.

The Whiskey's maximum gross weight is 14,750 pounds, and with its T700-401 twin powerplant rated at 3,380 shp, it has a top speed of 200 mph and cruises at 170 mph. With a full armament load, the AH-1W can hover out of ground effect at 3,000 feet. Protective measures include crew armor, dual radar warning, IR jammers, dual chaff/flare dispensers, and a fuel system designed to withstand 23mm shell hits. The Whiskey became the only attack helicopter to feature dual anti-armor capability, with the introduction of the AGM-114 Hellfire missile, and the first to qualify with the Sidewinder missile. Although both the AIM-9L Sidewinder and Stinger are heat-seekers, the decision on which to use is based upon the type of adversary aircraft; a Sidewinder would be best against a fast fixed-wing aircraft, while the shorter-range, smaller-warhead Stinger is best against helicopters.

The multi-mission AH-1W can also carry the AGM-65 Maverick and AGM-22A Sidearm (anti-radiation) missiles. A wide assortment of weapons can be carried to complement the M197 20mm cannon carried over from the AH-1T. At the onset of AH-1W production, the M197 was qualified to fire the Phalanx round, a powerful projectile that combines depleted uranium with tungsten steel to penetrate armor. Using an onboard laser designator as part of a Night Targeting System (NTS) that incorporates FLIR, the AH-1W can detect and attack targets at night. The first NTS-equipped AH-1Ws were sent to Bosnia in late 1996.

By bringing 37 AH-1Ts up to Whiskey standard and with new production, the Marine Corps set a goal of 230 AH-1Ws by 1997. As Whiskey Cobras arrived, they filled the ranks of 10 Helicopter Marine Light Attack (HMLAs); two in the 2nd Marine Aircraft Wing (MAW), five in the 3rd MAW, and three in the Reserve 4th MAW. The HMLA squadrons operate Whiskey Cobras alongside heavily armed UH-1N twin Hueys for close fire support. The HMLA typically carries 18 SuperCobras and nine UH-1Ns in its inventory.

The result of Bell's experiments with a more powerful engine in the AH-1T was the SuperCobra, which first flew on 16 November 1983. For its debut, the aircraft was painted with this striking black and gold scheme. The up-engined SuperCobra boasted a 15 percent power increase over the AH-1T. (Bell Helicopter)

Its rocket launchers filled with practice rockets, this Whiskey Cobra carries a single AGM-114 missile on its outboard Hellfire launcher. Mounted atop the stub wings are chaff/flare dispensers. Visible in the forward gunner/copilot's cockpit is the sighting unit slaved to the nose-mounted M56 TSU. (Bell Helicopter)

This AH-1W, BuNo. 162547, belonging to the HMLA-169 Vipers carries an AGM-122 Sidearm missile on its outboard missile rail. The Sidearm was designed for use against air defense radars. Note effectiveness of the high-contrast camouflage scheme in disguising specific structural features of the aircraft. (Bell Helicopter)

Wearing the name "Christine" across its nose, this TOW missile-armed AH-1W has screened engine air inlets. Unusual is the Whiskey's assignment to HMM-365 Skyknights, which is a medium helicopter CH-46E squadron. (Don Brabec)

A Whiskey Cobra test fires a Maverick air-to-ground missile. The Hughes AGM-65 Maverick is the only Western air-launched missile that out-ranges the Hellfire, having a 10-mile reach, but it is much more expensive. (Bell Helicopter)

The Marines sought the twin-engine Huey simultaneously with the twin-engine Cobras, for the same reasons: improved performance in hot and high conditions and safety over water. The Army, incidentally, was reluctant to get in on the twin-engine fervor less it detracted from its commitment to the AH-56A Cheyenne. During the 1980s, the AH-1W, along with the AV-8B Harrier and CH-53E Super Stallion, formed the air element of Marine Expeditionary Units. These specially trained and equipped units, which are special operations capable, operate from ships to conduct raids, evacuate civilians, provide security, and fly search and rescue for downed aircrew.

Knowing that one of the keys to maximizing the use of an airframe is the rotor system, Bell engineers during

the 1980s began independent studies of advanced blades and hubs. They concentrated on a bearingless and hingeless rotor system, called the Model 680. The system was 15 percent lighter than other systems and had 50 percent fewer parts. When a four-blade version was tried on a Bell Model 222, the aircraft showed remarkable maneuverability. Next, the system was installed on the first AH-1T, which had been converted to an AH-1W. Called the AH-1-4BW, or Four-Bladed Whiskey, the hybrid could carry more armament, thanks to an uprated transmission.

Other systems were tested or added, including night targeting, a revamped cockpit, an Auxiliary Power Unit (APU), detection and countermeasures gear, and GPS. Structural improvements included improved landing gear,

Originally built as the AH-1T prototype, BuNo 161022 also tested the four-blade Model 680 rotor system, becoming the AH-1W SuperCobra prototype. It is seen here in its AH-1T scheme and carrying a 19-tube rocket launcher. (Bell Helicopter)

Another twist on the AH-1-4BW was this wheeled, flat-plate canopy variant for the Turkish Land Forces. Armament includes Sidewinder and Stinger missiles and rocket launchers. (Ned Gilliand Collection)

In 1995, Bell proposed this extensively modified AH-1-4BW for the Marine Corps. Obvious is the switch to wide-track wheeled landing gear, wider wings, and a shrouded tail rotor, also called ducted fan, or fan-in-fin design. (Ned Gilliand Collection)

Bell's Model 412 was based on its Model 212 twin-engine Huey. The first examples rolled out in early 1981 and the first armed version was this demonstrator flown in 1982 with an XM-157 rocket launcher and podded dual 7.62mm machine gun. In June 1986, Bell proposed its 412SP (Special Performance) version, which included the 412AH (Attack Helicopter). The 412AH, along with the 412HP and EP, had greater takeoff weight, an improved transmission, and PT6T-3D powerplant. It was armed with a Lucas Aerospace under-nose turret housing a .50-cal. machine gun, which was aimed with a Sperry Head Tracker helmet sight system. (Bell Helicopter)

Besides 10 Marine Corps attack squadrons equipped with UH-1N twin Hueys, a number of Navy squadrons utilized the type. This UH-1N served Development Squadron Five (VX-5) at China Lake in 1980 for evaluation of the M93 minigun system. (U.S. Marine Corps)

The Navy steadily improved its Sikorsky H-60 fleet. This SH-60 of HSL-47 fires an AGM-114B Hellfire missile off the coast of San Clemente, California, in August 1999. (U.S. Navy)

a reinforced rotor pylon, and two additional wing stations. In 1987, Bell introduced the AH-1-4BW as the Viper. By the time it began flight testing in January 1989, the Marines planned to do the upgrades and keep the Cobra until 2025. In the twenty-first century the term Viper would be heard again, but in reference to a Cobra improved far beyond anyone's imagination.

Navy Gunship Improvements

Throughout the quarter century between the fall of Vietnam and the twenty-first century, the naval helicopter has not only grown and multiplied, its unique capabilities have been better understood so that its use has been maximized. With the reasonable perception during the 1980s that armed helicopters would engage each other over a land battlefield, the NATC explored aspects of aerial helicopter combat. Extensive tests of air-to-air weapons on helicopters by VX-5 had begun a decade earlier at China Lake.

The LAMPS program, which was a success from the beginning, took on the new Sikorsky SH-60B Seahawk in

Prematurely relegated to the past, Kaman's SH-2 Seasprite got a new lease on life beginning in 1985 as the SH-2G. Two Reserve Squadrons flew the Super Seasprite from 1993 to 2001, finally ending its career as the Navy's front-line, medium-weight ASW helicopter. Besides the AGM-119B Penguin anti-shipping missile seen here on BuNo 163214, the SH-2G was qualified with the Hellfire, Maverick, and Sea Skua missiles, plus a wide range of European weapons. (Kaman Aircraft Corporation)

1984. Not only could LAMPS helicopters search for and attack submarines, they could detect over-the-horizon surface targets. After successful helicopter air-to-surface missile firings during the Falklands War, the Navy re-examined its operational requirements for LAMPS helicopters to have that offensive capability. Studies led to the development during the late 1980s of the Norwegian-made AGM-119B Penguin Mk 2 Mod 7 air-to-surface fire-and-forget missile.

In 1987 operations against Libya, SH-60Bs remained airborne for strikes and radar coverage over the Gulf of Sidra. That same year, LAMPS III air teams arrived in the Persian Gulf to cover convoy operations. Throughout 1988, as part of *Operation Earnest Will*, the Seahawks shared the skies over the Gulf with Army special operations helicopters.

Kaman's line of SH-2 Seasprites, which was thought to have seen its heyday, remained in the Navy for anti-submarine work. With the switch to a more powerful engine in 1985, along with upgrades in electronic systems, the SH-2F became the SH-2G Super Seasprite. Since the conversion program began as the Cold War was ending, only 24 SH-2Gs were built, equipping two Reserve Squadrons, HSL-84 and HSL-94, which flew them throughout the 1990s. Sikorsky's Hawk series became the dominant ASW and SAR helicopter for the fleet, with improvements apparent in the SH-60F Oceanhawk and HH-60H Rescuehawk. Since these helicopters often operated over troubled waters, .50-cal. machine guns and miniguns became standard armament for crewmembers, in addition to Hellfire and Penguin missiles, and torpedoes.

Hits and Misses

Throughout this period, various gunship designs would come and go; some bore fruit, while others died on the vine. Aircraft manufacturers conducted some as private ventures, while others were concepts created in military think tanks.

The Bell Huey in Vietnam proved the value of assault transport helicopters. Although the Huey's legacy would continue, the Army decided even before combat operations ceased that the UH-1 series had to be replaced by something bigger and better. Discussions concerning the Huey's replacement had actually begun as early as late 1965. In January 1972, the Army announced its search for a new Utility Tactical Transport Aircraft System (UTTAS). Specifications called for a simple, tough, and reliable aircraft that could carry a crew of three, plus an 11-man infantry squad, and cruise at 200 mph. Power was to be derived from a pair of 1,500-shp GE T700-GE-700 turboshafts. Only minimal avionics were required, along with wheeled landing gear, manual blade folding, and sufficient armor.

Bell, Sikorsky, and Boeing Vertol submitted proposals, with Bell's Model 240 eliminated early in the process. Three prototypes each of Boeing Vertol's Model 179

During a 1970s competition for a replacement for the famed Huey, called UTTAS, Boeing Vertol submitted this Model 179, militarily designated YUH-61A (S/N 73-21656). The Army in August 1972 contracted for three prototypes, and an additional aircraft was built for company use. The YUH-61A first flew in November 1974, and eventually lost to Sikorsky's UH-60 Blackhawk. (Boeing Vertol)

(YUH-61A) and Sikorsky's Model S-70 (YUH-60A) competed until December 1976, when Sikorsky was declared the winner. A production order for UH-60A Black Hawks quickly followed and the type's widespread use mirrored that of the Huey. Boeing Vertol "navalized" one of its Model 179 prototypes, labeled it the Model 237, and submitted it in the Navy's LAMPS II competition. After it lost to Sikorsky's S-70, the design was dropped.

Since the Black Hawk could be fit with a sturdy External Stores Support System (ESSS) that incorporated stub wings for carrying 10,000 pounds of weapons, it was eyed as a cheaper alternative gunship to the expensive, sophisticated Apache. The idea became even more viable after tests showed that the ESSS could carry an extraordinary amount and variety of systems, including 16 Hellfire missiles; another 16 could be carried inside the aircraft.

Although the idea passed, six Black Hawks attained gunship status as MH-60L DAP (Direct Action Penetrator) with the Army's 160th Special Operations Aviation Regiment. Reportedly, a total of 37 MH-60Ls eventually were assigned to the Night Stalkers. Often, these are mistakenly

referred to as AH-60s, which designated an armed Attack Hawk export variant, which was discontinued. The MH-60L used a modified ESSS, which was originally developed for the U.S. Air Force special operations H-60, called the *Pave Hawk*. Depending on the mission, the MH-60L carried a potent mix of weapons, which consisted of an M230 30mm chain gun, direct-fire or crew-operated Dillon Aero M134D miniguns, Hellfire or Stinger missiles, .50-cal. machine gun pod, and rocket launchers. They were later fit with nose-mounted FLIR and terrain-following radar.

Probably the longest development program in the history of Army aviation involves the Comanche helicopter design, which grew out of another program. In 1982, the Army sought design concepts for a single helicopter to replace its aging UH-1 Huey, AH-1 Cobra, OH-6 LOH, and OH-58 Kiowa. The new helicopter, called Light Helicopter Experimental, or LHX, would assume the utility transport, scout, and attack roles performed by the four proven types. This tall order also dictated that the new aircraft be light and survivable, yet pack a powerful punch. It would feature the latest in electronics technology.

Four of the big names in the helicopter industry combined to form two teams to formulate proposals. Bell and McDonnell Douglas formed the "Super Team" and Boeing and Sikorsky made up the "First Team." The Super Team's design, whose strong points were its Model 680 composite rotor and McDonnell Douglas No Tail Rotor (NOTAR), never got beyond the drawing stage. In 1987,

specifications were changed, calling for only the scout and attack mission. Throughout the LHX program, the four companies brought their best to the table, creating numerous designs, many of which were futuristic wonders.

In 1991, the Boeing-Sikorsky team's design was named the winner. Officially designated the RAH-66 Comanche, the first of two prototypes

Although designed and built as the Huey's replacement, Sikorsky's H-60 series qualified as a gunship when packing the punch of 16 Hellfire missiles. Another 16 Hellfires could be carried inside the aircraft for quick landing and reloading. Making the large missile load possible was the external stores support system tested on the UH-60A Blackhawk. The ability of the ESSS to also carry fuel tanks, gun pods, and mine dispensers enhanced its appeal as a cheaper alternative to expensive sophisticated gunships. (Igor I. Sikorsky Historical Archives, Inc.)

During tests of the M-60L for special operations, the prototype evaluated the SUU-23 system with M61 20mm cannon. Outboard of the cannon is a 19-tube 2.75-inch rocket launcher, and inboard is a stationary or crew-operated gun unit. The stores system originally was developed for the Air Force special operations Pave Hawk, which explains the Air Force camouflage. (Igor I. Sikorsky Historical Archives, Inc.)

After Boeing Vertol's YUH-61A lost the UTTAS competition to Sikorsky, the firm entered this Navy version, called the Model 237, in the LAMPS II competition for a ship-based multi-purpose aircraft. The LAMPS II project, intended to replace the Kaman Seasprite, itself was canceled in 1972. The torpedo-armed prototype, seen here during ship trials, wore BuNo 162371, which was later assigned to a Sikorsky SH-60B. (U.S. Navy)

Although the Army passed on the idea of flying Blackhawks as gunships, the special operations community took advantage of the H-60's ESSS. A number of Blackhawks were converted to MH-60L Direct Action Penetrators (DAPs), which were tested with this weapon arrangement on the ESSS. Inboard of dual 19-tube Hydra 70 rocket launchers is a Belgian FN Herstal 12.7mm machine gun with three 70mm rockets. Undoubtedly, this is one of a number of weapon options for use by Night Stalker MH-60Ls. (Igor I. Sikorsky Historical Archives, Inc.)

The LHX Superteam flies together for the first time. The McDonnell Douglas/Bell Helicopter Textron team was comprised of AH-64A S/N 84-23258 for cockpit evaluation, Bell's fourth-built Model 222 with 680 rotor, and McDonnell Douglas's OH-6A S/N 65-12917 modified into the NOTAR (No Tail Rotor) prototype. (McDonnell Douglas Helicopter Company)

To kick off the LHX program, the Army in early 1983 began work on hands-off flying using the Model 249 Cobra. The crew of S/N 70-16019 is seen here demonstrating hands-off during Advanced Rotorcraft Technology Integration (ARTI) studies. (Bell Helicopter)

was rolled out on 25 May 1995 and made the first flight on 4 January 1996.

Its angular features built mainly of composite and radar-absorbing material gave the Comanche stealth qualities. Powered by two 1,432-shp T800-LHTEC-801 engines, the 11,000-pound RAH-66 cruised at 190 mph and had a top speed of 200 mph. Retractable landing gear and internal weapon bays not only streamlined the aircraft, they helped reduce its radar signature. It was intended that the roomy cockpit could, at times, be manned by one pilot; however, tests revealed that single-pilot missions were unsafe.

Each weapons bay door held three Hellfire or six Stinger missiles, and optional stub wings held an additional four Hellfires or eight Stingers. Comanche's standard weapon was a retractable chin turret housing a GE/GIAT 20mm cannon.

After industry giants Boeing and McDonnell Douglas merged in 1996, their engineers considered converting some Apaches to AH-64Es to serve as scouts until the

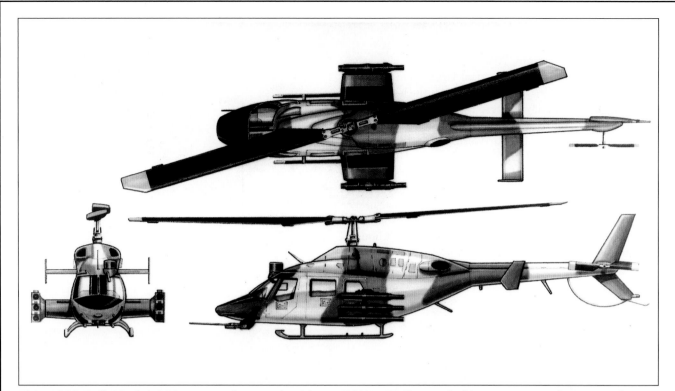

This 1983 Bell Model 222 proposal, armed with six TOW missiles and chin turret, was but one of many designs considered for the LHX program. (Ned Gilliand Collection)

Comanche arrived. Talks even raised the prospect that AH-64Es replace the Comanche, prompting the Army to reaffirm its stance on the Comanche.

After 2000, 13 new Comanches were to be built for additional tests. Delay of their construction spelled trouble, and in 2002 the program was restructured, lowering the original production estimate from 1,213 machines to 650. First deliveries of the RAH-66 were slated for 2006, but in February 2004 the Army canceled the Comanche program, citing the need to instead channel funds toward improving its existing helicopter fleet.

One of the aircraft used to test systems for the LHX and Comanche was Sikorsky's S-76, the development of which began in 1975. Designated in honor of the American Bicentennial, the S-76 was built with experience Sikorsky gained from its S-70 Hawk series. Initially aimed at the civil market, military versions of the S-76 were later introduced. Construction of the S-76B began in 1985 and spawned the AUH-76 Strike Eagle, which stood for Armed Utility Helicopter, S-76 design base. "Armed Utility" seemed a contradiction in terms, but Sikorsky was determined to showcase the aircraft's broad range of capabilities. Although Sikorsky took the low-cost high-performance AUH-76 on a broad marketing campaign, only the Philippine Air Force was interested enough to buy 16, which it armed with rockets and machine guns.

In 1985, a highly modified S-76 Sikorsky Helicopter Advance Demonstrator of Operator's Workload (SHADOW) was used for a MANPRINT study of the engineering interface between pilot controls and displays

The Boeing/Sikorsky LHX team proposed this futuristic design, which had its missiles housed in wing fairings. The LHX competition was begun to find a replacement for the Army Cobra, Huey, and Kiowa helicopters, while using the latest technology in glass cockpits and electronics. (Igor I. Sikorsky Historical Archives, Inc.)

to determine if the Comanche could operate with one pilot; the original LHX concept was aimed at developing a one-man aircraft. Grafted to the nose of the aircraft was a single-pilot advanced cockpit based on that intended for the Comanche. The study concluded that, for safety, the Comanche had to be a two-pilot aircraft.

The nature of mines places them near the top of the list of specialized ordnance. As such, they are seldom used, but when brought onto the battlefield, their deployment is carefully governed. Nevertheless, the capability exists to mass deploy them from Army ground vehicles and helicopters to disrupt movement of large enemy forces. Since mines are a politically sensitive issue, the helicopter-deployed M56 mine laying system of the Vietnam War required enhancement for precise placement and control. The answer lay in the M139 Air Volcano mine system that can be installed on a UH-60A/L helicopter. The system launches 160 canisters, each containing five anti-tank and one anti-personnel mine, for a total of 960 mines. At 138 mph, the Black Hawk can dispense the full load in 17 seconds. A vital feature of the mines is their ability to self-destruct by means of a timer that can be preset for 4 hours, 48 hours, or 15 days. When the Air Volcano was fielded in 1995, each aviation brigade was to receive three systems.

The YRAH-66 (S/N 94-0327) ended its test flying on 30 January 2002. The liberal use of glass surrounding its roomy cockpit gave pilots excellent visibility to perform the scout mission. (Igor I. Sikorsky Historical Archives, Inc.)

Sikorsky's S-67 Blackhawk was flown as a fan-in-fin flight test platform to establish design criteria for the RAH-66 Comanche. The S-67 was able to attain speeds sufficient to warrant dive brakes. The aircraft was reverted to conventional tail rotor design, but later was destroyed in an accident at the 1974 Farnborough Air Show. (Igor I. Sikorsky Historical Archives, Inc.)

The last feature added to the Comanche was the mast-mounted sight, which mirrored capabilities of the Apache. Comanche's canted and shrouded tail rotor is obvious in this view. (Igor I. Sikorsky Historical Archives, Inc.)

Stealth features are apparent in this mockup of the RAH-66 Comanche. The RAH-66 took on an all-business appearance even in its "dirty" configuration, with chin turret, landing gear, and weapons bay doors in open and down position. (Igor I. Sikorsky Historical Archives, Inc.)

The RAH-66 Comanche flies off the wing of an AH-64D Longbow Apache prototype. It was intended from early on that the Comanche team with the Apache to designate targets for the gunship. (Boeing)

Wearing civil registration N5415X on its tail, Sikorsky's Armed Utility Helicopter (AUH-76) Strike Eagle is armed with 16 TOW missiles. Other features include a mast-mounted sight, rescue hoist, and wire strike protection kit. The stars on the cabin door contain a letter for each of the eight countries in which Sikorsky promoted the Eagle. (Igor I. Sikorsky Historical Archives, Inc.)

This view of Sikorsky's AUH-76 Strike Eagle firing weapons shows the understatement in the "Utility" segment of the gunship's designation. Despite such dazzling displays across the globe, the Strike Eagle did not garner the level of interest that Sikorsky had hoped for. (Igor I. Sikorsky Historical Archives, Inc.)

A UH-60A of the Mississippi National Guard taxis for a practice mission with the Air Volcano mine system. The system's weight of 6,350 pounds brings the Blackhawk up to gross weight, which could require that fuel tanks not be topped off. Each tube of the Air Volcano system holds six mines. Four 40-tube units can be carried for a total of 960 mines. (Author's Collection)

The Combat Explorer was the military version of the McDonnell Douglas MD Explorer, which the company introduced in 1995. The twin-turbine aircraft was multi-mission, and easily converted to gunship armed with 70mm rockets and a .50-cal. machine gun unit. A chin-mounted FLIR and roof-mounted Nighthawk surveillance and targeting system complete the Combat Explorer's battle package. (McDonnell Douglas Helicopter Company)

CHAPTER EIGHT

SANDSTORMS

Sand Shark (S/N 67-15643) was an AH-1G that had been converted to an AH-1F Modernized Cobra. It is seen here in February 1991 during Operation Desert Storm wearing the markings of N Troop, 4th Squadron, 2nd Armored Cavalry Regiment, home-based at Fort Polk, Louisiana. Armament is four TOW missiles and two 19-tube M261 Hydra 70 rocket launchers. The M260 (7-tube) and M261 were introduced during the mid 1980s to replace heavier launchers that had been in use since the Vietnam War. (Werner Roth)

Prior to Iraq's invasion of Kuwait in August 1990, the United States had established a military presence in the region, which included armed helicopters. Three years earlier, under *Operation Earnest Will,* two MH-6 and four AH-6 Little Birds of the Army's Task Force 160 were sent to the Persian Gulf. Operating from ships and barges, the Night Stalkers located and attacked enemy boats that threatened shipping. On the night of 21 September 1987, three AH-6s silently approached to within 500 yards of the *Iran Ajr,* videotaped its crew shoving mines into the water, and then riddled it with rockets and machine gun fire. The world now had proof that Iran was mining the Gulf. After leaving three Iranian gunboats in flames two months later, TF 160 was replaced by *Prime Chance* OH-58Ds of 4th Squadron, 17th Aviation Regiment, whose skilled crews carried on the business of keeping harassment of shipping in check.

The Sea Cav Kiowas not only shared the crowded decks with Navy LAMPS I Seasprites or LAMPS III Seahawks, they teamed with them on missions. The LAMPS helicopter trailed a pair of OH-58Ds, using its search radar and vectoring the gunships, while also functioning as the search and rescue element for the flight.

Equipped with self-protection systems, including the ALQ-144 IR jammer and ALE-39 chaff/flare dispenser, LAMPS Mk III SH-60B Seahawks were the major U.S. air presence prior to the war, blanketing the Gulf with radar coverage. They were the eyes and ears of their mother ship, and provided instantaneous information to all commanders in the region. Sixteen SH-2Fs had also been equipped with the jammers and dispensers, plus an under-nose AN/AAQ-16 FLIR, missile warning system, new radios, and crew-operated machine guns. Called the Middle East Expeditionary Force package, these improvements allowed the aging Seasprites to operate in the Persian Gulf.

After President Bush ordered *Operation Desert Storm* in January 1991, A and B Troops of the 4/17 flew their OH-58Ds throughout the conflict; B Troop on the second day of the war claimed the first Iraqi prisoners of war from armed oil platforms, and on 26 January, a pair of Kiowas flew to an Iraqi-held island and liberated the first Kuwait real estate, taking 29 prisoners in the process. Two weeks later, Sea Cav crews entered Kuwait with U.S. Special Forces.

Throughout Desert Shield and Desert Storm, the Kiowas of 4/17 continued to operate from ships with Navy SH-60B Seahawks. During 1991, 12 Kaman SH-2F

A Hellfire missile-armed OH-58D flies near a burning oil well in the Middle East. The night vision goggles that Kiowa pilots relied upon were blinded by burning oil wells, but the Kiowa's FLIR housed in the mast-mounted sight allowed pilots to see about a quarter-mile ahead to avoid power lines. (U.S. Army)

LAMPS Mk I Seasprites in Iraq recorded the first operational use of the Kaman-developed ML30 Magic Lantern laser sub-surface mine detector.

Task Force 160 became a major participant in the conflict. Missions flown by the Little Birds included insertion

Troops of the 82nd Airborne Division inspect a captured Iraqi Mil Mi-24 armed with 57mm S-5 rocket pods and an AT-2 Swatter anti-armor missile during Desert Storm in March 1991. Such spoils of war became useful and realistic assets at U.S. training sites in the United States. (U.S. Army)

Coalition rotary-wing aircraft in Iraq included the PZL W-3W Sokol, such as this example of the Special Air Wing of the Polish Air Force. Equipped with 23mm cannons, the aircraft is being refueled at a Forward Area Refueling Point (FARP) in August 2003. (U.S. Army)

of Special Forces teams, attacks on key targets, and armed reconnaissance. It was revealed years later that Little Bird crews had hunted for and destroyed Scud missile launchers. Eleven launch vehicles were tracked and destroyed in their night lairs by 160th crews. During the Scud chase across western Iraq, the Little Birds were fueled by their special operations cousins, MH-47 Chinooks.

After U.S. Army AH-64A Apaches made their striking debut in the first hours of Desert Storm, they went on to log thousands of combat hours at readiness rates over 85 percent, often when foul weather kept other helicopters grounded. A total of 15 Apache battalions, consisting of nearly 280 gunships, flew over the deserts of Southwest Asia during the conflict. Demonstrating their power and versatility, Apaches, often equipped with extended-range fuel tanks, flew long-range surveillance, armed reconnaissance, and security missions, around the clock and in bad weather.

From August 1990 through March 1991, Apaches created an impressive scoreboard, having destroyed more than 800 tanks and tracked vehicles, more than 500 wheeled vehicles, 66 bunkers and radar sites, 14 helicopters, 10 fighter aircraft, and numerous artillery and air defense sites. The Apache is also credited with assisting in the capture of more than 4,500 prisoners of war. Apaches fired the closing shots of the war when they engaged Iraq's Republican Guard on 2 March, destroying 81 tanks and 23 other vehicles, and assisting in the capture of more than 3,200 prisoners of war. Apaches often flew with many of the deployed OH-58Ds, which designated targets for the gunships. The Kiowa Warrior flew NOE well ahead of the Apache, hiding behind objects or folds of the terrain, exposing only its mast-mounted sight. Using secure radios and laser technology, the OH-58D handed off target information to the Apache, which could pop up from hiding and strike from a distance.

The Kiowa Warriors accounted for one-tenth of the total 1,026 Bell helicopters that served in *Desert Storm;* 142 AH-1F/S Cobras participated in the conflict. A total of 91 Marine Corps Cobras were deployed, only seven of which were AH-1Ts; 24 were AH-1Js, and the remaining 60 were AH-1Ws. The Whiskeys, which operated from both land bases and shipboard, were armed mainly with rockets and Hellfire missiles, while Army AH-1Fs balanced their rocket loads with TOW missiles. Marine AH-1Ws, along with OV-10 Broncos, provided close air support, clearing the way for the fast-moving 1st and 2nd Marine Divisions.

The U.S. Air Force commitment of armed helicopters in Desert Storm consisted of MH-53J Pave Lows of the 20th Special Operations Squadron, six MH-60G Pave Hawks of the 55th SOS, and five special operations-modified MH-3Es of the Reserve 71st SOS. All fell under the Air Force Special Operations Command, and all were armed with crew-operated 7.62mm miniguns and .50-cal. machine guns.

After the 9-11 attack, America faced the challenges of new sandstorms. Under the umbrella of the Global War

The Kiowa has come a long way since its introduction during the Vietnam War. The OH-58D has undergone successive improvements, including upgrade of its transmission and Rolls-Royce 650-shp T703 engine for high-temperature conditions. For its light attack and armed scout roles, 10 weapon combinations are possible, thanks to quick-change pylons. Its weapons group comprises a .50-cal. machine gun, M260 rocket launcher, and two Hellfire or Stinger missiles. At the onset of Kiowa Warrior development, it was found to be more successful with artillery targeting than with helicopter gunships. First deployment of the OH-58D was in Desert Storm with the 82nd and 101st Airborne Divisions. (U.S. Army)

on Terrorism, a U.S.-led coalition in late 2001 kicked off *Operation Enduring Freedom – Afghanistan* to rid the country of Taliban control. Similar actions were taken in Iraq in 2003 as part of *Operation Iraqi Freedom*. These protracted wars drew a heavy and sustained commitment, which made ample use of helicopter gunships. A large number of aviation units took their turn deploying to the "sandboxes" to provide support of coalition forces. In both conflicts, Marine Light Attack Helicopter Squadrons (HMLAs) rotated with their combined inventory of AH-1Ws and UH-1Ns. In both operations, the Whiskey

Cobras flew in teams of two or four, maintaining a protective two-kilometer bubble around its Marine grunts. The ratio of AH-1Ws to UH-1Ns in HMLAs was 12 Cobras to 6 Hueys, with some squadrons later having 18 Cobras and 9 Hueys. A typical load-out for the Whiskeys is four Hellfires, four TOW missiles, and two M260 7-tube Hydra 70 rocket launchers, carrying a mix of blast-fragmentation warheads and flechette.

The Marines acquired the latest Hellfire missile, the AGM-114N. Having a thermobaric warhead, which is a form of fuel-air explosive, but more powerful, the missile has been known to collapse large buildings. Anti-armor Hellfires often bored through buildings and blast-fragmentation warheads didn't have the explosive shock power of the thermobaric type.

Besides the Navy helicopter's time-honored role of anti-submarine warfare, its SH-60 series has become more multi-mission capable. As such it is armed not only with

This SH-60F, BuNo 165259, was assigned to the USS John F. Kennedy in 2002 for deployment during Operation Iraqi Freedom. This Seahawk of Helicopter Anti-Submarine Squadron Five (HS-5) "Nightdippers" is armed with eight AGM-114 Hellfire missiles for the squadron's secondary missions of combat SAR and special warfare support. The Nightdippers' primary mission is ASW. The SH-60F was slated for replacement by the MH-60R with Penguin and Hellfire missiles. (U.S. Navy)

Called the ultimate special operations aircraft, the Sikorsky MH-53J/M equipped three special operations squadrons, in the United States, Great Britain, and Korea, when Desert Storm began. Four MH-53J Pave Lows, along with an Apache force, opened a corridor in Iraq's air defenses so that coalition aircraft could begin the campaign against Hussein's forces. After 9-11, the 20th SOS Green Hornets conducted operations in Iraq and Afghanistan, often working closely with special operations ground forces. Since MH-53s were modified from Vietnam-era C models, they were finally retired and replaced by the CV-22 Osprey. (U.S. Air Force)

In place of a .50-cal. machine gun, a Dillon Aero M134D minigun could be fired from the MH-53M's rear ramp. This 20th SOS gunner is connected to the aircraft with a safety strap during an extremely low level Helocast mission, during which special operations troops are dropped into water. (Sean Borland)

Given the MH-53's enormous size and payload, it could carry a large supply of ammunition for heavy weapons fired from the rear ramp and two waist window openings. This 20th SOS crewman demonstrates the .50-cal. machine gun mounted to the rear ramp of an MH-53M in Afghanistan. (Sean Borland)

torpedoes, but air-to-ground missiles, such as Hellfire and Penguin, and its crew scan for threats down the barrels of modern versions of the .50-cal. machine gun. The Air Force brought to the deserts and mountains of Iraq and Afghanistan its monstrous and highly sophisticated, and well-armed, MH-53M, the ultimate special operations aircraft. Army Apache and Kiowa teams hunt for and destroy targets in these regions.

In Afghanistan, the Royal Army's much-improved Westland Apache AH1 shares the angry skies with Army helicopter fire teams. In Iraq, the 1st Battalion, 227th Aviation Regiment of the 1st Cavalry Division's Combat Aviation Brigade gave the Longbow Apache its first taste of combat. Apache-Kiowa teams also came from brigades within infantry divisions, and from the 11th Attack Helicopter Regiment and the 101st Aviation Brigade. Besides the heavily armed AH-6 Little Birds of the 160th SOAR Night Stalkers, contracted civilian firms fly similar MD 530 helicopters, which often are as heavily armed.

Even in the deserts of Southwest Asia, the Huey gunship flies on, in a not-often-advertised role with the U.S. Department of State (DOS). Since counter-narcotics and counter-terrorism go hand-in-hand, the DOS's Bureau of International Narcotics and Law Enforcement Air Wing formed a fleet of Huey IIs. The UH-1H Huey's complete refurbishment to Huey II standard was done at BellAero of Ozark, Alabama, and includes an 1,800-shp T53-L-703 engine, which boosts gross weight to 10,500 pounds, even in desert conditions. With crews comprised mainly of former U.S. Army aviators contracted with DynCorp, 14 Huey IIs operate from DOS Air Wing bases at Kabul and Kandahar, Afghanistan. Heavily armed with modern Dillon Aero M134D miniguns and .50-cal. M240 machine guns, the Hueys fly in support of Afghan poppy eradication forces. While covering ground teams, a team of three Huey IIs is used, consisting of two gunships and a search and rescue aircraft. The Hueys arrived in Afghanistan in 2006, and are also used for similar tasks in Pakistan and South America.

Reminiscent of the Cobra and Loach Scout hunter-killer teams of the Vietnam War, this Hughes Apache and Bell Kiowa Warrior look for trouble near Tal Afar, Iraq, in 2006. The rocket-armed pair was from the 3rd Armored Cavalry Regiment. The Apache hails as the most advanced and most lethal helicopter in the world. Like most gunship designs worldwide, the AH-64A, and its improved AH-64D Longbow cousin, feature tandem, tiered seating for the pilot and gunner/copilot. (U.S. Army)

Armed with Hellfire missiles and 70mm rockets, an AH-1W prepares to lift off from a refuel/rearm site near Tikrit, Iraq, in 2005. The ace of spades on its engine housing identifies the SuperCobra as being assigned to HMLA-267 Stingers. (U.S. Marine Corps)

Armament technicians load Hellfire missiles on an AH-64D Longbow Apache in northern Iraq during June 2008. The Apache, of 1st Attack Reconnaissance Battalion, 1st Armored Division, was flying in support of Task Force Iron. (U.S. Army)

Department of State Huey IIs in Afghanistan wear either camouflage or this gray scheme with maroon trim. Markings consist only of an aircraft number on the nose and tail fin. Besides weapons, the Hueys are fully combat equipped with survivability systems, armored pilot seats, and armor surrounding vital components. Long-range fuel bladders are usually secured in the cabin. (Rob Neil)

On the External Stores Support System (ESSS) of this MH-60 DAP is a minigun and an M230 30mm chain gun. On the opposite side of the aircraft is a minigun and an M261 19-tube rocket launcher. In Iraq, the special operations DAPs used their weapons and advanced sensors to good effect against insurgents. (U.S. Army)

During Operation Desert Storm, the Marine Corps deployed four AH-1W squadrons. The Whiskey Cobras wore various camouflage schemes, with this brown and tan being the most effective. BuNo 162552 is armed with an M260 rocket launcher inboard, while the M261 outboard is loaded with M257 illumination rockets. (Bell Helicopter)

In the war in Iraq, captured helicopters determined to be airworthy were pressed into service as coalition aircraft. These Mi-17s at Joint Base Balad in 2008 are armed with 20-tube S-8 B-8M1 launchers for 80mm rockets. Like the Western 70mm rocket, the S-8 family of rockets was made available in a variety of warheads. Crew-operated M240 machine guns are mounted in cabin doorways. (U.S. Air Force)

Since narcotics and counterterrorism go hand-in-hand, the U.S. Department of State acquired 14 Huey IIs for its Bureau of International Narcotics and Law Enforcement Air Wing. Converted from Bell Model 205s (UH-1Hs), the heavily armed Hueys are involved with drug wars in South America and South Asia. In Afghanistan, the gunships are operated under contract by private firms, whose employees come mainly from the ranks of military aviation. The Huey IIs in Afghanistan arrived from the United States in January 2006, and were put to work supporting ground poppy eradication teams. Two aircraft armed with miniguns and M240 machine guns typically fly missions. One is designated the SAR aircraft, with the other flying cover. (Rob Neil)

CHAPTER NINE

TWENTY-FIRST CENTURY

Wearing a dazzling paint scheme, plus under-wing dummy armament and civil registration N998HF, this AH-1F flies with the Sky Soldiers at Fort Worth, Texas, in 2007. The group operates a flight of Cobras in aerial demonstrations and as recruitment advertisement for the Army. (Tim Perkins)

Wars, in their own sinister way, accelerate technology, yet it makes one wonder what the limits of technology, as they relate to attack helicopters, really are. Since crew safety is paramount, adversarial air defense systems have been sharpened, and aircraft have been developed that withstand stresses better than humans, military leaders have become more reliant upon the use of pilotless aircraft. These Unmanned Aerial Vehicles (UAVs), or Remotely Piloted Vehicles (RPVs), are nothing new, having first been tested during World War I, and then expanding into large scale target and training use during World War II. They became even more common as drones, and as Navy DASH platforms during the Vietnam War. They have developed to the extent they are sophisticated, multi-purpose craft whose widespread use in Iraqi and Afghan war zones is unprecedented.

Although UAVs, historically, have been fixed-wing aircraft, rotorcraft designs are, once again, becoming more prevalent. The large number of UAVs in use is classified according to roles, while new designs wait their turn on tests ranges. Technically qualifying as twenty-first century helicopter gunships, two UAVs fall under the expanded classification, Unmanned Aviation & Strike Weapon, or UAS.

Science Applications International Corporation and Advanced Technologies, Inc., both in Virginia, developed the Vigilante UAV/VTOL jointly. The Vigilante made history on 13 December 2004 by becoming the first VTOL unmanned aircraft under 2,330 pounds to launch 2.75-inch rockets in flight. The tests were conducted at Yuma Proving Ground, with an Army UH-1H controller aircraft flying nearby. Vigilante fires Hydra Universal Rail Launcher/Integral Intelligence (HURL/II) Hydra 70 rockets in 4-tube launchers; Hellfire missiles can also be launched from the UAV.

Developed by Northrop Grumman, the MQ-8B Fire Scout made naval aviation history when it deployed aboard the USS *McInerney* (FFG-8) in October 2009. As part of a series of deployments to learn everything about the Scout, the initial deployment involved counter-narcotics activities, while other assignments were planned to test the UAV's combat capabilities. Next on the Scout's schedule were missions flown from Littoral Combat Ships (LCSs) to evaluate its effectiveness with H-60 helicopters during surface warfare, mine counter-measures, and anti-submarine warfare.

The Navy remained active in armed helicopter development, tailoring its weapon needs to operations at sea. Its master helicopter plan at the beginning of the century

The wave of the future is said to be widespread use of unmanned aerial vehicles (UAVs) that can perform most missions historically performed by manned aircraft. The UAV Vigilante can be armed with a 4-tube HURL/II Hydra 70 rocket launcher or Hellfire missiles. It poses at Yuma Proving Ground with an equally interesting helicopter, UH-1H (S/N 72-21479), carrying control equipment on a universal weapons mount. (Advanced Technologies, Inc.)

The U.S. Navy remains active in armed helicopter development, tailoring its weapons needs to operations at sea. In July 2003, this Sikorsky SH-60B of HSL-51 fires an AGM-119 Penguin missile during aircrew certification off the coast of Okinawa. The squadron is based at Atsugi NF, Japan, but maintains a detachment at Kadena, Okinawa. (U.S. Navy)

The UAV Vigilante made history in 2004 by being the first rotary-wing aircraft in its weight class to fire 2.75-inch rockets. (Advanced Technologies, Inc.)

Northrop Grumman's small but potent MQ-8B Fire Scout began deployment with the 4th Fleet during late 2009. Initial tasks of the UAV involve counter-narcotics, with flights planned to test its combat capabilities. (U.S. Navy)

is the transformation of its seven helicopter types into a tightly focused force comprising two H-60s, the SH-60R and the CH-60S. The plan's twofold goal was to simplify logistics, maintenance, and training, thereby reducing costs, and to enhance the war-fighting capabilities of the helicopter fleet. By the time the Kaman SH-2G was retired from the Naval Reserve in 2001, the H-60 line of helicopters became dominant, with all armed variants given nose-mounted Texas Instruments FLIR units, and provisions for firing Hellfire missiles. The SH-60R is a remanufacture of existing H-60B, F, and H versions, while the CH-60S is new production. While optimized for littoral operations such as ASW and electronic missions, the SH-60R, when armed with Penguin and Hellfire missiles,

Enhanced miniguns come in a variety of versions, including those produced by Dillon Aerospace (M134D) and Garwood Industries (M134G). The GAU-17/A seen on this Navy UH-1N was initially an Air Force development as a flexible helicopter mount. The Navy also uses them as shipboard weapons. The GAU-17/A has a selectable firing rate of 2,000 or 4,000 spm. (U.S. Navy)

Weapons on this UH-1N in 2003 consist of M261 rocket launchers and crew-operated GAU-16/A .50-cal. machine guns. The gun is a lighter version of the vintage M2, and is mounted on the shock-absorbing defensive armament system. This November Huey features the latest electronic systems, including IR jammer (atop the engine cowl), radar warning receivers, chaff/flare dispenser, and nose-mounted Texas Instruments FLIR. (U.S. Navy)

Ominous skies seem an appropriate background for the debut of Bell's AH-1Z Viper and UH-1Y Venom for the Marine Corps. The Global War on Terrorism and Marine requirements prompted a decision at the beginning of the twenty-first century not only to convert AH-1Ws to Vipers, but also to begin new production. (Bell Helicopter)

can fly strike missions. The CH-60S, although dedicated to transport, CSAR, and special warfare support, is also capable of mine countermeasures.

In March 2009, one of four mine countermeasures systems under development by Northrop Grumman, the AN/AWS-2 Rapid Airborne Mine Clearance System (RAMICS) was successfully test fired. The RAMICS gun is a 30mm Mk44 Bushmaster II cannon built by ATK Armament Systems of Utah. After a mine is laser designated, the gun fires a tungsten supercavitating round, which has a unique design that allows it to maintain velocity underwater to destroy mines.

Outfitted with test instrumentation, a UH-1Y prototype performs a test flight in early 2003. The Viper and Venom have 84 percent commonality in components, which translates to tremendous cost saving, while extending the life of both airframes. (Mike Wilson)

The UH-1Y, BuNo 166475, test fires Hydra 70 rockets from its M261 launchers in March 2005. During the Venom's trial period, its engine exhaust areas were completely redesigned from vertically to horizontally arranged exhaust sections. (U.S. Marine Corps)

Air Test and Evaluation Squadron Twenty One (HX-21) at NAS Patuxent River, Maryland, was assigned AH-Zs BuNos 166772 and 166760. The squadron also had AH-1Ws BuNos 165359 and 163937, which were slated for conversion to Vipers. Here, BuNo 166760, armed with Hellfire missiles, undergoes FLIR integration tests at Pax River in April 2009. The air data sensor probe is pole-mounted immediately forward of the windscreen. (Mike Wilson)

A UH-1Y Venom prototype unleashes a salvo of Hydra 70 rockets in flat trajectory during a test high-speed attack run. As the latest in Bell's long line of Huey models, the AH-1Y and its partner AH-1Z are expected to serve Marine aviation well into the twenty-first century. (U.S. Navy)

The Marines knew they made a good decision in staying with the Huey and Cobra line of helicopters, but by the end of the twentieth century they also knew the aircraft required updating to better meet the Corps' pressing littoral warfare needs. The Corps chose not to wait for whatever aircraft resulted from a Joint Replacement Aircraft Study, then under way. Marine aviators found the twin-engine UH-1N the ideal all-weather, day-night helicopter for medical evacuation, forward air control, assault support, and special operations. The Marines expected its 100 UH-1Ns to remain in the fleet until 2014, or until something better came along. The engineering phase had already begun to upgrade AH-1Ws to AH-1-4BWs to keep 180 Cobras in service until 2025.

In 1997, Marine Corps officials decided to remanufacture its UH-1N and AH-1W Cobras under one H-1 Upgrade Program, rather than buy new aircraft. Besides the obvious benefit of having 84 percent commonality of major components between both aircraft, both types would be flown and maintained within the same eight HMLA squadrons. They would get new composite four-blade main and tail rotors, semi-automatic blade fold, an improved drive system and landing gear, a restructured rotor pylon, and a glass cockpit with integrated avionics. The rebuilt UH-1N Huey was designated the UH-1Y and the AH-1W Cobra became the AH-1Z. Early in 2009, they were officially named *Venom* and *Viper*, respectively. When Bell test pilot Monte Nelson and Marine Corps Maj Tony Randall lifted off in the first UH-1Y, named *Yankee One*, just three months after the 9-11 attack, the Marines knew their decision had been timely. On 8 January 2002, the needle of *Yankee One*'s airspeed indicator read 140 knots (161 mph), already faster than the maximum speed allowed of the UH-1N.

The first five aircraft, three AH-1Zs (BuNos 166477, 166478, and 166479) and two UH-1Ys (BuNos 166475 and 166476) arrived at NAS Patuxent River, Maryland, during April 2002. Marine Light Attack Helicopter Training Squadron 303 (HMLAT-303) at MCAS Camp Pendleton conducted crew training.

The Global War on Terrorism caused a surge in the operational tempo of the UH-1N, prompting the decision in April 2005 to switch from remanufacture of the UH-1N to new-build aircraft. The cost difference was marginal and Marine Corps' global commitments did not allow having a large number of Hueys out of service for the two-year rebuild. New production began in 2006, with the delivery of 123 Venoms to be completed in 2016.

The AH-1Z phase of the program, meanwhile, faced problems integrating the Target Sight System, a most critical factor in attack helicopters. The problem was ironed out and the Viper's rebuild plan was also changed. Instead of 180 AH-1Ws being rebuilt, 168 would be remanufactured and 58 would be new production, giving the Corps a total of 226 AH-1Zs. At the same time, to keep pace with the expanding ground combat force, three HMLA squadrons were added, and one reserve squadron deactivated. The Viper was slated to be operational by mid 2011, with the total number in service during 2017.

In mid 2009, three UH-1Ys deployed with the 13th Marine Expeditionary Unit to conduct anti-piracy operations off the coast of Somalia. The deployment was the driving factor in accelerating integration of the Advanced Precision Kill Weapons System (APKWS) with the Venom and Viper. Using a semi-active laser seeker, this revolutionary system gives the 2.75-inch rocket precision guidance after years of use as an area weapon only. In October 2009, the UH-1Y deployed in squadron strength with HMLA-367 to Afghanistan. The nine Venoms were equipped with improved FLIR, mission computers, and helmet sights. Six were fit with satellite communications (SATCOM), which proved useful in Afghanistan's mountain ranges.

Seen here in 2007, this OH-58D was to have already been replaced by a new Armed Reconnaissance Helicopter. Cancellation of that program, however, kept the Kiowa Warrior in place, pending a new search for a replacement. The OH-58D has recorded 200,000 combat flight hours. This example (S/N 93-0974) served the Arkansas National Guard. (Matt Ellis)

Nose panels of Number 974's XM296 .50-cal. machine gun's cage assembly displayed elaborate artwork. The ammunition box, which is positioned slightly above and rearward of the gun, holds 463 rounds, which gravity-feed the weapon. For transport in cargo aircraft, the gun unit can be stowed in a higher position to allow skids to be placed in a kneeling position. (Matt Ellis)

In the Army world of armed helicopters, at the beginning of the century, the retirement of Vietnam-era helicopters was accelerated to make available funds for improving the remaining fleet. About 600 National Guard and Reserve, and 400 active duty force helicopters were earmarked for retirement. All AH-1 Cobras were retired by the end of 2001, and all UH-1 Hueys were to be gone by 2004, six years earlier than previously planned. Only the Apache, Blackhawk, Kiowa, and Chinook would remain, with most attack helicopters assigned to the active duty force. It was hoped that the savings from retiring hundreds of aircraft could be used to accelerate the Comanche's arrival.

The first RAH-66s were to come off the assembly line in 2006, with deliveries totaling 62 per year. That plan took a dramatic turn when the Army ended the RAH-66 Comanche program in February 2004. Having spanned 13 years and with $8 billion invested in the project, Comanche's demise marked one of the largest cancellations in Army history. Contributing to the Comanche's end was not only the shift toward the use of unmanned aircraft, but the prospect that UAVs would eventually fly reconnaissance and attack missions.

Of great concern since the final months of the Vietnam War were surface-to-air missiles, or SAM. Another concern has been air-to-air combat. While the Apache represents the state-of-the-art of helicopter design, potential adversaries have not been standing idly by. Some nations have improved dated weapons, built new ones, and developed attack helicopters, such as the Mi-24, Mi-28, Havoc, and KA-30 Hokum. SAMs track and hit their target either by radar-tracking, heat-seeking, or laser-guided means. Most can detect any aircraft flying in the "SAM belt" between 1,000 and 20,000 feet. SAMs fired from shoulder launchers, called MANPADS, for Man Portable Air Defense Systems, have emerged as a major threat.

When introduced, the Apache was well equipped to detect and counter SAM threats, yet there was little defense against conventional line-of-sight weapons; and they were not fully capable of engaging in air-to-air combat. These, and other factors, emphasized the need for improvements, which led to the Apache Multi-Stage Improvement Program.

The First Block II Apaches, which featured upgraded digital communications and Air-to-Air Stinger (ATAS) missiles, were delivered to the Army in February 2003. When AH-64Ds deployed to Afghanistan for *Operation Anaconda*, beginning in 2003, the Army possessed more than 800 Apaches; 500 of those were AH-64As slated for upgrades, with deliveries to be completed by August 2006. Deliveries of new production Longbows began in 2007.

Continued use of the Army's special operations Little Bird speaks well for the dynamic H-6 airframe. The modern version, the MH-6M Mission Enhanced Little Bird, or MELB, shows off its firepower, which consists of Hellfire missiles, Hydra 70 rockets, and .50-cal. GAU-19 machine guns. (U.S. Army)

Powered by a Honeywell HTS-900 engine, the ARH-70 prototype makes a test flight in April 2007. Wearing a combination of Army markings, civil registration N44515, and the prototype numeral 1, the ARH-70 carries M260 rocket launchers, along with flight instrumentation. (Bell Helicopter)

Bell's entry for the Armed Reconnaissance Helicopter competition was this Model 407 demonstrator called the ARH-70. The Model 407 was based on Bell's 206L-3 LongRanger II introduced in 1977. The ARH-70 first flew in June 2005. Radar warning receivers and a FLIR unit are on the nose, while launchers carry dummy Hydra 70 rockets. (Bell Helicopter)

Block III improvements were slated for 2008 onward, which included increased digitization, the capability to control UAVs, and new rotor blades that would increase speed, climb rate, and payload.

In the Army's special operations community, the small but powerful and versatile A/MH-6 Little Bird continues to prove indispensable in pressing the war on terrorism and indulging U.S. interests. Lightweight universal mounts are part of an integrated weapons management system that allow the gunship AH-6M, or MELB to carry a wide variety of weapons. These include Hydra 70 rockets, .50-cal. GAU-19 machine gun, 7.62mm minigun, 40mm Mk 19 grenade launcher, and the Hellfire, TOW, and Stinger missiles. Planned expansion of the Little Bird force in 2009 included testing of a UAV, called the Unmanned Little Bird (ULB) demonstrator, the operational version of which is the A/MH-6X.

The Little Bird was on the verge of having a greater presence in the Army when it became the favorite in a competition aimed at improving the helicopter force. The age and attrition of Kiowa Warriors led to the Army's search in the new century for a new Armed Reconnaissance Helicopter (ARH). The program was one of a number made possible by the savings of canceling the Comanche program.

In response to the Army's Request for Proposals, two firms submitted bids; Boeing came in with an upgraded MELB, and Bell proposed a militarized version of its Model 407. Bell was announced the winner in July 2005, receiving a contract for 368 aircraft, the first four of which were to be pre-production aircraft; deliveries were to begin in 2006 and be completed in 2011. Army planners later increased that number to 512 to equip four Army National Guard attack helicopter battalions whose Apaches would be shifted to active-duty units.

Called the ARH-70, the Bell 407 is a derivative of Bell's 206L-3 Long Ranger II with a four-blade rigid rotor used on the OH-58D. The ARH-70 was to be single-pilot capable and be armed with Hydra 70 rocket launchers and a .50-cal. GAU-19 machine gun, although many weapons combinations were possible. The Honeywell HTS900 engine would give the ARH-70 a top speed of 161 mph.

Bell's ARH demonstrator (N91796) flew on 3 June 2005, and the second prototype (N44548) made the first flight of the actual ARH-70 on 20 July 2006. The program suffered its first setback when the fourth prototype (N445HR) was destroyed during a crash landing in February 2007. Production was delayed and cost overruns eventually led to cancellation of the ARH project in October 2008.

The changing world of the new century has kept the Air Force special operations community busy operating its force of mammoth MH-53M helicopters, which were heavily armed with miniguns and .50-cal. machine guns. When the 21st SOS turned in its MH-53M IV Pave Lows in 2007, it signaled the end of an era and the beginning of new multimission technology with the tilt-rotor CV-22B Osprey. The first Osprey for special operations arrived at Hurlburt in

2006, with 50 slated for delivery by 2017. Although the 1970s-vintage UH-1N gunship was removed from the Special Operations organization, they are still operated by the 6th SOS at Hurlburt Field, Florida. Since it is the unit's job to assess, train, and assist foreign air arms to defend their country, the 6th SOS possesses the aircraft types used by these governments. Among the mix of armed helicopters in the squadron's inventory are Soviet-built Mi-8 and Mi-17 helicopters, which are in abundance worldwide.

For the first time in the history of the U.S. Coast Guard, its helicopters began flying ocean patrols with standardized weapons. The crew-operated weapons are necessary elements of helicopter upgrades to keep pace with the Coast Guard's increasing role in law enforcement and anti-terrorist duties. To dramatically increase the Coast Guard's drug interdiction tallies, in 1999 two MH-90 Enforcers were armed to test the ability to catch fast boats suspected of carrying drugs in the Atlantic. Their success led to the lease in 2000 of eight short-range Agusta MH-68A Stingrays. They, in turn, were replaced by 10 EADS/Eurocopter HH-56C Dolphins, which had been upgraded to Multi-Mission Cutter Helicopters

having 40 percent more power. Enhanced electronics and two Turbomeca Arriel engines gave the Dolphin a top speed of 190 mph and a gross weight of 9,480 pounds.

Weapons packages varied according to aircraft and evaluations, but consisted mainly of crew-operated .50-cal. guns or various models of the M240 7.62mm machine gun. The latter is used to fire warning shots across the bow of vessels, usually go-fast drug smugglers, while either Barrett M107 or Robar RC50 .50-cal. guns with high-tech scopes are used by onboard snipers to disable the engines of vessels whose operators refuse to surrender.

The helicopters formed the USCG Helicopter Interdiction Tactical Squadron (HITRON) based at Cecil Field, Jacksonville, Florida. With the introduction of the Dolphin, in 2008 the helicopter element was labeled Airborne Use of Force (AUF). In the plans at that time was the conversion of 42 Sikorsky HH-60Js to MH-60T Thunderhawks, which would feature weapons and new engines, electronics, and cockpit. Unsurprisingly, armed Coast Guard helicopters began appearing at the San Francisco air station, a foreboding indicator of the challenges the American military faces in the new age.

U.S. Air Force MH-53s served until 2008 when the last of their breed, S/N 68-10369, seen here, was retired and replaced by special operations version of the CV-22 Osprey. This Pave Low IV flew the first mission of Operation Desert Storm while assigned to the 20th SOS, based at Hurlburt Field, Florida. The MH-53M operated with a crew of six, and was armed with three miniguns or .50-cal. machine guns. (U.S. Air Force)

The Air Force, through the 6th Special Operations Squadron at Hurlburt Field, continues its unique but vital mission of training members of allied air arms with aircraft familiar to their inventories. As such, the 6th SOS operates a number of those aircraft, some of which are unique to the Air Force. Since numerous countries assisted by the U.S government fly the Mi-17, the 6th SOS uses this aircraft, which is armed with S-8 unguided rocket launchers. (U.S. Air Force)

One of three weapons stations on the special operations MH-53Ms was this minigun mounted on the rear loading ramp of the aircraft. The position gave the gunner tremendous latitude in providing cover fire during commando operations. (U.S. Air Force)

In 2000, the U.S. Coast Guard, for the first time in its history, began flying armed helicopters. Flying from both East and West Coast air stations, the armed aircraft are necessary to keep pace with increases in terrorism and drug smuggling. Squadrons flying the aircraft are called Helicopter Interdiction Tactical Squadrons (HITRONs), which flew Agusta MH-68A Stingrays, such as this example. Perched in the aircraft's doorway is a gunner armed with an M240 machine gun. (U.S. Coast Guard)

Eight HITRON Stingrays were replaced by EADS/Euro-copter HH-56C Dolphins for coastal anti-narcotics and counterterrorism duty. Mounted in the doorway of this Dolphin pulling out of Air Station San Francisco is an M240 machine gun. (U.S. Coast Guard)

A Stingray aerial gunner trained in sniper skills takes aim with a precision .50-cal. machine gun. The M240 is used to fire warning shots across the bow of a suspect go-fast boat, while the .50-cal. disables the craft's engine. (U.S. Coast Guard)

CHAPTER TEN

GLOBAL GUNS

This ex-German Mi-24 HIND went to the Hungarian Air Force after the former East and West Germanys were rejoined. Hungary overhauled the Mi-24P in 2004, replacing its single nose-mounted 12.7mm gun with twin fixed 30mm cannon. Units mounted to the lower nose section comprise a missile control system. (Tamas Szorad)

The Boeing AH-6i Light Attack/Reconnaissance helicopter made its first flight during September 2009. Based on the highly successful special operations Little Bird, the AH-6i is intended for international customers. The prototype, registered N106HX, is seen here at the 2009 Dubai Airshow, its first showing outside of the U.S. Armament consists of miniguns on both sides, 4-tube directional guided rockets, and a joint air-to-ground missile. (Martin Bach)

When the value of the helicopter was realized during the 1950s, arming them became the endeavor of many air arms across the globe. Hardly fitting the term "gunship" as it is used today, often these were U.S.-built aircraft armed with rudimentary weapon systems. Early attempts by the French, for example, had machine gunners strapped into the stretchers mounted to the sides of Bell Model 47s. Governments having a profound interest in arming helicopters during this period watched closely French and U.S. developments.

While operational use of the helicopter gunship is largely credited to France's struggle for colonial rule during the 1950s, other nations had begun arming helicopters. After the Vietnam War proved to be the ultimate proving ground for armed helicopters, technology and the uncertainty of the Cold War gave rise to their further development. Of great concern to many nations was the threat of Soviet armor, resulting in greater attention given the helicopter as an anti-armor weapon. The superpowers took the lead, initiating armed helicopter programs that not only met their needs, but those of smaller nations with defensive, and offensive, ambitions. Many armed helicopters serve beyond their nation's borders, protecting national interests, or as coalition aircraft.

Although helicopters built by America's giants in the industry, such as Hughes, Bell, and Sikorsky, were popular exports, major firms abroad, such as Fuji, Westland, Mil, and Aerospatiale, made inroads in the industry. Many of the helicopters flown around the world retain their original designations from an era before corporate mergers and buyouts became commonplace. Some U.S. firms granted license to manufacturers abroad, allowing them to build their own line of the same basic aircraft. Smaller firms across the globe got in on the action, usually developing helicopters for use within their own borders, while supplying the air arms of neighboring countries. A mix of former Soviet bloc and Western-manufactured helicopters in some nations indicates their shift in alliance.

The silhouette of Bell's Huey helicopter, like that of its ubiquitous cousin, the Model 47, is recognized worldwide. Without question, the Huey's success since the 1960s accounted for the largest number of armed helicopters in the world; the governments of nearly 60 nations are known to have operated the series. With production figures topping those of the famed Douglas C-47 and B-24 bomber, the Huey was not only available in large numbers, it was easily converted to a weapons platform. Bell's Cobra, the world's first pure helicopter gunship,

During the Falklands War, Royal Navy 829 Squadron sent 10 Westland HAS.1 Wasps to the war zone. Although acquired as a shipboard ASW helicopter, the Wasps proved effective armed with AS.12 missiles. This aircraft, seen firing an AS.12, in April 1982 fired the missiles at the Argentine submarine ARA Santa Fe, scoring three hits. (Author's Collection))

Displayed in 1984 with this early version of the Royal Navy's HAS5 is (from left to right): AM39 Exocet missile, MAD, BAe Sea Skua missile, and BAe Sea Eagle missile. Trials of the Sea Eagle long-range anti-ship missile began in 1985 with Advanced Sea King, which was strengthened to carry two Sea Eagles. The Sea Skua entered service in 1982 and was carried by the Lynx. Seven were launched during the Falklands War, all of which scored hits on three Argentine ships. Twenty HAS5s of two Royal Navy squadrons maintained continuous ASW screen during the conflict. (Author's Collection)

Royal Navy Westland HAS2A Sea Kings, such as this example, serialed XV697, were initially painted Royal Air Force Blue. This Sea King was armed with four Mk-44 torpedoes while assigned to Number 824 Squadron at RNAS Culdrose. The unit was embarked on Fort Grange from May to October 1982 for the Falklands conflict. Westland-built S-61 Sea King variants were also used extensively in civilian applications for everything from big city inter-airport passenger transportation to ferrying oil workers to offshore drilling rigs in the North Sea. (Author's Collection)

The Westland Lynx AH.7 is an improvement of the AH.1 begun during the late 1990s. This TOW missile-armed AH.7 of the British Army is seen in 2005. (Jenny Coffey)

Recognizing the need for a dedicated attack helicopter for its border war, South Africa turned to its own Denel Aerospace firm, which developed the AH-2 Rooivalk, which is Afrikaans for Red Kestrel. Only 12 were built and placed in service with 16 Squadron of the SAAF, beginning in 1999. This prototype is displayed at the Dubai Airshow. (Emiel Sloot & Luc Hornstra/STAS)

along with improved variants, would also be in great demand. Beginning in the 1980s, foreign governments became less reliant upon America's Mutual Defense Assistance Program (MDAP), turning instead to regional helicopter firms that had come into their own.

As defense manufacturing became more globalized and sophisticated aircraft systems became more abundant, it was not unusual for multiple firms to have a hand in the development of a single aircraft type. Given the realities of smugglers, border clashes, protracted guerilla wars, and terrorism, to name a few, the global demand for armed helicopters remains high. For foreign governments that seek attack helicopters built in America, the political climate must be conducive to the acquisition, especially concerning high-end types such as the Apache. Here, then, in broad geographic terms, is a look at the world inventory of armed helicopters.

Helicopter types that have flown the African continent are as diverse as the 53 nations that form its expanse. Besides Western and Soviet types, African air arms acquired a wide variety of helicopters. While South Africa operates helicopters of various origins, noteworthy is its only attack helicopter, the Rooivalk, only 12 of which were built by the local firm Denel.

Among Asian nations, Japan and South Korea maintain the largest and most modern of Asian air arms. Both received large numbers of helicopters from U.S. stocks,

with Japan's Fuji Heavy Industries licensed to build Bell Cobra variants. South Korea's fleet of McDonnell Douglas MD-520MGs is kept low-profile to prevent North Korea from mimicking them with its similar armed versions. North Korea also flies the Mi-24. Although China's People's Liberation Army Air Force is the third-largest air force in the world, it places less importance on the attack helicopter, having less than 90 aircraft. The majority are Z-9s, Z-10s, and Z-11s made in China, plus French Gazelles. The Republic of China Air Force, meanwhile, ensures the defense of Taiwan with two attack battalions of AH-1W Cobras. In Southeast Asia, the Royal Thai Air Force inherited a number of U.S. helicopters, mainly Bell Hueys, following the war. The RTAF also operates a small number of AH-1 Cobras. Laos and Cambodia rely upon armed Mi-8s, while the Philippines Air Force favors the MD520MG. India's armed forces have long been equipped with Soviet-manufactured helicopters, many of which are being replaced by the MBB-influenced and heavily armed Dhruv produced by India's Hindustan Aeronautics Ltd. (HAL). The Indian Navy found the Sea King the best aircraft for its ASW force.

In Oceania, Australian Army Aviation operates a single attack helicopter, the Tiger Armed Reconnaissance Helicopter (ARH), armed with 20mm cannon, Hellfire missiles, and 70mm rockets. Although The Royal New

After the Sri Lankan Air Force acquired a number of Bell 212s during the 1980s, 12 were converted to gunships to support commando operations. Seen on this Model 212 is a universal weapons mount on its hard points, along with two machine guns in the cabin, a .50-cal., and an M240. (Author's Collection)

Beginning in 1990, the Philippines Air Force (PAF) increased its fleet of Model 500 helicopters with 22 MD500 Defenders. Standard armament for the type was an M260 rocket launcher and .50-cal. gun opposite. The PAF operates eight squadrons equipped with the MD-520MG. (McDonnell Douglas Helicopter Company)

Of three ASW helicopter squadrons in Taiwan's navy, one is equipped with 12 Hughes Model 500MD/ASWs ordered in 1977. The other squadrons fly the Sikorsky S-70C. The 500MD/ASW is fully equipped for anti-submarine duty, complete with torpedo and flotation gear. The MAD is deployed on a cable from its pylon mount. (Hughes Helicopters)

Through assistance from the Soviet Union, China began production of its modest helicopter force with the Zhishengji-5 (Z-5), first built in 1958. Based on the Mi-4, 545 Z-5s were built by the Harbin Aircraft Factory for China's People's Liberation Army Air Force and civil aviation. The armed variant had a 12.7mm machine gun on the belly and racks to carry two unguided missiles. Although influenced by Sikorsky's S-55, Mil's Mi-4 was on a par with the S-58 in terms of size and performance. An Mi-4M tactical variant with ventral cannon or 76mm anti-tank gun was introduced in 1968. (Olaf Bichel)

Zealand Air Force maintains a UH-1H squadron in the tactical role, its Hueys, and the NH90s slated to replace them, are armed with door guns only.

In the Middle East, even before the Israeli Air Force (IAF) came to rely upon Huey helicopters, it armed Bell 47s, beginning in 1965. Armed with SS-10 missiles, 68mm rockets, and .50-cal. machine guns, the small helicopters saw extensive use in the assault role. They were put to the test in the 1967 Six-Day War, and phased out the following year. Popular with the IAF was a line of AH-1 Cobras of various models, beginning with the AH-1Q. Of particular interest is the assistance given Israel by founder of the co-axial rotor system, Peter Papadakos, in continuing the QH-50E drone for classified surveillance. The IAF boasts

the most powerful attack helicopter force in the region, having three Apache squadrons. Turkey, Saudi Arabia, and United Arab Emirates fly the Apache as well. A cooperative effort between Sikorsky and the Israeli government in 2008 demonstrated the Armed Black Hawk (ABH) proof-of-concept helicopter for the new Battlehawk. Armed with the latest in sensors, laser-guided rockets and missiles, and a 20mm cannon turret, the Battlehawk will be made available as a retrofit kit or new-build.

Before the Islamic revolution of 1979, Iran had received 202 International AH-1Js, 62 of which were TOW missile equipped. Some were kept airworthy for defense against Iraq, with the government eventually leaning toward the acquisition of Eastern Bloc aircraft. Iraq during

To fight terrorists during the 2007 siege of Nahr al-Bared, the Lebanese Army modified this Bell 205 with racks from Mirage III jets to carry a 750-pound Mk-117 and Mk 82 500-pound bombs. The Hueys were also armed with French Matra 68mm SNEB rockets. (Author's Collection)

Deliveries of Bell Cobras to Israel began in 1977 and progressed through the AH-1G, Q, S, E, and F models. This TOW missile-armed AH-1S, decorated with a fitting motif, was assigned to the IAF base Tel-Nof/Ekron. (Yuval Lapid)

During the 1982 Peace for Galilee campaign, the Syrians lost several anti-armor Gazelle gunships, which were armed with four HOT missiles and two 20mm cannons. This was one of two that were recovered in Lebanon by Israeli Air Force CH-53s. Both Gazelles were made flyable, with this SA 432L displayed at the IAF Museum at Hatzerim AFB, wearing both IAF and Syrian Air Force insignia. (Yuval Lapid)

Compared to other HIND variants, the Mi-35P features fixed landing gear and shorter stub wings with two hard points each. Armament options are 16 9M114 Shturm-V or 9M120 Ataka guided anti-armor missiles; B8V20-A rocket launchers for 20 unguided 80mm S-8 rockets; APU-68 UM3 launchers with two or four 240mm unguided S-24 rockets; and 23mm gun units. On the lower right nose section of this Cyprus Mi-35P is a twin-barrel GS630-2 cannon. The Mi-35P cockpit is NVG-compatible. (Emiel Sloot & Luc Hornstra/STAS)

The Cypress Air Force Command took delivery of four Aerospatiale SA.342L1 Gazelles in 1988. These fill the anti-armor role armed with four HOT missiles. Having a range of 2.5 miles, the missile is guided by the pilot through an infrared M397 targeting system mounted atop the cabin. The HOT missile (high subsonic optically-guided) was a French-German venture developed by Euromissile beginning in 1978. It is the counterpart to the U.S. TOW missile. (Emiel Sloot & Luc Hornstra/STAS)

the mid 1980s purchased more than 50 McDonnell Douglas Model 500s and 530Fs. More than half of them were still in use at the 2003 invasion. Iraq, like many Middle Eastern nations, used a mix of aircraft obtained from a number of sources. With allied assistance, the Iraq Air Force struggled to re-establish its helicopter force, having only a small number of Mi-17 attack helicopters at the time of the U.S.-led invasion. The Air Force set as its goal the acquisition of additional Mi-17s and helicopters in use with the U.S. Army. Bahrain, whose air force was not established until 1977, carries more than 20 helicopter gunships on its inventory, while Jordan continues to fly a mix of AH-1S/Fs into the twenty-first century. Syria operates more than 100 attack helicopters, most of them Mil aircraft.

South American governments have long had a need for attack helicopters, given the region's propensity for civil war. The gunships of many nations saw combat, including Argentina, Peru, Colombia, Mexico, Guatemala, El Salvador, Honduras, Nicaragua, and possibly Ecuador. Predominant in most air arms were U.S.-built helicopters, especially Hueys; however, Peru, Venezuela, Brazil, and Cuba operated Mil types as well. During El Salvador's civil war from 1979 to 1992, its air force received about 80 UH-1Hs and 24 UH-1Ms, which engaged in heavy combat with guerilla forces; many were shot down. Some Hueys, along with Alouette IIIs, were modified to carry 250- and 500-pound conventional bombs.

America's commitment in the war on drug trafficking in Latin America produced large assistance packages that included helicopters, including gunships. The Huey's distinctive rotor sound was common in Colombia until augmented by Blackhawks, some of which were attack versions. Since the late 1960s, the Colombian military has acquired nearly every model in the Hughes/McDonnell Douglas family of helicopters, many of which served as gunships. Bolstering the infusion of military hardware into

the country in support of *Plan Colombia* were 33 UH-1Ns in 2000, along with the upgrade of 50 UH-1Hs to Huey IIs, and an additional 25 Huey IIs in 2002.

The 1982 Malvinas/Falklands war spotlighted the air assets of Argentina and Great Britain. Although when Argentina invaded the Falklands and South Georgia, it had no attack helicopters, the military added weapons to many of those used for other purposes. A small number of Bell 212 Hueys were armed with four 7.62mm machine guns, along with UH-1Hs, Alouette IIIs, Agusta A-109s, and CH-47 Chinooks. The Argentine Army quickly took possession of Police BO-105 helicopters to arm them, but the modification did not occur. During the conflict, the Argentine Navy used all five of its S-61D-4 Sea Kings for ASW duty. The six helicopter types used by Great Britain during the conflict, Wessex, Scout, Sea King, Lynx, Wasp, and Gazelle, carried some form of weaponry. The Wasp successfully fired AS-12 missiles, the Gazelle fired SNEB rockets and machine guns, and the Lynx was armed with the AS-12 and Sea Skua missiles, and torpedoes.

The Mexican military is all business when it comes to armed helicopters, having 31 Mil types and 20 MD 530Fs in its air force, along with nearly 30 Mils, 6 MD 902s, 11 Bolkow Bo-105s, and 2 Eurocopter Panthers in its navy. All have provisions for mounting miniguns and rockets for counter-narcotics operations. The Brazilian Air Force took delivery of 12 Mi-35Ms beginning in 2009, and its army has a large force of Eurocopter Panthers and Fennecs, as well as Helibras (Eurocopter-licensed) HB-350s. The Philippine Air Force has long maintained two attack squadrons of MD-520MG Defenders.

Armed helicopters remain an important asset in the air forces of Europe, which, for decades filled its attack inventories with U.S.- or Soviet-built helicopters. In the twenty-first century, popular among European air arms is the French Tiger, which is considered the equivalent of

Void of markings other than an aircraft number, this UH-1M came from U.S. Army stocks as part of the massive infusion of U.S. military aid to El Salvador during the 1980s and 1990s to combat rebel forces. Besides being armed with the XM-21 system familiar to U.S. Army gunships, the Mike model has an IR-suppressing upturned exhaust and armor panels over the engine. (Emiel Sloot & Luc Hornstra/STAS)

This UH-1H of the Argentine Army in 1988 is armed with SNEB 68mm rockets and a large machine gun in the crewman's well. Among about 20 UH-1Hs, nine saw heavy use during the Falklands conflict. The only other armed helicopters used by Argentina in the war were three Agusta A-109A Hirundos, two of which were captured and one destroyed. (Author's Collection)

The oldest helicopters in the Brazilian Navy are 10 Sea Kings: six Sikorsky SH-3Hs acquired from the U.S. Navy in 1970, and four Agusta models acquired in 1984. Agusta upgraded the Sikorsky aircraft, re-designated SH-3As in Brazilian service, in 1987, with one of the major modifications being the installation of launchers for Exocet anti-shipping missiles. The missile enhances its anti-shipping mission, which is secondary to ASW using sonar, Mk-46 torpedoes, and Mk 9 depth charges. (Author's Collection)

Ten of these Sud Aviation/Aerospatiale SA.319B Alouette IIIs were delivered to the Chilean Navy during the late 1970s. A development of the SA.316B, the Alouette III's torpedo normally was balanced by a 2.75-inch rocket launcher on the opposite side of the aircraft. More than 75 countries ordered 316 and 319 variants. (Author's Collection)

In 1973, Squadron 007 of the Spanish Navy began flying eight AH-1Gs for armed coastal patrol. By 1985, half were lost in crashes, three were returned to the United States, and one was placed in storage. Spain was first to acquire exported Cobras, with deliveries later made to Bahrain, Israel, Japan, Jordan, Pakistan, South Korea, Thailand, and Turkey. (Bell Helicopter)

An Italian Army A.129CBT Mangusta (Mongoose) of the 5th Aviation Regiment flies over northern Italy near its home base Casarsa della Delizia. Twenty-first century upgrades expanded the Mangusta's role beyond anti-armor. The type was first deployed in Iraq in 2005, and in 2007 a detachment deployed to Afghanistan. Ammunition for the cannon was fed through a long chute attached to the aircraft's left side. (Emiel Sloot & Luc Hornstra/STAS)

Featuring angular lines like the U.S. Apache, the Eurocopter Tiger HAP is one of three versions. France ordered 70 for combat support and 10 for anti-armor, deliveries of which began in 2003. France planned a total procurement of 215 Tigers. Besides the Tiger's under-nose 30mm GIAT 750-spm cannon, it can be armed with four Mistral or Stinger missiles, Euromissile HOT 3, and Trigat-LR anti-tank missiles. Two pods of 22 SNEB 68mm rockets and the FN Herstal HMP-400 gun pod can also be carried. Seen at the 2009 Dubai Airshow, this Tiger HAP of 5 RHC, ALAT wears French civil registry since it was leased for demonstration. (Martin Bach)

In 1999, this MBB B0-105 of the German Heeresflieger was painted with a special color scheme incorporating the distinctive emblem of Army Aviation Regiment 26, which was renamed Combat Helicopter Regiment 26. The aircraft is armed with Franco-German HOT missiles, which have a range of 2.5 miles. This excellent Messerschmitt-Bolkow-Blohm helicopter also served in a variety of civilian aerial roles from law-enforcement and medevac flying ambulance to passenger carrying and light utility transport. (Martin Bach)

In 1969, Germany ordered 23 Westland HAS.41 Sea Kings to replace its H-34 fleet. Re-designated Mk 41s, they were to be upgraded with four Sea Skua anti-shipping missiles, beginning in 1986. The program was canceled with Germany's reunification and demise of the Warsaw Pact. Accordingly, images of armed helicopters of the German Navy are rare. All Mk 41s were assigned to MFG-5 at SAR Base Kiel-Holtenau to protect northern regions and the North and Baltic seas. The large nose radome houses Mk.3 Seaspray radar. (Press and Information Center German Navy)

This SE.3130 Alouette II, which is armed with SS-11 missiles, is displayed at Roth Air Base, Germany, to commemorate its arrival in 1962. The Alouette was the first German Heeresflieger aircraft type assigned at Roth, where they formed Army Aviation Regiment 26. On the helicopter's nose is the emblem of the regiment, which later was designated an attack helicopter unit. (Martin Bach)

America's Apache. France took possession of 80 Tigers, beginning in 2008, some of which it committed to combat in Afghanistan in 2009. Deliveries of 24 Apaches to the Spanish Air Force began in 2008. Germany ordered 80 UHT, or armed multi-role, Tigers, and 22 armed reconnaissance ARH versions went to Austria. The British Army operates eight AH1 Apache squadrons, rotating at least one through Afghanistan. Apaches augment the British Army's force of Gazelles and Lynx, which have gone through a number of improvements over the years.

The Italian Air Force has long favored its force of about 50 BredaNardi 500E Defenders, while the Italian Army operates nearly 140 Agusta (Bell-licensed) variants, and 60 Mangusta state-of-the-art attack helicopters. Among the former Eastern Bloc countries, Poland operates the largest gunship force, with more than 40 Mi-24 and Mi-35Ps.

At the 1991 collapse of the Soviet Union, the Soviet Air Force had more than 3,000 helicopters. As military assets were divided among the new Russian states, the new Russian Air Force gained the lion's share with 305 attack helicopters, two-thirds of which were Mi-24s, with the remainder being a mix of Kamov Ka-50s and -52s. Russia made plans to double that number, mainly with Mi-28s, by 2015. The future world political climate will determine how many gunships of the Mil line of helicopters will be categorized as friend or foe. Regardless, America will strive to maintain the most powerful and technologically advanced attack helicopter force in the world.

Romania's first attack helicopter came from its own Intreprinderea Aeronautica Romana (IAR) which license-built Aerospatiale's SA. 330L Puma beginning in 1974. In 1994, IAR contracted with Israel's Elbit Systems Ltd. to upgrade Pumas to the Search Optronic Combat Anti-Tank (SOCAT) version. Carried on the SOCAT's four armament stations are UB-16-57 rocket pods or Rafael Spike ER anti-tank missiles on the outer racks. The rocket launcher carried 16 55mm S-5 rockets. On the cabin door is the emblem of the 90th Air Transport Base from which two squadrons of SOCATs operate. Four-aircraft Puma

SOCAT attachments deployed to Bosnia-Herzegovina in 2004 and 2006. An electro-optical pod with FLIR and video system is mounted above the aircraft's Nexter THL-20 20mm gun. (Emiel Sloot & Luc Hornstra/STAS)

An ungainly creature, this Mi-24 of the Hungarian Air Force is armed with a 12.7mm nose gun. Pods under its nose are control systems for anti-tank missiles, with the smaller unit on the left side an antenna, with the right side pod an optical device. The system is called Raduga, for "Rainbow." The large wing pod is a Hungarian-developed radiation monitoring unit. Hungary operates the Mi-24D, V, and P models.
(Tamas Szorad)

This Mi-24V of the Czech Air Force in 2006 appeared with this eye-catching blue scheme with tiger artwork. Armament is a 12.7mm nose gun and six wing stations that could carry 5,300 pounds of a wide variety of ordnance. (Martin Bach)

While similar to the Mi-8, the Mi-17 is differentiated by its tail rotor on the left side, engine intake shields, and six external racks, compared to the Mi-8's four. This Mi-17, with auxiliary fuel tanks on its center racks, deploys special operations troops. (Tamas Szorad)

The Polish-built PZL W-3 Sokol first flew in 1979, but was not operational until 1985. This model shows off its wares, which includes a fast-rope for deploying special operations troops. Air arms of Myanmar and the Czech Republic also operate the Sokol. (Olaf Bichel)

The air force of Czechoslovakia operated 30 Mi-24Vs. When the nation split into the Czech and Slovak republics on 1 January 1993, 20 Mi-24Vs went to the Czech Air Force, and the remainder to the Slovak Air Force. The Czech Republic later received six Mi-24Vs from Russia. Number 0812 was one of six sold to the re-established Afghan Air Force in 2008. (Emiel Sloot & Luc Hornstra/STAS)

Kamov's Ka-50 Hokum (Werewolf), along with the Ka-52, comprised one-third of the Soviet Union's attack helicopter force when the USSR dissolved in 1991. The Hokum is fully capable of air-to-ground and air-to-air attack, having a 30mm cannon in its nose, and under-wing stations for multiple launchers mounting 20 80mm rockets, two eight-round clusters of AT-9 Whirlwind anti-tank missiles, and air-to-surface and air-to-air missiles. (Alexei Mikheyev)

While the Russian-built Mi-28 Havoc could never win a beauty contest, it made up in muscle what it lacked in looks. The twin-engine gunship sports a 2A42 30mm nose cannon, and four wing stations for carrying a mix of ordnance including 16 modified AT-6 Spiral anti-tank missiles, four UV-20-57 multiple launchers for 55mm rockets or UV-20-80 multiple launchers for 80mm rockets, or four air-to-air missiles. (Olaf Bichel)

BIBLIOGRAPHY

Books

Adcock, Al. *H-3 Sea King In Action.* Squadron/Signal Publications, Inc. 1995.

Brandt, Robert J. and Davies, William J. *The Piasecki H-21 Helicopter.* Trafford. 2007.

Brown, David A. *The Bell Helicopter Textron Story.* Aerofax, Inc. 1995.

Fails, William R. Lt. Col. USMC. *Marines and Helicopters 1962-1973.* History and Museums Division Headquarters, U.S. Marine Corps. Washington, D.C. 1976.

Hobson, Chris and Noble, Andrew. *Falklands Air War.* Midland Publishing. 2002.

Lundh, Lennart. *Sikorsky H-34: An Illustrated History.* Schiffer Publishing, Ltd. 1998.

Macy, Ed. *Apache.* Atlantic Monthly Press. 2008.

McGuire, Francis G. *Helicopters 1948-1998: A Contemporary History.* Frank L. Jensen, Jr. 1998.

Mutza, Wayne. *Kaman H-43.* Schiffer Publishing, Ltd. 1998.

Rawlins, Eugene W. Lt. Col. USMC. *Marines and Helicopters 1946-1962.* History and Museums Division Headquarters, U.S. Marine Corps. Washington, D.C. 1976.

Young, Ralph B. *Army Aviation in Vietnam 1961-1963.* The Huey Company, Inc. 1999.

Young, Ralph B. *Army Aviation in Vietnam 1963-1966.* The Huey Company, Inc. 2000.

Publications

Bolino, John V. and Toia, T. S. *LAMPS MKIII: The Early Years.* Rotor Review. Winter 1992.

Colucci, Frank. *Clementine and the Big Mothers.* Air Enthusiast No. 20. Dec. 1982 – March 1983.

Ellerin, Norm. *LAMPS MKIV – Historical Perspective.* Rotor Review. Winter. 1992.

Galdorisi, George CDR. *LAMPS MKIII…Battle Group Asset.* Rotor Review. Winter 1992.

Gunther, Carl R. *The First Whirly Aboard.* THE HOOK. Fall 1985.

Harvey, David S. *A Clear Path Ahead.* Rotor & Wing. January 1997.

Kerr, John N. and Crabtree, James A. *Helicopter Technological Progress.* Vertiflite. July-August 1975.

Kirby, Reid. *Operation Snoopy: The Chemical Corps' People Sniffer.* Army Chemical Review. January-June 2007.

Machat, Mike. *Bring in the Choppers: The Evolution of the Modern Military Helicopter.* Wings. October 2003.

Miller, Richard A. VADM USN Ret. *LAMPS Granddaddy.* Rotor Review. Fall 1991.

Nikolaus, Lt. JG Larry D. *End of Big Mothers.* Naval Aviation News. August 1975.

Phillips, Thomas LCDR USN Ret. *Scramble Seawolves.* Rotor Review. Winter 1992.

Rosier, Bill JO2. *Seawolves on the Prowl in Vietnam.* Naval Aviation News. January 1967.

Sikorsky, Sergei. *The Dorsey Controversy.* Flight Journal. April 2003.

Thomason, Tommy. *Helicopters and Carriers.* THE HOOK. Winter 1981.

Weseleskey, A. E. LCDR. *The Seawolf Helicopter Pilots of Vietnam.* U.S. Naval Institute Proceedings. October 1972.

Wheeler, Howard A. Commander. *The Naval Helicopter: A Machine for Many Missions.* Naval Aviation News. May-June 1985.

DSN-3 Helicopter Completes Destroyer Tests. Aviation Week & Space Technology. April 8, 1963.

Hughes: Masters of Attack. Defense & Foreign Affairs Digest. August 1978.

Military Aviation. Flying Review International. April 1966.

Government Publications

Browning, Robert M. Jr. *The Eyes and Ears of the Convoy: Development of the Helicopter as an Anti-submarine Weapon.* Coast Guard Historian's Office. September 1993.

Troxell, Harold M. *LAMPS DESTROYER/ HELICOPTER SYSTEM.* Naval Air Development Center, Warminster, Pennsylvania. 8 June 1973.

AH-1 Priority Aircraft Subsystem Suitability Intensive Review, Final Study Report. U.S. Army Aviation Center, Fort Rucker, Alabama. 30 June 1975.

Advanced Attack Helicopter Final Report. Source Selection Evaluation Board, U.S. Army. June 1973.

Advanced Attack Helicopter Task Force Report. United States Army Combat Developments Command, Alexandria, Virginia. July 1972.

Final Report Project No. 54-66-11 UH-1E Armament Door Mount. Marine Corps Landing Force Development Center, Quantico, Virginia. 19 May 1967.

Final Report of the Special Task Force for AAH/ASH/HELLFIRE Test Integration. Headquarters, U.S. Army Test and Evaluation Command, Aberdeen Proving Ground, Maryland. (nd).

Joint Operational Evaluation of Armed Helicopters. Department of the Army. 29 July 1963.

Lessons Learned – Advanced Attack Helicopter. Department of Research and Information, Defense Systems Management College, Fort Belvoir, Virginia. July 1983.

Military Potential Test of the UH-2A Helicopter – Report Number A688130, 25 October 1963. Army Aviation Test Board, Fort Rucker, Alabama.

Report of Test Project No. AVN 362 Evaluation of the 2.75-inch (Modified) Aerial Rocket Weapons System (H-34), 27 February 1962. United States Army Aviation Board, Fort Rucker, Alabama.

Other Documents

Pember, Harry. *The Story of the VS-300: The Aircraft that launched an Industry.* Igor I. Sikorsky Historical Archives, Inc. (nd).

Armament OH-6A Helicopter. Hughes Tool Company, Aircraft Division, Culver City, California. (nd).

Introduction to the History of the Navy HA(L)-3. Vietnam Helicopter Pilot's Association. (nd).

U.S. Navy Riverine Operations. Warplane No. 76.

INDEX

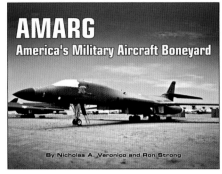
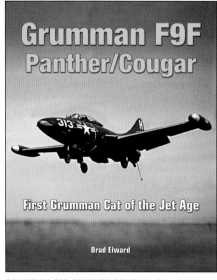
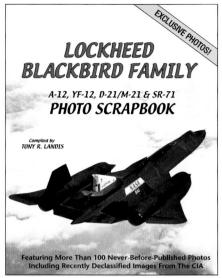
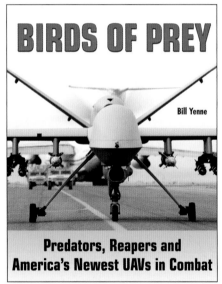
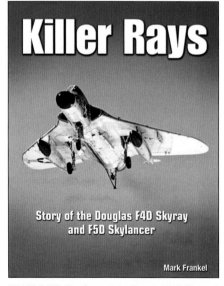
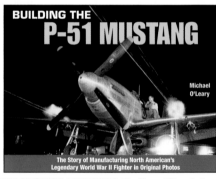